Affective Learning and Serious Games

Kaoru Sumi

CRC Press
Taylor & Francis Group
Boca Raton London New York

CRC Press is an imprint of the
Taylor & Francis Group, an **informa** business
A SCIENCE PUBLISHERS BOOK

First edition published 2026
by CRC Press
2385 NW Executive Center Drive, Suite 320, Boca Raton FL 33431

and by CRC Press
4 Park Square, Milton Park, Abingdon, Oxon, OX14 4RN

Library of Congress Cataloging-in-Publication Data (applied for)

ISBN: 978-1-041-32262-7 (hbk)
ISBN: 978-1-041-32264-1 (pbk)
ISBN: 978-1-003-78273-5 (ebk)

DOI: 10.1201/9781003782735

Typeset in Times New Roman
by Prime Publishing Services

Preface

In a world where technology and education intertwine, the way we learn and interact with information is undergoing a profound transformation. This transformation is deeply influenced by nonverbal communication, human-computer interaction through emotions, emotion expression, emotion recognition, and persuasion techniques. These topics are not only inherently fascinating but also pivotal in creating innovative educational systems.

Humans have a natural tendency to perceive emotions even in artifacts. The behavior of a robot, whether through gestures, movements, or simulated expressions, can evoke emotional reactions in us. This innate response lays the foundation for intuitive interactions with technology. Imagine a world where computers, robots, and other digital artifacts understand and respond to our emotions. Such interactions have the potential to revolutionize the way we learn, communicate, and solve problems.

Games, on the other hand, captivate people of all ages. Beyond entertainment, games offer a powerful medium for interaction and engagement. Serious games, in particular, take this concept further by addressing real-world issues and fostering learning through immersive experiences. They enable users to learn visually, emotionally, and experientially, making education not just effective but enjoyable.

This book explores the exciting fields of affective learning, serious games, and next-generation educational technologies, shedding light on recent research and its implications for the future of education. These emerging disciplines leverage emotional engagement and game-based learning to enhance educational outcomes. In addition, innovative approaches to language education are introduced, such as using etymology and animation to support elementary students in learning English. Affective learning uses emotional cues to create responsive, human-like interactions in educational systems, while Serious Games harness the power of gaming to teach through simulated experiences. Together, they represent a promising direction for the future of learning.

Structure of the Book

This book is structured into four main parts, each focusing on a key area of innovation:

1. Affective Learning

This section examines how emotional intelligence is integrated into educational systems, fostering more human-like and responsive interactions. Key topics include:

- **Intelligent Tutoring Systems:** How adaptive systems use affective interaction to guide learning, similar to human teachers.
- **Avatars in Online Education:** Investigating the role of avatars in creating engaging and effective online learning environments.
- **Emotion-Driven Story Generation for Game-Based Learning in Virtual Environments:** Exploring how emotions can shape narratives in immersive educational contexts.

2. *Affective Interaction*

This section focuses on the role of emotional exchanges in enhancing learning experiences and behavior changes. Highlights include:

- **Pet-Type Artifacts:** Exploring how emotional expressions in robotic systems can influence human behavior.
- **Human-Robot Interaction in Learning:** Examining how robots can serve as empathetic and intuitive learning companions.
- **Observation of Student Behavior:** Understanding emotional cues to create adaptive educational environments.
- **Persuasive Information Media:** Examining how emotional and culturally tailored media—such as avatars and video content in immersive environments—can enhance persuasion and influence educational engagement.

3. *Serious Games*

The third section highlights the use of games as tools for solving social challenges and enhancing learning through immersive environments. Topics include:

- **SNS Etiquette through Simulated Experiences:** Teaching responsible online behavior using games that replicate social networking scenarios.
- **Anti-Bullying Education:** Designing systems that foster empathy by allowing players to experience the perspectives of both bullies and victims.
- **Sports Training and Cognitive Development:** Enhancing athletic performance and spatial cognition through virtual reality training systems.
- **Game with a Purpose:** Developing a Visual Effect Dictionary through gameplay that captures context-sensitive interpretations of visual effects, combining engagement with semantic knowledge construction.

4. *XR and Beyond: The Future of Learning*

This section explores how emerging technologies—such as virtual reality (VR), mixed reality (MR), and digital twins—are transforming education. These chapters present immersive environments and advanced interaction models that support deep engagement with complex subjects and simulated scenarios. Topics include:

- **Immersive STEM Learning:** Using mixed reality to visualize mathematical and scientific concepts.

- **Generative Art in Education:** Applying MR in programming and creative expression.
- **Geography Education through Digital Twins:** Combining real-world mapping with VR for spatial learning.

Purpose of the Book

This book aims to inspire readers to explore the transformative potential of emotional engagement and game-based learning in education. Whether you are a student eager to discover cutting-edge educational tools, a researcher investigating affective computing, or an educator seeking innovative methods, this book offers a wealth of knowledge and inspiration.

As you journey through these chapters, you will uncover how emotions, technology, and games are converging to reshape how we learn, interact, and grow. From fostering digital literacy on social networking platforms to improving spatial cognition through immersive simulations, the systems described here illustrate the immense possibilities of integrating affective technologies, game-based learning, and next-generation tools such as XR and digital twins into education.

Let us embark on this exciting exploration of **Affective Learning, Affective Interaction, Serious Games, and XR and Beyond**, unlocking new pathways for creating engaging, intuitive, and impactful learning experiences.

Contents

Part 4
XR and Beyond: The Future of Learning

Part 1
Affective Learning

Emotions are fundamental to how we learn, communicate, and make sense of the world. In the realm of education, leveraging emotions can foster deeper engagement, enhance retention, and create more personalized learning experiences. Affective learning focuses on the integration of emotional intelligence into educational systems, transforming the way we approach teaching and learning.

This part delves into groundbreaking research and applications that explore the intersection of emotions and education. The chapters investigate diverse approaches to affective learning, such as intelligent tutoring systems that adapt to learners' emotional states to guide them more effectively, avatars that contribute to engaging online learning environments and enhance learning effectiveness, and emotion-driven story generation for game-based learning in virtual environments, enabling experiences tailored to individual users. By addressing both the cognitive and emotional dimensions of learning, these chapters reveal how technology can bridge the gap between human-like interaction and digital education.

By examining these innovations, educators and researchers can uncover practical insights into creating systems that not only understand but also respond to the emotional needs of learners. This paves the way for a future where education is more intuitive, adaptive, and impactful.

These contributions highlight the core principles and potential of affective learning in modern educational environments.

1 Intelligent Tutoring System using Affective Interaction

1. Introduction

This chapter outlines the background and motivations for our research. It provides an overview of student modeling in intelligent tutoring systems, emphasizing the affective aspect of student modeling and its potential application in computer programming education.

1.1 Intelligent Tutoring Systems and the Student Model

Over the years, intelligent tutoring systems (ITS) have garnered significant research attention for their ability to support student learning. These systems not only deliver content but also adapt feedback to individual needs, aiming to replicate the personalized nature of one-on-one human tutoring. Human tutoring, as Bloom (1984) demonstrated, achieves an unparalleled effect size of 2.0 in improving student performance—equivalent to two standard deviations in test scores. However, scaling this approach is impractical due to the need for individual tutors. ITS research has focused on replicating this success, though no system has yet achieved the same level of effectiveness. VanLehn (2011) highlights key factors behind human tutoring's success: personalized activity selection, motivational dialogues, and timely feedback. These require an understanding of the student's state, referred to in ITS as the "student model." This model encompasses knowledge, skills, cognitive processes, and emotional states, enabling systems to tailor interventions effectively.

Despite advancements, ITS has yet to fully replicate the complexity of human tutoring. Baker (2016) suggests shifting focus from replicating human tutors to designing systems that complement and enhance teachers' capabilities. Examples include Lumilo, providing real-time student data via smart glasses, Zuvio IRS, enabling instant classroom responses, and Course Signals, offering performance analytics.

Central to all approaches is the student. Whether augmenting teachers or acting as tutors, ITS must effectively model students to deliver meaningful interventions. For educators, understanding the student's perspective remains vital, driving ongoing exploration of this essential element in ITS research.

1.2 Affective Student Modelling

Our work emphasizes the affective aspect of student modeling, focusing on the emotional experiences students encounter during learning. Studies have shown that emotions correlate with improved performance (Rodrigo et al., 2009; Daniels

DOI: 10.1201/9781003782735-2

et al., 2009) and self-regulated learning (Mega et al., 2014; Cho et al., 2015). Human tutors effectively influence students' emotional states through motivational dialogues, enhancing learning outcomes.

Several studies have explored enabling intelligent tutoring systems to detect and respond to students' emotions. A comprehensive review by Feidakis (2016) highlights emotion-aware systems utilizing video, sensor data like voice and EEG signals and system interaction logs for emotion detection. Each method has pros and cons; for instance, EEG signals require specialized hardware, which may be inconvenient or impractical in natural learning settings.

Emotions in Programming

Programming-focused tutoring systems face unique challenges compared to conventional ITS. Unlike traditional systems, where students interact with learning materials and a virtual tutor, programming involves tasks like writing, testing, and debugging code. As a result, standard emotional cues such as voice, interaction logs, and facial expressions may be less applicable in this context. Studies indicate novice programmers experience varied emotions while coding, including engagement, confusion, frustration, and boredom (Bosch & D'Mello, 2017). In our research, students solved programming exercises and later reported their emotions during the session. Those who completed more exercises frequently reported feeling engaged, as shown in Figure 1.

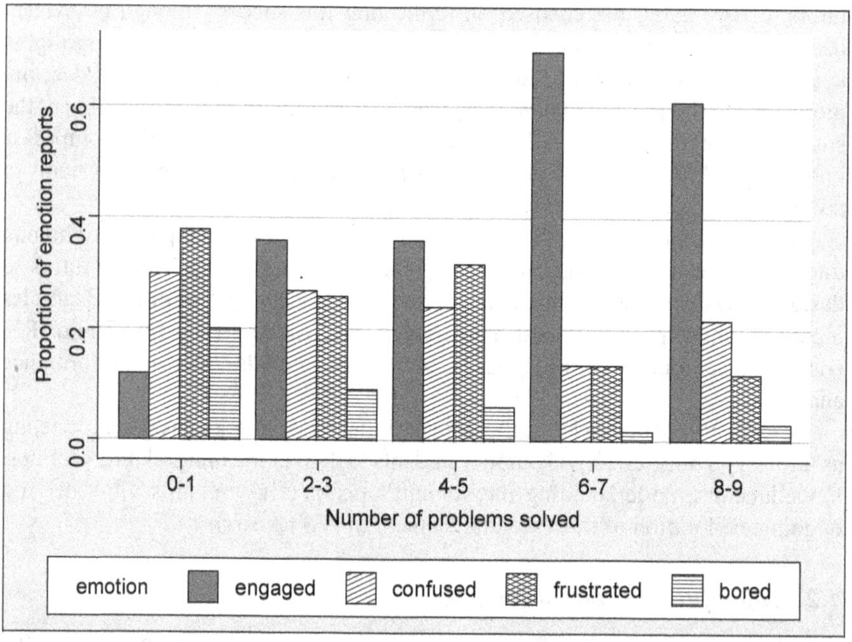

Fig. 1 Proportion of self-reported emotions among students at varying performance levels.

Inferring student emotions in programming contexts is valuable but challenging. A recent study by Bosch, Chen & D'Mello (2014) revealed difficulty in detecting fixed-point emotion judgments from facial features, with classifiers barely outperforming chance. However, certain expressions, like AU04 (lowered eyebrows), are linked to confusion and frustration, as supported by earlier research (Grafsgaard, Boyer & Lester, 2011). AU04, part of the Facial Action Coding System (Ekman & Friesen, 2003), offers insights into detecting emotions via facial muscle movements.

In our studies, we found that log features, combined with facial features, effectively predict student affect and enhance performance (Tiam-Lee & Sumi, 2019). Data from programming sessions annotated with emotional states revealed notable trends. AU04 (lowered eyebrows) was strongly associated with frustration. Document changes (insertions or deletions in code) were more frequent during engagement, while code compilations occurred more often during moments of confusion and frustration. These patterns are illustrated in Figure 2.

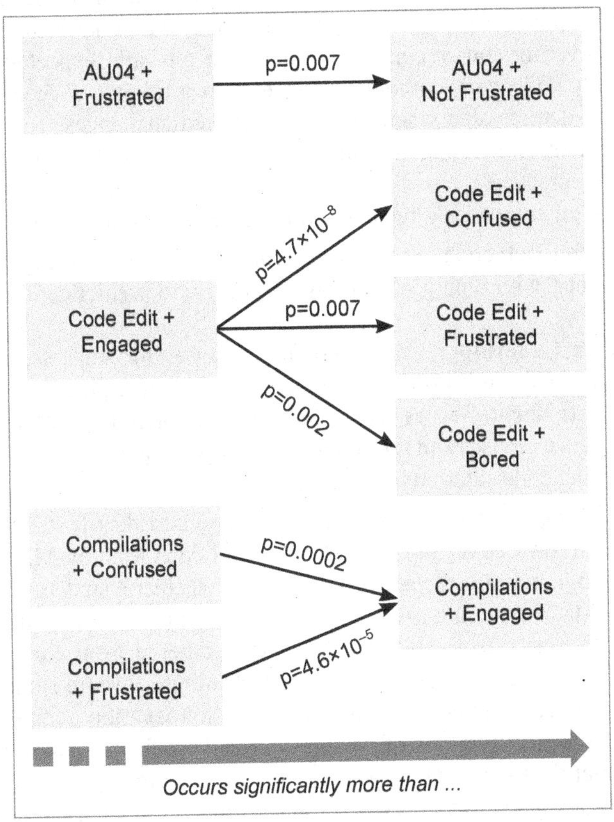

Fig. 2 Trends from programming session data highlighting significantly more frequent combinations (left) compared to others (right), with p-values from the signed Wilcoxon test provided.

In our work, we leverage these correlations to develop systems capable of detecting and responding to student emotions during programming exercises.

2. System for Learning Programming with Adaptive Feedback

As part of our research, we have developed a real-time system that adapts to students' emotional states during programming exercises. This section introduces the system and outlines the adaptive feedback it offers to enhance coding practice.

Our system offers real-time adaptive feedback when it detects student confusion (Tiam-Lee & Sumi, 2018a). It is designed to assist students improving their programming skills, specifically those learning introductory concepts such as basic coding statements, variables, expressions, conditional statements (if-else), and loops.

Practice plays a vital role in learning coding (Barros, Estevens, Dias, Pais & Soeiro, 2003). Although introductory programming involves fewer concepts compared to other domains, mastering the ability to combine these concepts into syntactically correct code demands practice. Since classroom lectures are better suited for covering course content, students are typically expected to practice independently. However, without guidance from a teacher or mentor, students may become demotivated when facing unexpected challenges. To address this, the system offers an automated solution to help resolve student confusion during programming practice.

The system comprises three main modules, as shown in Figure 3:

1. **Confusion Detector:** Utilizes data from a webcam recording the student's face, along with typing and compilation logs, to predict confusion in real-time.
2. **Problem Generator:** Creates coding exercises for students, adjusts their difficulty, and offers problem-specific guides when required.
3. **User Interface:** Serves as the primary interaction point for students, displaying exercises and providing tools for writing, testing, debugging, and submitting code solutions.

The confusion detector employs generative models to identify student confusion in real time (Tiam-Lee & Sumi, 2017). Using Hidden Markov Models (HMM) trained on programming session data, it predicts whether a student is engaged or confused. HMMs were chosen for their ability to represent the sequential nature of time-series data effectively. The data were gathered from eleven freshmen during programming sessions lasting forty-five minutes, where students tackled exercises without tutor intervention to elicit confusion at various points. Afterward, each student labeled intervals of engagement and confusion. These labels were used to extract time series data, incorporating log features (typing, compilations, submissions) and facial features (facial expressions captured via webcam).

Determining whether a student is confused involves constructing real-time time series data and comparing the likelihood of the sequence being generated

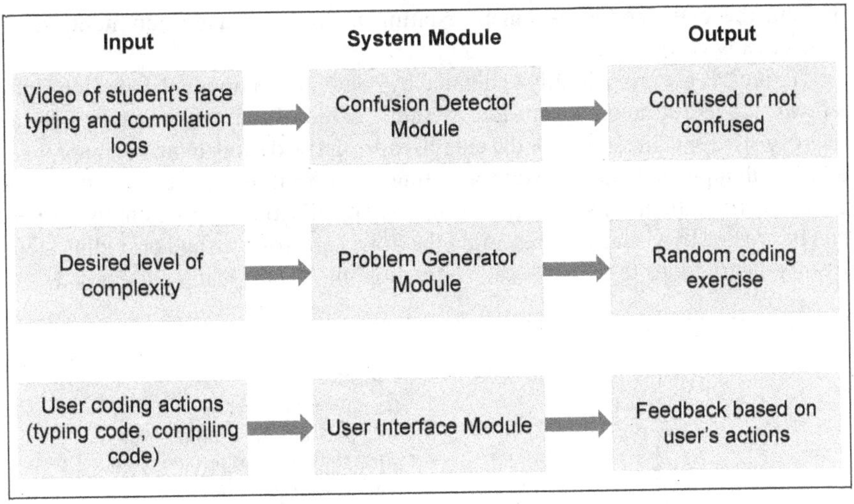

Fig. 3 Modules of the system for programming practice.

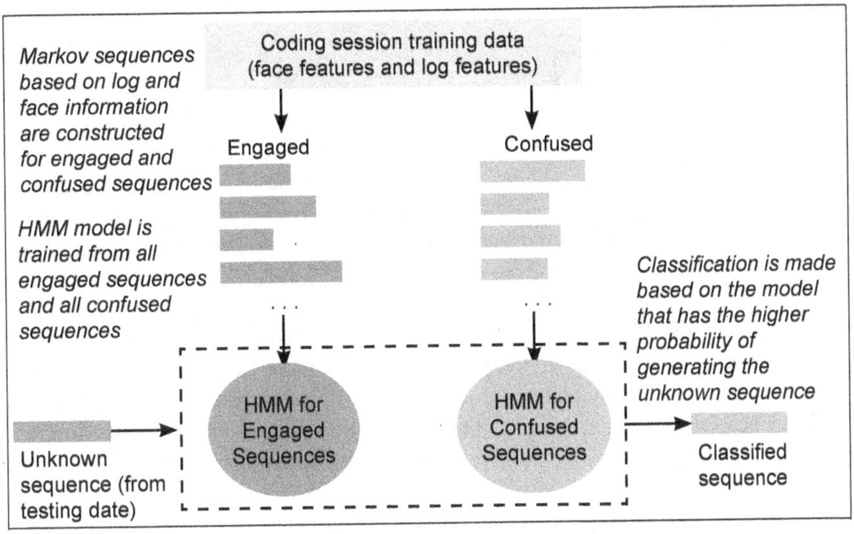

Fig. 4 Confusion detector model training and classification process.

by the HMM trained on engaged sequences versus the HMM trained on confused sequences. The model with the higher probability is chosen as the system's prediction of the student's current emotional state, as illustrated in Figure 4.

The problem generator creates coding exercises automatically, requiring students to write the body of a function based on provided specifications. These specifications consist of computational operations described in natural language, making the exercises a task in translating natural language commands into syntactically correct code.

Exercises are procedurally generated by combining individual operations into a flowchart-like structure (Tiam-Lee & Sumi, 2018b). From this structure, natural language text specifications for the exercises are derived using template mappings, along with input and output cases for testing. Figure 5 illustrates an example of an exercise structure and its corresponding text specifications. Additionally, guides can be created by visually representing the flowchart structure and providing step-by-step instructions to translate each operation into syntactically correct code.

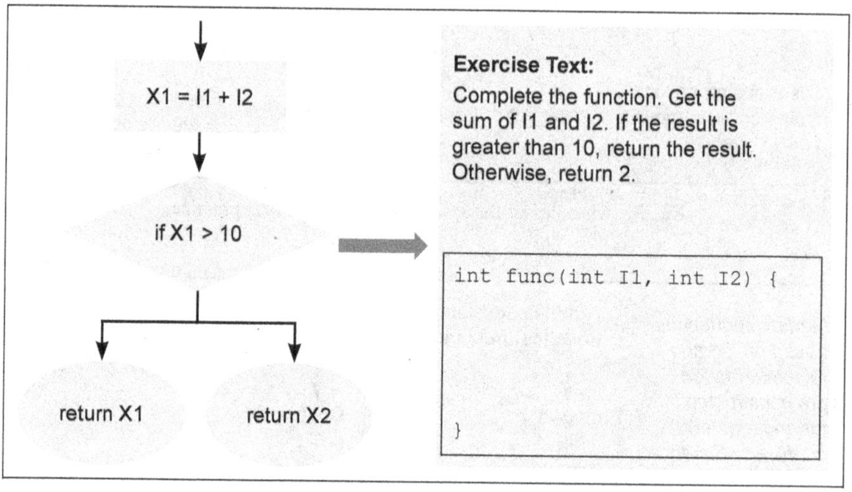

Fig. 5 Example of a randomly-generated exercise structure and the corresponding text specifications.

Figure 6 illustrates the user interface. The upper-left panel displays the exercise specifications, while the lower-left panel provides an interface for students to write their code. Students can test the code by inputting sample values for function arguments, compiling and running it to view results. Syntax errors are highlighted with corresponding messages, whereas successful execution shows the function's return value. Once students are confident in their code's accuracy, they can submit it for automatic evaluation against predefined input test cases.

The right panel of the user interface displays interventions when student confusion is detected. In the upper section, a dialog box appears, prompting students to confirm if they would like a guide for the problem. If accepted, the guide is presented in the lower section as a flowchart, detailing the steps required to solve the problem.

These three modules align with the main components of an intelligent tutoring system as outlined by Nkambou, Mizoguchi, and Bourdeau (2010). The emotion detector represents the student model, capturing real-time student states during system interaction. The problem generator corresponds to the domain model,

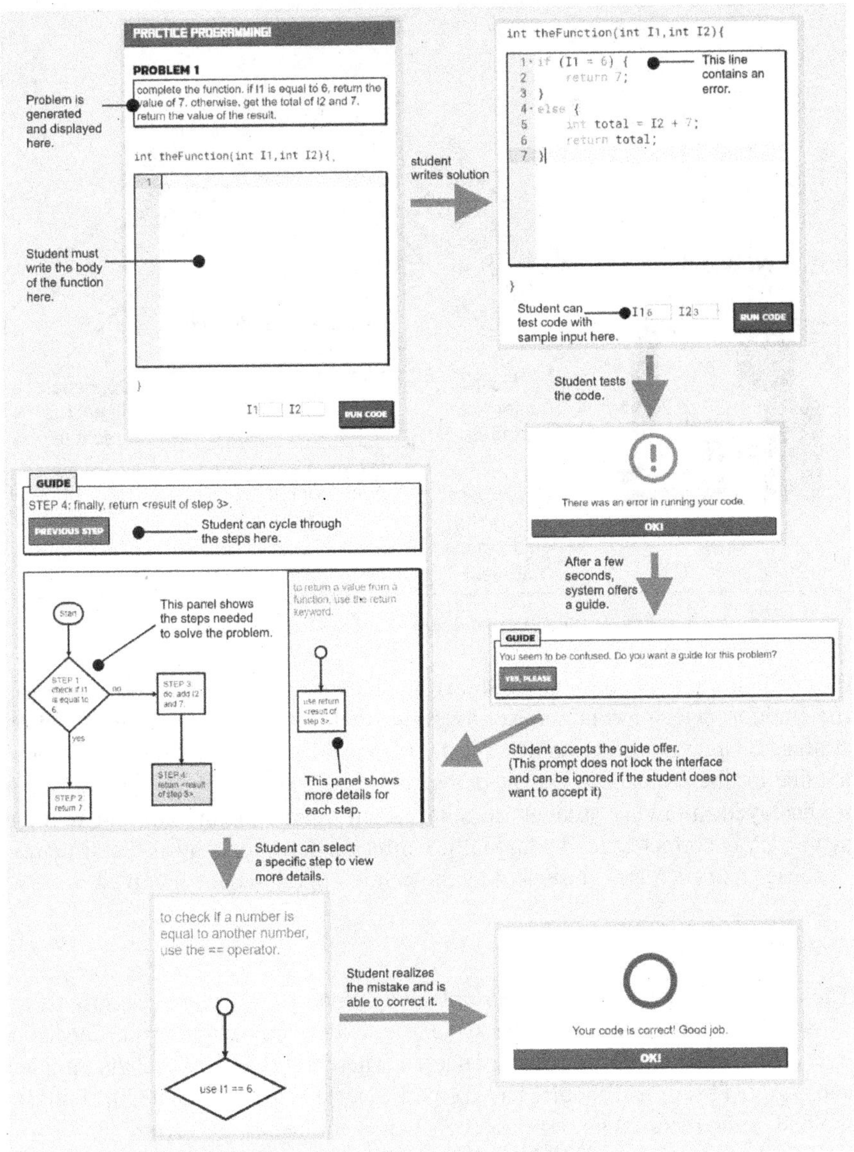

Fig. 6 User interface and operation.

defining exercise scope and feedback types. The user interface matches the user interface model, facilitating direct interaction with students. While the tutoring model is not a separate module, its role in providing interventions is reflected in the integration of the other three modules, as summarized in Figure 7.

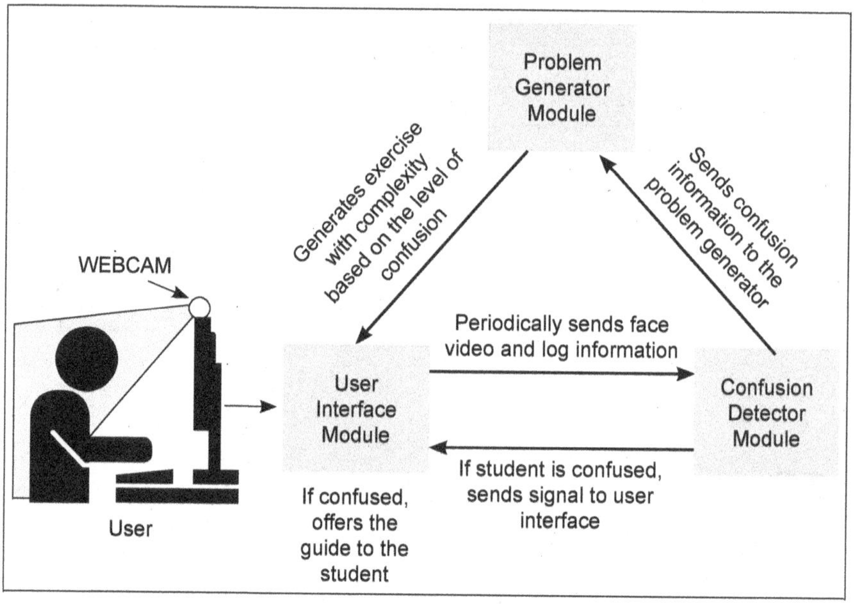

Fig. 7 Summary of operation of system modules.

At first, no interventions are shown to students. As they work on exercises, the emotion detector continuously assesses whether they are likely engaged or confused. Upon detecting confusion, the system intervenes by offering students a guide for the problem. If accepted, a visual representation of the solution steps is displayed, allowing students to select each operation for hints on writing syntactically correct code. Additionally, confusion detection adjusts the difficulty of subsequent exercises, measured by the number of operations involved.

System Evaluation

The system was evaluated with 35 university students, split into two groups of 17 and 18. Both groups used the system, but only the second group received interventions when confusion was detected. These interventions included guides and adjusted exercise difficulty based on the detected emotional state. In contrast, the first group received no response, even when confusion was identified.

Each student interacted with the system for forty minutes, without any human intervention, allowing the system to independently facilitate practice sessions. Following the session, students completed a questionnaire. Their responses, along with system usage logs, were analyzed to evaluate the impact of adaptive feedback on programming practice. The findings from this experiment are discussed in this section.

Student Performance

Students who received emotion-based adaptive feedback outperformed those using the plain system, solving an average of 13.5 exercises compared to 6.33. Figure 8 illustrates the distribution of problems solved across the two groups. A student's t-test confirms that this difference is statistically significant at $\alpha = 0.05$ ($p = 0.0018$).

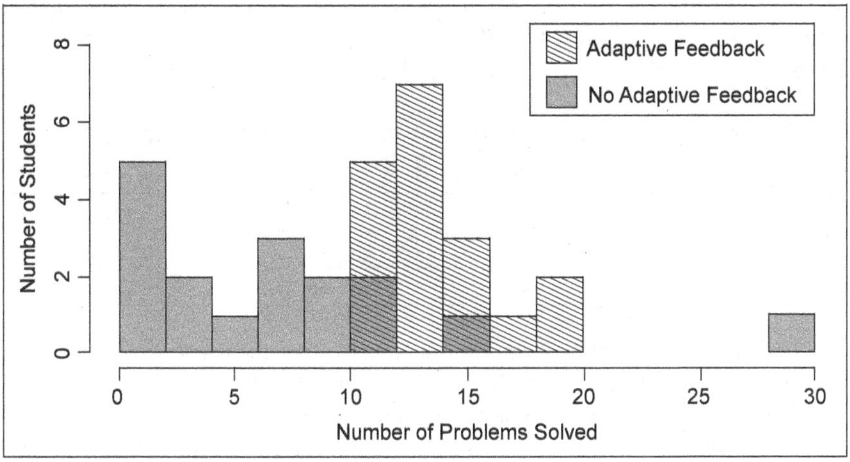

Fig. 8 Number of problems solved across the two groups.

Across different difficulty levels, students who received emotion-based adaptive feedback consistently outperformed their counterparts. This difference was statistically significant at $\alpha = 0.05$. Table 1 provides a detailed comparison, showcasing the percentage of problems solved across both groups. These findings emphasize that offering guides in response to detected confusion effectively aids students in completing more exercises.

Table 1 Percentage of problems solved across different difficulty levels across the two groups.

Difficulty	*No adaptive feedback*	*Adaptive feedback*	*p value (level of significance)*
All	53.05%	90.23%	0.00016
1	55.11%	98.61%	0.00007
2 – 3	70.53%	97.42%	0.01
4 – 6	51.62%	94.42%	0.041

2.1 *Confusion and Guides*

For each instance where the system detected confusion (restricted to one point per problem—the first occurrence of detected confusion), a corresponding item was included in the post-test questionnaire. This item presented a replay snapshot of the moment, along with the preceding 30 seconds. Participants were asked to report their emotional state at that time by selecting one of three options: "very confused," "somewhat confused," or "not confused at all." This process was conducted for both the group receiving adaptive feedback and the group without it. Based on self-reports, out of 135 instances where the system detected confusion, participants identified themselves as "very confused" or "somewhat confused" in 105 cases, resulting in a precision rate of 77.78% for the system's confusion detection. Table 2 provides a summary of these findings.

Table 2 Self-reports on moments when confusion was detected by the system.

	Very confused	*Confused*	*Not confused*
Adaptive feedback	23	37	20
No adaptive feedback	26	19	10
Total	49	56	30

For the group receiving emotion-based adaptive feedback, the acceptance rate of guides offered during detected moments of confusion is outlined in Table 3. Notably, students accepted the guides 65% of the time even when they reported feeling "not confused." This behavior underscores the need for accurately understanding student states to ensure that interventions are delivered at the most suitable moments.

Ideally, teachers should offer assistance only when students truly need it. Making the guide available from the outset risks fostering undesirable habits, where students might rely on it immediately rather than attempting to solve the exercise independently. In 38 instances where students viewed the guide, exercises were successfully solved within three minutes. Exploring the effects of always-available guides versus state-dependent guide offerings remains an intriguing area for future research, though it has yet to be empirically examined in this study.

Table 3 Acceptance rate of guides versus the actual emotion that was reported (adaptive group only).

	Accepted	*Not Accepted*	*Total*
Very Confused	19	4	23
Somewhat Confused	19	18	37
Not Confused	13	7	20
Total	51	29	

2.2 *Experience Perceptions*

Student perceptions of the system were assessed based on two criteria: (1) the level of enjoyment during the exercises and (2) their usefulness for programming practice. For each criterion, participants rated their experience on a 5-point Likert scale, with 1 signifying "very much," 3 indicating "neutral," and 5 meaning "not at all." The summarized results are presented in Table 4.

Table 4 Summary of Results from the Student Experience Perceptions Questionnaire Across the Two Groups.

	How fun/engaging were the exercises?					*How helpful were the exercises in programming practice?*				
	1	2	3	4	5	1	2	3	4	5
Adaptive feedback	4	9	2	3	0	2	12	3	1	0
No adaptive feedback	2	7	3	5	0	2	8	4	3	0
Total	6	16	5	8	0	4	20	7	4	0

A higher proportion of students receiving emotion-based adaptive feedback rated the exercises as "very fun" or "fun" (72.22%), compared to 52.94% of those without adaptive feedback. However, this difference was not statistically significant at $\alpha = 0.05$. Similarly, 77.78% of students with adaptive feedback found the exercises "very helpful" or "helpful," whereas only 58.82% of those without adaptive feedback shared this view. Here too, the difference was not statistically significant at $\alpha = 0.05$.

Although these results suggest the potential benefits of emotion-based adaptive feedback in programming practice, the lack of statistically significant differences between the groups might stem from the simplicity of the system's interventions. Section 4 explores future research directions, including the development of more sophisticated emotion-based interventions.

In addition to the quantitative responses, students were invited to share free-form qualitative feedback about their experience with the system. A selection of these comments is summarized in Table 5.

Students who received adaptive feedback highlighted the usefulness of receiving hints during challenging moments, noting that the guides were effective in resolving confusion. They reported that the guides improved their understanding of the exercises, helped them recall forgotten concepts, and provided a clear visualization of the target program's structure. However, some students expressed concerns that the guides were overly revealing, often coming close to providing the complete solution. Offering suitable hints in programming education is a crucial aspect for future research. Section 3 delves deeper into this topic, exploring strategies to optimize hint delivery for effective learning.

A student who received adaptive feedback remarked in the comments that he could "practice at his own pace," likely due to the system's dynamic adjustment of exercise difficulty based on his state. However, a recurring observation among participants was that the exercises felt overly repetitive and lacked engagement. This stems from the nature of the exercises, which emphasize translating abstract computational operations into code rather than focusing on logic formulation to tackle more compelling, real-world problems.

Table 5 Some free-form comments provided by students who used the system.

Category	*Feedback*
Offering of Guides (Mode B group only)	It was nice that the system gives hints during times of trouble.
	The guide is useful.
	The guides come up when I am having trouble.
Quality of the Guides (Mode B group only)	By looking at the visualization, I was able to grasp the structure of the program better.
	The figure was easy to understand.
	The guide helped me remember little things that I forgot.
	I feel it would be better if I had more specific programming tips.
	It was almost like an answer guide.
Exercises	The problems were too similar with one another.
	The same types of problems come up.
	It tends to get monotonous.
	It is useful only for beginners.
	There were many simple problems.
	I think it is useful as a reconfirmation of basic knowledge.
	Because it gets harder and harder, I can do it at my own pace. (w/ adaptive feedback)
	You can practice in the pace you are comfortable with. (w/ adaptive feedback)

3. Discussion

3.1 Potentials of Emotion-Based Feedback

Emotion-based feedback enables computer learning systems to consider both the cognitive and emotional states of students, addressing an often-overlooked aspect of learning. While learning is typically viewed as a cognitive process, the emotional dimension is equally vital, as numerous studies have shown its significant influence on various aspects of student learning.

The system developed in this study demonstrated the potential benefits of this type of feedback within a learning context. Learning is both a cognitive and emotional experience, shaped by factors such as engagement, motivation, and boredom. In domains like programming, where students spend long hours writing code and experiencing diverse emotions, acknowledging and addressing their emotional state becomes crucial for effective learning.

Emotion-based feedback enhances tutoring systems in multiple ways. First, it enables systems to address a broader range of learning scenarios. Unlike traditional tutoring systems, which focus exclusively on cognitive aspects—responding only to the correctness of a student's answers—emotion-based feedback incorporates the student's emotional state (e.g., boredom or frustration). This inclusion broadens the scope of interventions, allowing tutoring systems to cater to a wider variety of learning situations. Second, it enriches the student model in learning systems by enabling the tracking of not just cognitive progress but also emotional progress. This deeper understanding allows learning systems to tailor content and modify intervention strategies based on the learner's current mood.

Finally, affective tutoring systems offer a more humanlike learning experience. The ability to convey emotional understanding—a key strength of human tutors—is often absent in automated systems. Part of the effectiveness of human tutoring lies in the emotional feedback tutors provide. When implemented effectively, emotion-based feedback can improve students' interaction with learning systems, fostering greater engagement and a sense of support. However, designing such systems requires careful consideration, as overly humanlike artificial agents may provoke negative reactions due to the uncanny valley effect. This topic is explored further in the next section.

3.2 Challenges in Affective Tutoring Systems

A fundamental aspect of affective tutoring systems is detecting the student's emotional state. Although many studies have examined affect detection in learning environments, the challenge intensifies in domains where emotions are expressed in a more naturalistic manner, such as programming, where social interaction is minimal. Several obstacles in emotion detection hinder the development of a fully accurate model of affect.

First, data collected outside controlled laboratory settings tends to be noisy. In this study, video recordings of students' faces were analyzed to extract emotion-related information using a machine learning-based image processing tool that detects facial expressions frame-by-frame. Despite empirical evaluations indicating reasonable accuracy, real-world conditions—such as occlusions, lighting changes, unexpected student movements, or differences in ethnicity compared to the training dataset—can introduce noise, complicating emotion classification. Other approaches, such as heart rate monitoring or electroencephalogram (EEG) signals, have also been utilized to infer student emotions, but these methods are similarly susceptible to noise and variability.

Second, emotion is inherently ambiguous,presenting unique challenges when studied. While many research efforts categorize emotions into distinct groups, emotional experiences are, in reality, fluid and continuous, with multiple emotions often occurring simultaneously. Collecting ground-truth data on emotions demands careful consideration of labeling methods. Self-reports, frequently utilized in studies including this one, provide direct insight into participants' feelings—acknowledging that individuals are the most reliable judges of their own emotions. However, self-reports are vulnerable to biases, memory limitations, and the Hawthorne effect, where participants alter their behavior due to observation. Alternative strategies, such as employing multiple external observers to classify emotions using predefined criteria, also hold merit. An example of this approach has been proposed by Baker, Rodrigo, and Ocumpaugh (Ocumpaugh, 2015). Finally, feedback mechanisms in affective tutoring systems must be thoughtfully designed. While offering feedback for specific emotions may seem simple, identifying the most suitable type and timing of feedback is essential for effectively managing students' emotional states. Additionally, for systems employing affective agents, designers must address the "uncanny valley" phenomenon, where artificial agents with highly humanlike features can provoke discomfort rather than fostering positive engagement (Mori, 2012). Further research is necessary to investigate these effects and to optimize emotion-based feedback strategies for tutoring systems.

4. Directions for Future Work

The field of affective tutoring in programming education presents numerous opportunities for exploration. In practice, learning systems are comprised of various sub-components that must collaborate seamlessly to effectively support students in their educational journey. This section delves into prospective research directions and outlines future areas of investigation within this domain.

4.1 Emotion Detection

Emotion detection becomes particularly challenging in domains where affect is displayed in a more limited and naturalistic manner. In the system discussed earlier, a model was implemented to detect confusion within a programming practice environment; however, this model has its limitations. Firstly, it only supports binary classification between two emotions: engagement and confusion. Other emotions, such as frustration and boredom, were excluded due to their infrequent occurrence in the training dataset. Secondly, the model's generalizability remains uncertain. An intriguing avenue for future research would be to examine whether the display of affect varies across different test subjects. While this seems likely based on the model's performance, it has not yet been empirically explored.

4.2 Feedback and Content Generation

Another promising research avenue involves identifying the most suitable types of feedback for specific learning scenarios. In educational contexts, feedback may take the form of motivational dialogue, hints, or other nudges aimed at regulating the student's emotional state. Investigating the impact of various feedback types on different emotional states could yield valuable insights. For motivational dialogues, it is essential to examine both the appropriate dialogue style and the level of interaction (i.e., how students might respond to such prompts). In the case of hints, considerations should include the nature of the hint and strategies for effective generation. These factors may vary depending on the domain (e.g., programming). Furthermore, the timing of feedback delivery warrants thorough exploration. Another intriguing research direction is the development of learning content customized to the student's emotional state. For example, if a student displays signs of boredom, content could be dynamically adapted to enhance engagement and maintain interest.

5. Conclusion

In this chapter, the integration of affective models to improve a learning system for programming was explored, showcasing the potential of emotionally adaptive systems to enhance students' learning experiences. Furthermore, the chapter outlined the capabilities of affective tutoring systems, as well as the challenges and prospective research opportunities in this domain.

Further Reading

For those seeking an in-depth examination of this research, the original study is highly recommended: [DOI= 10.1007/978-3-030-22244-4_4].

2 The Impact of Avatars Used in Online Education on Learning Effectiveness

1. Introduction

Over the past decade, education has experienced a significant transformation, with online learning environments becoming more immersive, interactive, and socially engaging. This evolution has been accompanied by the growing use of avatars, digital representations that act as visual, social, and psychological proxies in virtual spaces. Commonly featured not only in entertainment and gaming platforms but also in educational contexts, avatars enhance presence, facilitate communication, and enable identity exploration across cultural and geographical boundaries.

With the rise of accessible virtual platforms like Cluster, Mozilla Hubs, and VRChat, attending events in the metaverse has become a commonplace activity for many users. From academic conferences and art exhibitions to university open days and social gatherings, individuals now frequently participate through avatars from remote locations. These platforms enable real-time interaction, navigation of virtual spaces, and communication via embodied digital personas, opening up new avenues for engagement beyond the constraints of physical location. The COVID-19 pandemic notably accelerated the normalization of avatar-mediated interaction, solidifying virtual presence as a key feature of both academic and professional domains.

This widespread adoption of avatars for remote participation unlocks new opportunities for learning while presenting critical research challenges. Specifically, the characteristics of avatars, such as their appearance, behavior, and perceived personality, could significantly shape learners' experiences within virtual educational settings, especially in online or metaverse-based learning. Although avatars are known to enhance presence and motivation, the psychological and social dynamics they introduce are still not fully understood.

One promising avenue for examining these dynamics is the field of Human-Agent Interaction (HAI), which explores how people interact with artificial entities like virtual agents and avatars. Research in HAI has revealed that design elements such as gender, demeanor, and communication style in virtual agents can significantly impact users' trust, engagement, and learning outcomes. However, most existing studies have concentrated on avatars in instructional roles, like virtual tutors or animated educators. Less emphasis has been placed on avatars as peers or on the implications of learners embodying avatars themselves. Additionally, there is a notable gap in understanding how the perceived personality traits of avatars influence learning processes in social, collaborative, or metaverse-based educational environments.

DOI: 10.1201/9781003782735-3

This study seeks to fill this gap by investigating how avatar-based representations impact learners' engagement and performance in immersive learning environments. Specifically, it examines the effects of avatar personality traits on educational experiences, both during interactions with such avatars and when learners embody them. By exploring the intersection of avatar design, learner psychology, and virtual social presence, this research aims to advance the field of digital learning and Human-Agent Interaction (HAI), providing valuable insights into designing avatar-mediated education that fosters effective and inclusive learning in the metaverse.

2. Related Work and Theoretical Background

In recent years, immersive virtual learning environments have become increasingly prevalent, enabling learners to interact not only with content but also with one another through digital self-representations. As these environments continue to develop, understanding how learners engage with and are influenced by avatars, both their own and those of others, has become essential. This chapter examines the theoretical and empirical foundations of avatar-mediated learning, organized into five core areas: (1) avatars in educational environments, (2) social presence and affective learning, (3) human–agent interaction and pedagogical agents, (4) the Proteus effect and identity representation, and (5) a synthesis of research findings and existing gaps.

2.1 Avatars in Educational Environments

Avatars, digital embodiments of users in virtual environments, serve as more than mere visual proxies; they are socially and psychologically active elements of the learning process. In educational contexts, avatars enable learners to express their identity, participate socially, and foster a sense of presence. Embodying an avatar has been shown to enhance learner engagement, autonomy, and persistence in tasks, particularly within immersive and collaborative environments (Makransky & Mayer, 2022). The customization of avatars can further benefit learners, particularly when avatars embody aspirational or identity-affirming traits. For instance, research by Kao and Harrell (2017) revealed that students demonstrated deeper engagement with programming tasks when their avatars aligned with their cultural or gender identities. This personalization boosts motivation and helps reduce barriers, especially for underrepresented groups in STEM. Additionally, recent studies emphasize the importance of avatar personality and behavior extending beyond appearance. Kim and Baylor (2006) found that virtual agents perceived as conscientious or friendly fostered trust and team effectiveness in collaborative learning tasks. These findings underscore how avatar traits—whether chosen by learners or pre-assigned—can influence the social and cognitive dynamics of online education. In essence, avatars function as both identity constructs and social facilitators. They go beyond simply representing users, playing a vital role in shaping how learning experiences are perceived and navigated.

2.2 Social Presence and Affective Learning

One key function of avatars in educational environments is enhancing social presence, the sense of "being with others" in a mediated space (Short, Williams, & Christie, 1976). Social presence significantly influences learner satisfaction, motivation, and engagement. Avatars contribute to this by facilitating expressive interaction, spatial positioning, and behavioral realism (Biocca et al., 2001; Oh, Bailenson, & Welch, 2018).

Closely connected is the concept of affective learning, which examines how emotions impact attention, motivation, and information retention. Increasingly, research recognizes the critical role of emotion in learning. D'Mello and Graesser (2012) highlighted that during complex tasks, learners experience a dynamic range of emotions, curiosity, frustration, and confusion, among others. Systems like Affective AutoTutor, which monitor and respond to these emotional states, have shown improved learning outcomes by maintaining engagement through emotional regulation.

The theoretical foundation of affective computing further underscores these findings. Picard (1997) introduced the idea of building machines capable of recognizing and responding to human emotions. Hudlicka (2003) expanded on this by proposing frameworks for intelligent agents to model user emotions and adapt accordingly. These systems reduce frustration and foster emotional resilience, especially in self-paced or feedback-intensive environments.

As such, avatars and emotionally responsive agents not only enhance cognitive outcomes but also promote learners' psychological well-being and foster a sense of connectedness.

2.3 Human–Agent Interaction and Pedagogical Agents

Human-Agent Interaction (HAI) examines how individuals engage with artificial intelligence agents, frequently represented as avatars, in instructional settings. In educational research, these agents may serve as instructors, mentors, or peers. Although the distinction between avatars (controlled by users) and agents (autonomous entities) is valuable, both impact learner behavior by leveraging social signaling, behavioral modeling, and perceived credibility.

Early research by Moreno et al. (2010) demonstrated that students achieved deeper learning when engaging with animated pedagogical agents compared to passive instruction. The inclusion of social cues, such as eye contact, voice inflection, or gestures, stimulated more active cognitive processing, a phenomenon termed the social agency effect.

Baylor and Kim (2004) expanded on this by identifying distinct pedagogical roles for agents: expert, motivator, and mentor. Their study highlighted that factors like agent gender, demeanor, and role significantly influenced learners' outcomes and attitudes. Further research by Kim and Baylor (2006) revealed that relatable agents (e.g., those aligned with a learner's gender or ethnicity) enhanced motivation, particularly for students from underrepresented groups.

However, these effects are complex. Kim and Baylor (2006) also noted that learners' perceptions of agent authority were shaped by gender cues, potentially reflecting internalized cultural biases. Krämer, Simons, and Kopp (2007) found that nonverbal behaviors, such as warmth and rapport-building, were pivotal in fostering learner receptiveness, regardless of gender.

In a study of stereotype threat in virtual math instruction, Chang, Luo, Walton, Aguilar, and Bailenson (2019) found that female students subjected to sexist nonverbal behaviors from a male instructor avatar performed notably worse compared to those taught by neutral avatars. This supports Steele's (2011) assertion that environmental cues, referred to as identity contingencies, can signal exclusion and adversely affect academic performance.

Positive effects can also emerge from counter-stereotypical modeling. Rosenberg-Kima et al. (2008) found that young women engaging with competent, relatable female agents in STEM fields experienced increased self-efficacy and interest. Likewise, Bages, Martinot, and Marine (2016) showed that narratives featuring successful female role models improved girls' math performance and emotional engagement.

Together, these findings highlight that the traits of agents and avatars impact learning through both affective and social-cognitive mechanisms, with gender serving as a central yet context-dependent factor.

2.4 The Proteus Effect and Identity Representation

The Proteus effect, introduced by Yee and Bailenson (2007), describes how individuals unconsciously adjust their behaviors to align with the traits or stereotypes associated with their avatars. For instance, users given taller or more attractive avatars often exhibit more assertive or social behaviors, reflecting internalized social expectations.

This phenomenon holds particular significance in education. Learners embodying avatars characterized by traits like diligence, attentiveness, or professionalism may internalize these attributes and demonstrate enhanced academic engagement (Yee & Bailenson, 2007). In immersive environments, where visual embodiment is reinforced through real-time interactions, such shifts in identity can positively impact motivation, confidence, and performance.

However, the extent of the Proteus effect is influenced by context and user expectations. Chang et al. (2019) noted that changing learners' avatars could not counteract the adverse effects of stereotype-driven environments; the behaviors of surrounding avatars (e.g., biased instructors) played a more substantial role. This highlights the importance of social dynamics, which extend beyond self-representation in shaping the learner experience.

The Proteus effect also aligns with broader theories, such as Bem's (1972) self-perception theory and Tajfel and Turner's (2004) social identity theory, which suggest that individuals adapt their attitudes and actions based on observed or implied roles. In educational design, this emphasizes the potential of avatar manipulation to support identity but also underscores the risk of unintentionally reinforcing negative stereotypes.

Steele (2011) argued that learners thrive when their environment conveys respect and anticipates their success, a concept known as identity safety. By implementing inclusive avatar systems that encourage diverse self-expression and showcase equitable role models, designers can foster psychological safety, thereby enhancing cognitive and emotional learning outcomes.

2.5 Summary and Research Gap

The reviewed literature highlights that avatars and virtual agents significantly impact learning through mechanisms like social presence, emotional engagement, self-perception, and identity representation. Far from neutral tools, avatars convey social cues, model behaviors, and shape how learners perceive themselves and others.

Notably, the gender, personality, and behavioral traits of avatars play a critical role in influencing learner responses, which vary based on identity, subject matter, and social context. Some learners benefit from avatars that mirror their characteristics, while others are motivated by avatars demonstrating competence, authority, or empathy.

Despite the depth of existing research, key gaps persist. Most studies have concentrated on instructor agents or explored short-term effects in controlled settings. Limited attention has been given to peer avatars or co-present avatars with diverse personalities, particularly within collaborative, open-ended, or metaverse-based educational environments.This study addresses these gaps by examining the influence of nearby avatars' personality traits, such as diligence or disengagement, on learners' academic engagement and performance. It also investigates how these social dynamics intersect with learner identities and behaviors. By leveraging foundational theories, the study aims to contribute meaningful insights toward designing socially responsive, emotionally intelligent, and inclusive avatar-based learning frameworks.

3. Methodology

This chapter details the methodology used to explore how the personality traits of avatars, both self-embodied and co-present, impact learners' academic performance, motivation, and sense of identification in metaverse-based educational settings. Anchored in Human–Agent Interaction theories and the Proteus effect, the study investigates the psychological outcomes of embodying various avatar personalities and the effects of adjacent avatars exhibiting contrasting behaviors. A controlled virtual classroom, built using the Cluster platform, served as the setting for participants' engagement in two learning sessions across diverse experimental conditions and academic disciplines.

3.1 Experimental Platform and Environment

The experiment utilized the metaverse platform Cluster, selected for its accessibility and compatibility with custom-built environments developed through Unity and the Cluster Creator Kit. These tools facilitated the creation of a highly controlled yet immersive learning environment, allowing precise manipulation of avatar positioning, behavioral scripts, and instructional media. Participants were placed in a specially designed virtual classroom that simulated a standard online lecture setting. In this environment, they were assigned avatars representing either distinct personality traits or a neutral role, positioned near another avatar with defined characteristics. The learning sessions featured virtual lectures delivered by a teacher avatar, followed by post-lesson comprehension tests and self-report questionnaires. The setup was carefully designed to foster focus while maintaining ecological validity for metaverse-based educational scenarios.

3.2 Experimental Design

The study adopted a within-subjects design, where each participant was exposed to two of the four experimental conditions. These conditions were crafted to analyze the impact of avatar embodiment and the social influence of nearby avatars. The four conditions were as follows:

- **Diligent Avatar Condition**: Participants embodied an avatar characterized as conscientious, responsible, and high-performing.
- **Lazy Avatar Condition**: Participants embodied an avatar depicted as distracted, unmotivated, and academically underachieving.
- **Near-Diligent Avatar Condition**: Participants embodied a neutral avatar seated next to an avatar exhibiting diligent behavior.
- **Near-Lazy Avatar Condition**: Participant embodied a neutral avatar seated next to an avatar displaying disengaged behaviors.

The adjacent avatars' personality traits were conveyed through scripted dialogue and nonverbal cues but did not involve direct interaction with participants during the instructional phases. Participants attended two distinct learning sessions, each involving a different avatar, condition and academic subject. To account for potential order effects and subject-specific biases, the sequence of conditions and subjects was counterbalanced across participants. The chosen academic domains, mathematics and biology, were selected to represent varying cognitive demands and sensitivities to stereotypes.

3.3 Participants

Forty-three participants were involved in the experiment, comprising 27 males and 16 females, aged between 16 and 23 years ($M = 19.86$, $SD = 1.29$). All participants were either university students or recent graduates, recruited through academic mailing lists and social platforms. Eligibility criteria specified that participants should lack advanced prior knowledge of the instructional topics and possess basic familiarity with 3D navigation in digital environments. To ensure comparability across conditions, participants completed a brief questionnaire regarding their gaming experience and prior exposure to virtual platforms. Each participant undertook two experimental sessions, with each session featuring a distinct avatar condition and subject domain. Assignments to specific condition pairs were randomized and counterbalanced to mitigate systematic biases.

3.4 Learning Content and Instructional Procedure

The mathematics content centered on modular arithmetic, chosen for its conceptual difficulty and its relevance to documented stereotype threat effects among female learners. This instruction was followed by a true-or-false comprehension test consisting of 30 items, administered within a five-minute time limit. In contrast, the biology content focused on deep-sea organisms, a neutral academic subject selected to minimize domain-specific anxieties. The associated test also included 30 true-or-false items, but with a three-minute limit.

Instruction for both subjects was delivered via pre-recorded video lectures, presented by a teacher avatar. To avoid confounding variables linked to gender or species-based stereotype associations, the teacher avatar was designed as a non-human figure—typically a dog or another neutral character. Participants attended the lecture while seated in the virtual classroom and subsequently moved to the testing area to complete the comprehension assessments.

Before each session, participants received a brief description of the avatar's personality traits and behaviors. For Near-Avatar conditions, this included observing a scripted monologue or a demonstration of the adjacent avatar's behavior. After this initial exposure, participants completed a self-efficacy questionnaire and a short measure assessing their identification with the assigned avatar or their learning role. Following the instructional phase and comprehension test, a final questionnaire explored their experiences with the avatar interaction, perceived lesson difficulty, and subjective feelings of motivation and presence.

3.5 Measures

Multiple data points were collected to evaluate the impact of avatar personality conditions. Learning performance was measured using comprehension test scores, which reflected the number of correct answers in subject-specific quizzes. To assess motivational beliefs, participants completed a self-efficacy scale adapted from the General Self-Efficacy Scale (Schwarzer & Jerusalem, 1995). Psychological alignment between learners and their assigned avatars was examined through an avatar identification scale, adapted from Rosenberg-Kima et al. (2008). Additionally, participants' individual personality traits were assessed using the Japanese version of the Ten Item Personality Inventory (TIPI-J), designed to capture the Big Five dimensions.

These measures facilitated the analysis of both primary effects of avatar personality and potential interaction effects between participant traits and avatar conditions.

3.6 Procedure

Each participant took part in two experimental sessions conducted consecutively within a single sitting. At the start of the first session, participants underwent a tutorial on navigating the virtual environment using their assigned avatar. Following this, they completed a pre-experiment questionnaire that gathered demographic information, assessed their prior experience with virtual environments, and measured baseline personality traits.

Following the tutorial, participants were introduced to the avatar condition for that session. In the embodiment conditions, they adopted an avatar with predefined personality traits. In the Near-Avatar conditions, participants retained a neutral role but were exposed to the behavioral cues of a nearby avatar. This exposure included a brief scripted interaction or observable behavior, designed to establish the personality of the co-present avatar. Participants then moved on to the instructional phase, where they attended a short lecture delivered by the teacher avatar. After the lesson, they proceeded to a separate virtual room to complete the comprehension test. Upon finishing the test, participants completed questionnaires evaluating their self-efficacy, identification with the avatar, and overall impressions of the learning experience.

The second session followed the same structure as the first, but utilized a different avatar condition and subject domain. This design enabled the investigation of within-subject differences across conditions while effectively reducing carry-over effects.

4. Results

This chapter presents the study's findings derived from statistical analyses of test performance, self-efficacy, and avatar identification across the four avatar personality conditions. The data were examined to investigate both the primary effects of avatar personality traits and the moderating influences of learner characteristics, such as gender and dimensions of the Big Five personality model.

Participants' comprehension test scores varied across the four avatar conditions. In both academic domains, mathematics and biology, the Diligent Avatar Condition produced the highest average scores, while the Lazy Avatar Condition yielded the lowest. Participants in the Near-Diligent Avatar Condition outperformed those in the Near-Lazy Avatar Condition, though the difference was less pronounced than in the embodiment conditions. These findings indicate that avatar personality traits, whether embodied or co-present, can impact academic performance in virtual learning environments.

Regarding self-efficacy, while descriptive trends aligned with test scores, no statistically significant differences emerged across avatar conditions in mathematics

($p = 0.61$) or biology ($p = 0.41$). This suggests that although participants might have subjectively perceived variations in confidence or engagement, these differences did not meet statistical thresholds required for interpretation as robust effects.

In terms of avatar identification, no significant correlation was observed between conscientiousness and identification in the Diligent Avatar Condition. However, in the Near-Diligent Avatar Condition, particularly within the biology subject, a moderate positive correlation emerged between conscientiousness and identification scores. No notable effects were identified for openness to experience in any condition. Additionally, in the mathematics domain, no statistically significant differences in identification scores were found across avatar conditions. While some participants, especially those with low neuroticism, reported a sense of mismatch when embodying the lazy avatar, these observations were anecdotal and lacked quantitative significance. Furthermore, the single-item measure for avatar identification limited its reliability and interpretive depth. An exploratory analysis of gender revealed no statistically significant interaction effects between avatar condition and participant sex. Although some trends indicated that female participants might have reported lower self-efficacy or test scores in the Lazy or Near-Lazy Avatar Conditions, these patterns were not supported by inferential statistics and should be interpreted with caution. Further research is necessary to determine whether such tendencies represent consistent gender-based sensitivity to avatar-mediated social cues.

Lastly, the analysis of personality traits highlighted a noteworthy finding regarding openness to experience. Among participants with low openness, a significant performance difference was observed in mathematics between the Near-Diligent and Near-Lazy Avatar Conditions. Specifically, participants with lower openness performed significantly better when seated near a diligent avatar compared to a lazy one. This suggests that individuals with lower openness, who may have a preference for predictability and structure, are more responsive to social modeling cues in immersive settings. No comparable patterns were detected among participants with high openness.

5. Discussion

This chapter examines the implications of the experimental findings, integrating them with established theories and prior research in educational technology, Human–Agent Interaction (HAI), and avatar-mediated learning. It begins with a concise review of the key results, followed by an analysis of their significance within the frameworks of the Proteus effect, social modeling, learner identity, and individual differences.

5.1 Summary of Findings

Learners with low openness to experience showed a statistically significant improvement in mathematics performance when placed in the Near-Diligent

Avatar Condition compared to the Near-Lazy condition. This finding highlights a potentially valuable interaction between personality traits and avatar-mediated social cues.

The study investigated how avatar personality traits, whether embodied by the learner or co-present, affect learning outcomes within a virtual classroom environment. While comprehension test scores were generally higher in the Diligent Avatar and Near-Diligent Avatar Conditions and lower in the Lazy Avatar and Near-Lazy Avatar Conditions, these differences were not statistically significant for the overall participant sample. As such, while the observed trends suggest the potential influence of avatar context on performance, they remain inconclusive.

Self-efficacy ratings, gathered through self-reports, similarly did not show statistically significant differences across avatar conditions. Although some descriptive trends hinted at a subjective increase in confidence in diligent contexts, these patterns were not statistically robust.

Regarding avatar identification, most conditions demonstrated stable, moderate levels of identification. However, a notable exception was observed in the Near-Diligent Avatar Condition during the biology task, where a moderate positive correlation emerged between conscientiousness and avatar identification. No significant effects were found for openness to experience, and there were no significant differences in identification scores across avatar conditions in the mathematics domain.

5.2 Implications for Avatar-Mediated Learning

These findings contribute to the existing literature on the Proteus effect (Yee & Bailenson, 2007), which posits that individuals internalize the traits of their avatars and adjust their behavior accordingly. While prior research has primarily emphasized direct embodiment, the present study highlights that simply being in proximity to an avatar exhibiting high or low diligence can also shape learner outcomes. This observation aligns with Bandura's (1977) social modeling theory, which suggests that individuals learn not only through self-perception but also by observing and interpreting the behaviors and intentions of others. The results also highlight the concept of social presence, a learner's perceived sense of "being with others" in a mediated space, which is a critical component of virtual learning environments (Short et al., 1976; Biocca et al., 2001). In line with these theories, the presence of a diligent, peer-like avatar may have created a socially facilitative atmosphere that increased learners' attention, motivation, and perception of academic norms, even without direct interaction. These effects were especially pronounced among individuals low in openness, learners who often seek external structure or behavioral cues to guide their actions. This underscores the potential of avatar-mediated contexts to scaffold engagement for students who might otherwise face challenges in less structured environments.

Regarding **avatar identification**, while the study did not reveal widespread statistical effects, the moderate correlation between conscientiousness and identification in the Near-Diligent Biology condition underscores the idea that alignment between user traits and avatar cues can enhance psychological engagement. This finding supports previous research on agent-persona congruence (Baylor & Kim, 2004; Rosenberg-Kima et al., 2008), which suggests that learners identify more strongly and are more motivated when avatars reflect their own personality traits or values, especially in educational contexts.

5.3 Designing for Individual Differences

The finding that learners low in openness benefited most from the Near-Diligent condition highlights the potential of personalizing **avatar environments** to support diverse learners effectively. This aligns with Hudlicka's (2003) research on affective modeling, which emphasizes the importance of designing systems that dynamically respond to users' emotional and cognitive profiles. Tailoring virtual contexts to align with learners' dispositions can improve not only cognitive performance but also emotional resilience and sustained engagement.

This insight also suggests the feasibility of adaptive avatar systems that modify peer behaviors or presence based on individual learner profiles. For instance, learners with low openness may thrive in structured settings with high-achieving peer avatars, whereas those with high openness might excel in exploratory environments that encourage autonomy and creativity.

Such design implications are particularly significant for **metaverse-based education**, where elements like spatial positioning, avatar behavior, and identity flexibility can be adjusted in real time. Incorporating socially supportive avatars, whether embodied by learners or co-present, offers an affordable yet impactful method for creating inclusive and psychologically safe environments, where learners feel respected and supported in their identities (Steele, 2011), as well as emotionally engaging contexts that maintain motivation and cognitive effort (D'Mello & Graesser, 2012).

5.4 Reconsidering the Role of Self-Efficacy

While self-efficacy is frequently regarded as a reliable predictor of academic success, shaping learners' effort, persistence, and engagement (Bandura, 1977), it can also be influenced by the design of intelligent learning environments that respond to learner emotions and behavior (McQuiggan et al., 2008). However, its lack of statistical variation across conditions in this study warrants further consideration. One possibility is that the single-task structure or short-term exposure constrained the emergence of differences in this variable. Alternatively, the effects of avatars might exert a stronger influence on behavioral or affective outcomes rather than on self-reported efficacy measures.

Future research could benefit from adopting longitudinal designs, incorporating physiological indicators of engagement (e.g., heart rate variability), or utilizing more detailed self-efficacy instruments. Such approaches could provide deeper insights into subtle shifts in learners' confidence and resilience within avatar-mediated environments.

5.5 Implications for the Design of Metaverse-Based Learning Environments

The findings of this study provide valuable guidance for shaping future educational experiences within the metaverse. As virtual spaces become increasingly interactive, immersive, and socially dynamic, the behavioral and psychological roles of avatars must be recognized as central to instructional design, moving beyond aesthetic or technical considerations. First, the results support the notion that avatar-based social cues, such as diligence or disengagement, can influence learning outcomes not only through self-embodiment but also via co-presence. Incorporating purposefully modeled peer avatars into virtual classrooms can promote social norms, offer subtle guidance, and enhance learners' sense of structure and motivation. Notably, these peer avatars do not necessarily need to engage directly with learners; their mere presence and demeanor can act as environmental scaffolds.

Second, the interaction between avatar conditions and personality traits, particularly openness to experience, points to the promise of adaptive personalization for future systems. Metaverse-based learning platforms could dynamically tailor or recommend avatar configurations (e.g., diligent peer presence, collaborative partner, autonomous learner mode) based on user profiles, affective states, or learning goals. This approach mirrors advancements in **affective and intelligent tutoring systems** (D'Mello & Graesser, 2012; Hudlicka, 2003) while extending these innovations to the identity-rich realm of the metaverse.

Moreover, it is crucial for educators and designers to consider the sociocultural signals conveyed by avatar features, including gender, race, posture, and expression. As prior research has shown, such features can serve as implicit cues that either affirm or threaten learners' identities (Chang et al., 2019; Bages et al., 2016). For instance, biased nonverbal behavior by avatars has been shown to hinder academic performance among female students (Chang et al., 2019), while relatable role models can enhance motivation and engagement (Bages et al., 2016). These elements can activate stereotype threat or identity contingencies, especially for underrepresented groups.

In conclusion, effective metaverse learning environments should integrate socially expressive avatars, adaptive personalization systems, and thoughtfully modeled peer interactions to foster educational spaces that are psychologically attuned and pedagogically impactful.

5.6 Limitations and Future Directions

Although the present study provides valuable insights into avatar-mediated learning, several limitations must be considered.

First, the sample size (n = 43), while sufficient for preliminary exploration, reduces the statistical power to detect smaller effects and complex interactions (e.g., gender × condition × personality). Future research should aim to replicate this design with larger, more diverse populations, including international participants and learners from varied educational backgrounds and levels.

Second, the experimental sessions were short and focused exclusively on mathematics and biology. Although these subjects were chosen for their contrasting emotional and cognitive demands, the findings may not generalize to other domains, such as language learning or creative fields. Moreover, all avatars were scripted and non-interactive; future studies could investigate the effects of more dynamic or conversational avatars.

Third, some dependent variables, particularly **avatar identification and self-efficacy**, were assessed using brief self-report measures, which may not capture the full depth of psychological constructs. Employing multi-item validated scales, behavioral engagement metrics, or biometric indicators (e.g., eye-tracking, galvanic skin response) could yield more robust measures of learning experiences in future research. Another limitation relates to the **cultural specificity** of the study. Conducted within a Japanese-language version of Cluster, the avatars were designed to align with cultural norms, enhancing ecological validity for the target population but potentially limiting cross-cultural applicability.

Looking forward, several promising research directions emerge. Longitudinal studies could explore the sustained effects of avatar presence and personality on engagement and learning retention. Adaptive avatar ecosystems, capable of responding to learners' behaviors and preferences in real time, could transform immersive education. Lastly, ethical and psychological considerations around avatar manipulation, such as the reinforcement of stereotypes or over-reliance on artificial cues, warrant deeper investigation.

6. Conclusion

This study explored the impact of avatar personality traits, whether embodied by the learner or co-present in virtual environments, on educational experiences in metaverse-based settings. Grounded in theories of Human–Agent Interaction, the Proteus effect, and social modeling, the research examined how avatar behavior might influence learning through subtle social cues.

Although most performance differences across avatar conditions were not statistically significant, a notable pattern emerged: learners low in openness to experience exhibited significantly better performance in mathematics when seated near a diligent avatar compared to a lazy one. This underscores how even non-interactive avatars can act as quiet yet effective influences on learning behaviors, particularly for students who benefit from structured environments and social modeling.

This phenomenon mirrors everyday classroom dynamics. For instance, a student who is cautious or less inquisitive may benefit simply by sitting next to a focused, motivated peer. Similarly, virtual learners can be affected by the presence and demeanor of nearby avatars, even if those avatars are not actual people.

These findings emphasize that avatars can be more than just decorative or self-expressive tools. Thoughtful avatar design has the potential to foster motivation, communicate academic norms, and create psychologically supportive learning spaces. As the metaverse continues to evolve, this opens new avenues for crafting educational experiences that are not only immersive but also socially intelligent.

Column 1: Gender and Virtual Learning Environments

Subtitle: How Avatar Gender Affects Motivation, Confidence, and Inclusion in Digital Classrooms

In virtual classrooms, avatar gender extends beyond simply reflecting a learner's identity; it can actively shape how others perceive and interact with them. Research demonstrates that the perceived gender of an avatar can significantly impact learners' motivation, engagement, and academic performance.

The Gender Perception Effect in Education

Research indicates the following trends:

- Male avatars are frequently linked to authority and expertise in STEM disciplines (Yee & Bailenson, 2007).
- Female avatars, particularly as role models, can bolster self-efficacy and confidence among female learners in STEM fields (Kao & Harrell, 2017).
- However, studies also reveal that female avatars are occasionally perceived as less authoritative in subjects traditionally dominated by males (Moreno et al., 2010).

Beyond Binary Gender: Customization and Identity in the Metaverse

Avatars in the metaverse differ from static agents in traditional systems through their high degree of customization. This opens doors to more inclusive and personalized educational experiences:

- The use of gender-neutral or self-selected avatars may help learners reduce stereotype threat, addressing biases prevalent in STEM education.
- Empowering students to choose avatars that reflect their identity or aspirations can increase engagement and improve learning outcomes.
- Future educational platforms can incorporate avatars that dynamically adapt in voice, appearance, and interaction style, fostering inclusivity and meeting diverse learner preferences.

Implications for Future Learning Design

Building on these insights, educational system designers should:

- Offer diverse and customizable avatar options to accommodate varied learner identities and promote personalization.
- Present avatars in ways that counter stereotypes, fostering equity and a sense of belonging among learners.
- Investigate cultural and individual perceptions of avatars, advancing beyond binary gender frameworks.

As technology progresses, gender-neutral AI tutors and adaptive avatars may pave the way for learning environments that engage all learners, regardless of gender or background.

Column 2: The Future of Learning in the Metaverse

Subtitle: Beyond Avatars, Creating Intelligent and Adaptive Learning Ecosystems

While avatars remain central to the metaverse, the future of education lies in the development of fully adaptive, emotionally responsive ecosystems, moving beyond static digital representations and paving the way for immersive, personalized learning experiences.

AI-Driven Tutors and Affective Learning

Research in affective computing (Picard, 1997) highlights that emotionally responsive systems enhance both attention and retention. When applied to education in the metaverse these advancements offer transformative potential:

- AI-powered tutor avatars can tailor their teaching styles to learners' expressions, tone of voice, and interaction behavior.
- Emotionally responsive avatars have the ability to detect student engagement levels, dynamically adjusting pacing and encouragement to sustain motivation.
- Tools like eye-tracking and biometric feedback can identify signs of confusion or frustration, enabling timely interventions to prevent disengagement.

Expanding Learning Beyond the Classroom

The future of education in the metaverse will embrace multi-sensory and immersive experiences, including:

- *Interactive Simulations:* Virtual labs providing a safe environment for students to perform science experiments without real-world risks.
- *Immersive History:* First-person experiences of historical events, fostering deeper emotional and intellectual connections.
- *AI-Powered Research Agents:* Virtual assistants capable of helping students gather, summarize, and analyze information in real time streamlining the learning process.

Bridging the Physical and Digital Divide

To ensure metaverse education is accessible to all learners, the following strategies should be implemented:

- Develop cloud-based platforms optimized for low-bandwidth connections, making virtual education viable in areas with limited internet access.
- Support multiple input methods, including voice, text, and gesture, to facilitate inclusive and diverse participation.
- Promote affordability of AR/VR hardware, ensuring students in underserved communities have access to immersive learning tools.

Conclusion: A Metaverse Education for Everyone

Metaverse-based education has the potential to transcend novelty and become an essential aspect of learning. By integrating adaptive AI tutors, emotionally intelligent avatars, and immersive learning tools, we can build an educational future that is inclusive, personalized, and globally accessible.

3 Emotion-Driven Story Generation for Game-Based Learning in Virtual Environments

1. Introduction

Game-based learning, known for its interactivity and immersive environments, enhances education by enabling active engagement with content rather than passive consumption. Widely applied in training simulations, STEM, and language learning, game-based learning has been shown to improve learner engagement and conceptual understanding by leveraging real-world scenario simulations to foster deeper understanding (Kapp, 2012; Plass et al., 2020).

While game-based systems often excel in incorporating user actions and decisions, they frequently overlook the empirically supported role of emotions in shaping learning outcomes, memory, and self-reflection (Pekrun, 2006; D'Mello & Graesser, 2013). Emotions significantly impact cognition, influencing attention, motivation, and retention (Immordino-Yang & Damasio, 2007). Studies in affective computing and educational psychology show that emotionally charged experiences foster stronger memory and deeper engagement (Picard, 1997; Brierley et al., 2007; Ferré et al., 2015). However, the integration of real-time emotional tracking in educational games remains limited.

This study explores how real-time emotional and behavioral data can enhance learning in virtual environments. It presents an emotion-driven story generation system that captures players' emotions and actions to generate personalized narratives. Using technologies like Affdex and the Facial Action Coding System (FACS) (Ekman & Friesen, 1977; Magdin & Prikler, 2017) alongside Oculus Touch controllers, the system dynamically creates stories influenced by user interactions (Sumi & Sato, 2022).

The study examines whether reviewing emotionally enriched experiences enhances self-reflection and learning. It focuses on how emotion-informed narrative feedback affects learners' memory retention and engagement.

The research has two key goals: developing an interactive story generation system that crafts dynamic narratives based on users' actions and emotions, and assessing whether reviewing emotional and behavioral histories enhances reflection and long-term learning. By integrating experiential learning with emotional feedback and narrative review, it explores how real-time emotion tracking can enrich game-based education.

DOI: 10.1201/9781003782735-4

2. Related Work

This section highlights prior research on emotion-driven storytelling in game-based learning, focusing on three key areas: automatic story generation systems, emotional integration in interactive systems, and the use of affective computing in education.

2.1 Automatic Story Generation and Interactive Narratives

Early story generation systems like TALE-SPIN relied on rule-based methods and fixed plot structures, achieving coherence but lacking emotional depth or interaction (Dehn, 1981). Later innovations included systems like Dramatica (Anne & Huntley, 2004), which served as a narrative design framework rather than an interactive engine, and Façade (Mateas & Stern, 2003), which enabled player-driven narratives but offered limited emotional adaptation. Critical reviews, including Sousa (2000), emphasized challenges in achieving meaningful creativity in early AI-driven models like BRUTUS. Recent advancements in narrative generation have introduced planning-based methods for adaptive storylines. To support more adaptive and emotionally resonant narratives, Chang and Soo (2009) developed a planning framework for game narratives, introducing a structure capable of dynamic story progression. Building on this, Hernández et al. (2014) applied artificial intelligence techniques to generate emotion-driven stories, enabling characters and events to reflect users' affective states. León and Gervás (2014) emphasized creativity in non-deterministic, simulation-driven narratives, paving the way for personalized dynamic stories, though real-time emotional adaptation remains rare.

2.2 Emotion in Interactive Systems and Games

Affective computing has advanced interactive storytelling by enabling systems to detect and respond to emotions (Picard, 1997). Tools like Affective AutoTutor (D'Mello & Graesser, 2013) use emotionally intelligent dialogue to boost motivation and cognition. Emotional input has been shown to affect narrative agents' behaviors (Cavazza et al., 2009) and shape dynamic storylines through character emotions (Kaptein & Broekens, 2015). Emotion-aware systems often rely on scripted responses or generic emotional input. Passive interaction models (Gilroy et al., 2012) and affective characters (Neill & Riedl, 2016) expanded design possibilities but focused on NPC emotions over learners' experiences. Yannakakis and Togelius (2011) proposed experience-driven procedural content generation, using player feedback to adjust game elements, but most implementations focus on optimizing gameplay difficulty or pacing rather than integrating emotional content into narrative structures. As a result, its application to narrative learning for emotional reflection remains limited.

2.3 Emotion Recognition in Educational Contexts

Emotional engagement plays a vital role in memory and motivation (Pekrun, 2006; Immordino-Yang & Damasio, 2007), and systems utilizing emotional recognition via facial, physiological, or behavioral cues are gaining attention for personalized instruction (Kotsia et al., 2016; Magdin & Prikler, 2017). This is because emotions modulate attention and cognitive processing, making emotionally charged experiences more memorable and engaging. However, most systems focus on adjusting pacing or difficulty based on stress levels rather than fostering emotional reflection. For instance, Booth (2009) explored emotion-driven AI in *Left 4 Dead*, which adapted enemy behavior but excluded narrative content. Similarly, affective gaming environments emphasize gameplay dynamics over reflective learning (Kotsia et al., 2016). While Kolb's (2014) experiential learning highlights the importance of reflection, linking emotional experiences to narrative review for education remains underdeveloped. This is partly because most systems prioritize cognitive outcomes or gameplay dynamics, rather than supporting learners in processing and interpreting their own emotional journeys. Research shows that emotional framing enhances recall (Brierley et al., 2007; Ferré et al., 2015; Schmidt, 2012), but applying this in real-time personalized learning is still a challenge.

2.4 Research Gap and Direction

Although story generation, affective computing, and emotion-aware education offer valuable insights, few systems integrate these elements into a unified framework for reflective, emotion-driven learning. This study aims to address this gap by combining real-time emotional tracking with story generation to foster reflection, memory retention, and engagement through personalized narratives.

3. A Game-Based Story Generation System for Emotion-Driven Reflective Learning in Virtual Spaces

This chapter introduces a system that integrates game-based experiential learning with emotion-driven story generation to create an immersive, reflective virtual environment. By recording and transforming learners' emotional and behavioral data into personalized narratives, the system promotes reflection, self-awareness, and memory retention.

3.1 System Overview and Architecture

The system integrates a virtual learning environment with a lightweight, real-time narrative engine. Within the environment, players explore emotionally evocative scenarios, interact with objects such as vending machines and unusual creatures, and make decisions that elicit affective responses. During gameplay, facial expressions are recorded using Affdex and the Facial Action Coding System (FACS), capturing seven core emotions, namely joy, fear, anger, sadness, surprise, disgust, and contempt. Simultaneously, Oculus Touch controllers log physical actions like grasping or throwing items.

A key feature of the system is its ability to generate short, emotionally resonant narratives that reflect the learner's in-game behaviors and affective states. The narrative engine uses a template-based text generation approach, mapping specific emotion labels to descriptive modifiers such as adverbs or metaphors. For example, retrieving a drink while surprised might yield the sentence: "You nervously took the cola out of the vending machine, unsure of what would happen next." These simple narrative templates are selected and customized based on variables such as object type, emotion intensity, and interaction sequence.

By connecting actions to feelings through emotionally tagged narratives, the system encourages learners to reflect on their decisions and emotional responses. This integration supports deeper self-awareness, emotional learning, and memory retention.

3.2 Design of the Virtual Environment

The virtual space resembles a realistic office with an open workspace and break room, offering familiar yet flexible settings for exploration. While rooted in everyday realism, it incorporates fantastical elements to inspire curiosity and interaction. A key aspect of the space includes interactive objects like a vending machine, desk, and copy machine, allowing players to engage in diverse ways that evoke emotional and behavioral outcomes.

The environment includes a "Black Hole" mechanic inspired by the short film The Black Hole. Players can use this tool at any time during gameplay to access objects inside otherwise unreachable spaces, such as taking a drink or coins from a vending machine, or retrieving hidden items from inside machines and furniture.

The system does not assign moral value to the use of the Black Hole. Instead, it passively records how players use it and what emotions accompany those interactions. For example, a player might use the Black Hole to extract an item and then express surprise or fear after accidentally grabbing a cockroach. These emotionally marked moments are recorded and reflected back to the player in narrative form.

This interplay between object manipulation and emotional shifts forms the core of the system's reflective learning model, weaving actions and emotions into a narrative that captures both what players did and how they felt.

3.3 Learning Through Emotion and Behavior

A key feature of the system is recording players' emotional and behavioral histories to enhance reflection, self-awareness, and long-term learning. By reviewing the automatically generated narrative logs, based on synchronized in-game actions and facial emotion data, learners can identify decision-making patterns and emotional tendencies, such as cautious reactions to uncertainty.

Emotional memory research indicates that strongly emotional experiences enhance retention compared to neutral ones. By embedding emotion-linked events, such as retrieving an unexpected object or reacting with fear or joy, into first-person narratives, the system reinforces cognitive connections and fosters durable learning.

Additionally, decision-making in the game environment promotes critical thinking, encouraging players to evaluate consequences, explore options, and reflect on their motivations for deeper understanding.

3.4 Benefits and Challenges

The system enhances engagement and personalization by tailoring narratives to each learner's actions and emotions. By generating unique stories based on real-time data, this individualized approach boosts motivation and immersion, as learners see the story as a reflection of their journey.

Narrative reviews further encourage self-awareness and deepen connection to the content. However, challenges remain, such as ensuring narrative coherence across diverse emotional inputs and managing data privacy in affect-sensitive systems.

4. Experiment

This chapter outlines an experiment evaluating the effectiveness of an emotion-driven story generation system. It focused on enhancing player engagement, self-reflection, and memory retention. Eighteen male computer science students, aged 22 to 25, participated, with no prior experience in emotion-based storytelling. Each 30–40 minute session included a briefing on the experiment's structure and voluntary participation. None opted to withdraw.

4.1 Experimental Procedure and Setup

The experiment was conducted in a lab with a desktop computer, Oculus Touch controllers, and a webcam for emotion recognition. The virtual office environment included interactive features like a vending machine, desk, documents, and a "magical tool" for retrieving items. Participants completed a five-minute tutorial to practice navigation, controller use, and tool operation, with no mention of emotion or story generation to avoid bias. Following the tutorial, participants engaged in a ten-minute free-play session, during which Affdex software recorded their facial expressions and the Oculus Touch controllers tracked their actions. Following the session, the system generated a personalized narrative based on the collected data. Participants reviewed the story to evaluate its accuracy in reflecting their experience, then completed a questionnaire and semantic differential (SD) ratings to assess the story's interest, emotional depiction, and reflection support.

4.2 Data Analysis and Observations

The study analyzed behavioral logs, emotional recordings, questionnaire responses, and SD ratings using descriptive statistics, chi-square tests, and factor analysis to uncover patterns. While participants found the system intuitive, some struggled with interactions like using the "magical tool" or identifying actions during the tutorial. Emotion detection was generally reliable, though neutral expressions were occasionally misclassified, which altered story tone. Most participants found the narratives engaging and reflective, aiding memory recall and increasing awareness of emotional patterns and decision-making tendencies. They felt more connected to the learning process and motivated to explore alternative actions. The results show that integrating real-time emotional and behavioral data into personalized narratives supports learning and fosters immersive educational experiences.

5. Results

This section outlines the experiment's findings on participants' engagement, memory retention, reflection, and overall learning experience with the game-based story generation system, based on questionnaire responses, SD ratings, and qualitative feedback.

5.1 Engagement and Story Experience

The study aimed to assess the system's ability to generate engaging, reflective stories. Questionnaire results showed that over 80% of participants felt the stories accurately captured their actions, and nearly 75% believed their emotions were effectively represented. Participants appreciated the personalization, with comments highlighting how the emotional inclusion made the experience feel unique and immersive. Semantic differential (SD) ratings confirmed the system's dynamic and emotionally engaging nature, offering a distinct experience compared to traditional games. However, some noted issues with facial emotion recognition, where neutral expressions were misclassified, which impacted narrative tone. Suggestions included enhancing emotion detection and expanding in-game object variety to enrich gameplay and story complexity.

5.2 Memory and Reflection

The experiment examined how emotionally annotated narratives supported memory recall and reflection. Nearly 90% of participants reported clearer recall of in-game events, attributing this to the inclusion of emotional details. One participant noted, "The story clearly reminded me of my reaction," highlighting how emotional context enhanced memory. Participants described the stories as immersive, not just action logs, with emotional elements creating realism and fostering reflection. Many recognized how emotions shaped their decisions, gaining insight into their behaviors. These findings align with research on emotional memory, showing that emotion-driven storytelling enhances recall and supports reflective learning.

5.3 Usability and Areas for Improvement

While participants found the system intuitive and engaging, some usability issues were noted. About one-third felt the tutorial lacked coverage of all possible actions, causing confusion during gameplay, particularly with the magical tool and gesture-based operations. Emotion recognition occasionally misclassified neutral expressions, slightly altering narrative tone. To improve, participants suggested enhancing the tutorial with demonstrations, refining emotion detection to capture subtle expressions, and expanding in-game objects and interactions.

Recommendations included adding branching story paths, more complex scenarios, and alternative environments to boost engagement and replayability. These insights provide clear directions for enhancing the system's educational potential.

5.4 Summary of Findings

The experimental results demonstrate that the system successfully created engaging, personalized narratives that enhanced emotional involvement and memory retention. Participants felt the stories reflected their in-game experiences, with emotional annotations adding authenticity and immersion. The study revealed that emotionally enriched storytelling fostered self-reflection, offering insights into decision-making and emotional responses, supporting both learning outcomes and metacognitive awareness. However, limitations were noted in tutorial design, emotion recognition accuracy, and interaction range. Participants expressed a desire to re-engage, provided these areas are improved. In conclusion, the emotion-driven system demonstrates promise in combining affective computing and experiential learning, with potential for further development to enhance reflection, engagement, and memory retention in virtual education.

6. Discussion

This section discusses the significance of the findings, positioning them within existing literature and theoretical frameworks, while also exploring broader implications, limitations, and future directions for emotion-driven game-based learning.

The results confirm that combining real-time emotion detection with behavior tracking enhances learning by fostering memory retention, self-reflection, and emotional engagement. These findings are consistent with prior research in affective computing (Picard, 1997), emotional memory (Brierley et al., 2007; Ferré et al., 2015), and experiential learning (Kolb, 2014).

Emotionally annotated narratives allowed participants to recall in-game events more vividly, suggesting that integrating emotional data with narrative structure strengthens the encoding of both affective and contextual information. This aligns with the neuroscience literature on amygdala-hippocampal interactions in emotional memory (Immordino-Yang & Damasio, 2007).

Moreover, the system's personalized storytelling approach motivated learners to replay scenarios, explore alternative emotional responses, and reflect on behavioral outcomes, echoing principles from experience-driven content generation (Yannakakis & Togelius, 2011). The dynamic adaptation of narratives based on user emotion and interaction patterns differentiates this system from static storytelling approaches (Cavazza et al., 2009; O'Neill & Riedl, 2016), fostering ownership, immersion, and self-guided exploration.

Beyond narrative recall, the study highlights the pedagogical potential of virtual environments to support decision-making, ethical reasoning, and exploratory learning. Possible future applications include emotionally responsive simulations in STEM (Plass et al., 2020), historical role-playing (Sumi & Sato, 2022), or moral education (Pekrun, 2006).

However, several limitations must be noted. The system currently recognizes only seven discrete emotions (Ekman & Friesen, 1977), omitting nuanced states such as confusion or satisfaction. Additionally, the learning context is confined to a static office environment, limiting narrative diversity. Expanding to more interactive and context-rich environments would support deeper learning.

The study's short-term design also precludes conclusions about long-term effects on memory or behavior. Future work should incorporate longitudinal designs and leverage multi-modal emotional data, such as voice, heart rate, or galvanic skin response (Kotsia et al., 2016), to better adapt the learning experience in real time.

In conclusion, this research demonstrates the educational value of emotion-driven narrative systems. By integrating affective sensing with interactive storytelling, such systems offer scalable tools for enhancing memory, reflection, and engagement across diverse domains of virtual learning.

7. Conclusion

This study explored the integration of real-time emotional recording into game-based learning, showing that personalized narratives based on players' actions and emotions enhance engagement, reflection, and memory retention. Results confirmed that emotionally enriched narratives improved recall and supported emotional memory theories. Participants praised the system's interactivity and personalization, highlighting its ability to create meaningful learning experiences.

7.1 Summary of Key Contributions

This study contributes to game-based learning and emotion-aware educational technology by demonstrating the feasibility of real-time narratives with emotional data. Integrating facial emotion recognition and action tracking, the system created adaptive, immersive stories that enhanced engagement. Emotional recording improved memory retention, self-awareness, and reflection, highlighting its value as a learning aid. The findings emphasize how emotion-driven virtual environments support trial-and-error learning, reflection, and ethical reasoning, offering safe spaces for exploration and deeper understanding.

7.2 Future Research Directions

This study highlights the potential of emotion-driven storytelling in virtual learning while identifying areas for improvement. Enhancing emotion recognition with multi-modal inputs like heart rate or vocal cues could improve precision. Long-term research is needed to assess sustained effects on memory, decision-making, and learning transfer. Expanding to complex educational scenarios like simulations or ethical dilemmas would demonstrate versatility, offering personalized experiences tailored to learners' needs. This research paves the way for emotionally intelligent tools, fostering effective and personalized virtual learning.

Further Reading

For a detailed analysis of this research, refer to the original study at [DOI=10.3389/frai.2022.874106].

Column: The Role of FACS in Emotion-Driven Learning

Subtitle: Toward Adaptive Learning Through Multimodal Emotion Recognition

The Facial Action Coding System (FACS) analyzes facial muscle movements to infer emotions, enhancing engagement and reflection in emotion-driven learning by linking emotional responses to educational experiences.

1. FACS and Emotion-Based Learning Systems

FACS captures emotional reactions during gameplay and integrates them into narratives, creating personalized and immersive educational journeys that reinforce memory and self-awareness.

2. Beyond Facial Recognition: Multi-Modal Emotion Analysis

Relying solely on facial expressions limits accuracy. Future systems could use multi-modal emotion recognition by incorporating physiological, behavioral, and cognitive signals for deeper emotional understanding.

1. Physiological Emotion Recognition
Electroencephalography (EEG): EEG sensors track emotional arousal, cognitive workload, and attentional states via brain activity. For example, theta waves increase during cognitive stress, while alpha waves indicate relaxation. Emotion-aware systems could use EEG to dynamically adjust task difficulty based on engagement or fatigue. Heart Rate Variability (HRV): HRV data reveals stress, excitement, and relaxation levels. Reduced HRV may indicate anxiety or cognitive overload, suggesting pacing adjustments in learning. Galvanic Skin Response (GSR): GSR measures subtle electrical changes in the skin from emotional arousal (e.g., fear, excitement). High arousal might prompt systems to slow content delivery or reinforce difficult concepts.

2. Behavioral and Speech-Based Emotion Recognition

- Voice Analysis: Variations in tone, pitch, and speech rate reveal emotional states. High pitch and fast speech rate suggest excitement, while low tone and slow speech may indicate boredom. Systems could adapt delivery methods accordingly. Posture and Body Movement: Motion tracking detects physical signs of emotions, like restlessness from frustration or confident expansive postures. Hesitation may prompt supportive feedback or adaptive guidance.
- Eye-Tracking: Pupil dilation, blinking, and gaze fixation reflect interest and engagement levels. Frequent eye shifts may signal the need for interactive prompts or clarification.

3. Gesture Recognition for Emotion Detection

- Hand and Arm Gestures: Actions like crossed arms (discomfort), open palms (engagement), or hesitant movements (confusion) provide emotional clues for systems to adjust strategies.
- Head Movements: Patterns such as nodding (agreement), tilting (curiosity), or shaking (disagreement) enhance real-time feedback and storytelling. Micro-Gestures: Subtle actions, like fidgeting or tapping, may indicate anxiety or distraction, allowing systems to optimize engagement. Multi-modal emotion inputs help systems: Adjust difficulty (e.g., reduce complexity during cognitive overload detected via EEG or HRV). Enhance engagement strategies (e.g., add interactivity if body posture signals disengagement).
- Adapt narratives (e.g., increase empathy when voice analysis detects frustration).

Challenges & Future Directions: While promising, multi-modal emotion recognition faces challenges:

- Sensor Fusion: Synchronizing EEG, HRV, and FACS to avoid conflicting assessments.
- Privacy Concerns: Addressing ethical issues surrounding biometric data security and consent.
- Accessibility: Developing non-invasive, user-friendly solutions for broader adoption.

Further research should focus on lightweight emotion-tracking systems and ethical AI standards to ensure data security while advancing adaptive learning experiences.

Column: The Importance of Emotional Recording in Learning

Subtitle: How Emotion-Driven Learning Enhances Memory and Engagement

Emotions are crucial for memory retention and effective learning. Research indicates that emotionally impactful experiences are encoded more deeply in memory than neutral ones (Brierley et al., 2007; Ferré et al., 2015). Integrating real-time emotional data into educational tools transforms abstract knowledge into meaningful, lasting impressions.

1. Emotional Recording and Memory Retention

The proposed system combines real-time emotion tracking with gameplay actions to create personalized narratives. For instance, a surprise during gameplay might appear in the story as: "You nervously took the cola out of the vending machine."

This approach allows learners to:

- Reflect vividly on experiences by linking actions with emotions.
- Strengthen memory retention through emotional connections.
- Boost engagement, making learning immersive and personal.

These findings support psychological theories, emphasizing that emotionally charged events enhance memory recall and improve learning outcomes.

2. Beyond Education: Applications in Other Fields

The potential of emotion recording extends far beyond game-based learning, offering applications such as:

- Corporate Training: Emotion-tracking tools can assess stress levels during decision-making exercises, enabling the creation of adaptive leadership programs.
- Mental Health and Therapy: Patients can use these tools to track emotional fluctuations, supporting cognitive behavioral therapy (CBT) and mindfulness practices.
- VR/AR Training Environments: Emotionally adaptive virtual simulations can adjust scenarios to user emotions, making them ideal for medical training, emergency response preparation, and skill-based education.

3. Ethical Considerations and Future Prospects

While emotion-driven learning holds immense potential, it also brings critical privacy and ethical concerns:

- How should emotional data be securely stored and protected?
- Who can access this data, and how should its use remain responsible?
- How can unintended biases in AI-driven emotion analysis be avoided?

As virtual learning tools become increasingly adaptive, ethical guidelines and user consent mechanisms must prioritize transparency, security, and fairness. Integrating emotional recording into AI-driven learning environments could transform education by creating engaging, personalized, and reflective experiences that bridge the gap between knowledge and understanding.

Part 2
Affective Interaction

At the heart of human interaction lies emotion—an intrinsic force that shapes how we communicate, perceive, and learn. In the field of education, leveraging emotional interactions has opened new avenues for creating intuitive, adaptive, and persuasive learning environments. Affective Interaction explores how systems can recognize, respond to, and even simulate human emotions to foster deeper engagement and meaningful connections in learning.

This part highlights innovative approaches that harness emotional interactions to enhance educational experiences. Chapters explore how emotional expressions in pet-like artifacts can influence behavior change, how observing students' behavior can inform adaptive teaching strategies, and how culturally aware media can employ persuasive emotional techniques to captivate and motivate learners. Additionally, this part delves into the realm of human-robot interaction, investigating how robots can serve as empathetic and intuitive companions in educational settings.

By integrating emotional intelligence into technology, these chapters reveal the transformative potential of affective interaction in reshaping how we learn and teach. From fostering behavior change to creating emotionally aware learning systems, the research presented here underscores the critical role of emotional connection in education's future.

4 Pet-type Artifact That Promotes Behavior Change through Emotional Expression

1. Introduction

Persuasive Technology, as defined by Fogg (2002), investigates how digital systems such as computers, robots, and interactive environments influence human attitudes and behaviors. Its applications span from fitness trackers that encourage physical activity, to smart home systems that promote energy-saving, and intelligent tutoring systems that enhance learning motivation.

While persuasive robotics has often focused on humanoid robots and embodied conversational agents (ECAs) that influence behavior through facial expressions, speech, and gestures (Breazeal, 2003), these methods tend to rely on explicit instructions and can impose social pressure on users. In contrast, pet-like artifacts, inspired by animals, use nonverbal cues, such as gaze, movement, and posture, to deliver more intuitive and less intrusive forms of persuasion. For example, a robotic dog might whimper near a pile of trash or glance toward the user to subtly encourage tidying up.

Pet-like artifacts offer three main advantages over humanoid robots in the context of behavior change. First, they provide subtle prompts using body language and spatial positioning, gently nudging users without overt commands, like a dog glancing at a mess to suggest cleaning. Second, they enable emotional communication through tail wagging, ear movement, and posture, eliminating the need for complex facial expressions or speech (e.g., Wada & Shibata, 2007; Robinson et al., 2014). Third, their non-human appearance fosters low-pressure interactions, encouraging voluntary user responses without the burden of social expectations.

While prior studies have highlighted the emotional support roles of pet-like robots, such as reducing loneliness among the elderly, their potential for intentional behavior change remains underexplored. This study aims to address that gap (e.g., Wada & Shibata, 2007; Wada et al., 2005; Robinson et al., 2014).

Dogs, in particular, are exemplary models for persuasive design due to their adept nonverbal communication skills. They express needs through gaze, posture, tail movement, and vocalizations, which humans are naturally attuned to interpret. For instance, a dog might alternate its gaze between a person and an object—such as a leash, food bowl, or door, to indicate a specific desire, a behavior known as gaze alternation. Similarly, subtle shifts in body orientation, like turning partially toward an object or sitting near a location, can effectively draw human attention without explicit signals.

DOI: 10.1201/9781003782735-6

Tail wagging patterns also convey emotional states: a high, fast wag may indicate excitement, while a low, slow wag can signal uncertainty or appeasement. Posture and vocalizations, such as whining when ignored or barking near a target, further reinforce communicative intent.

Research by Miklósi et al. (2000) and Lakatos et al. (2012) has demonstrated that even untrained individuals can interpret these signals with high accuracy. Furthermore, Maginnity and Grace (2014) found that canine cues such as gaze alternation and body orientation are particularly effective at eliciting responsive behavior in humans, likely because they resemble familiar human-child communication strategies. These intuitive, evolutionarily grounded signals make dogs compelling models for designing emotionally expressive, low-pressure persuasive agents. Building on these insights, this study implements such behaviors in a virtual dog-like artifact, designed to convey emotions such as sadness, confusion, and joy purely through motion.

This approach connects to the field of affective learning, which emphasizes emotional engagement over direct instruction. Emotionally expressive companions can show concern or joy to reinforce desirable behaviors and mediate social cues like turn-taking. By leveraging emotional signals, such systems foster stronger user-artifact connections and support positive learning outcomes, especially in informal or home-based settings.

The goal of this study is to investigate how emotionally expressive, pet-like artifacts naturally influence user behavior. Key questions include identifying which emotional expressions (e.g., sadness, joy) are most effective, understanding how movement complexity affects interpretation, and testing whether nonverbal cues alone can prompt user action without verbal instructions.

To explore these questions, we developed a dog-shaped virtual agent capable of displaying six emotional states through body movements and vocalizations. The system was evaluated in Mixed Reality environments. The research contributes to the fields of affective computing, human-robot interaction (HRI), behavioral psychology, and persuasive design. The broader vision is to enable emotionally intuitive companions that assist in areas like education and caregiving—fostering cooperation through emotional resonance rather than reliance on commands.

2. Related Work

This chapter reviews prior research that informs the design and implementation of emotionally expressive pet-like artifacts for behavior change. It is organized into five key areas: emotional expression in persuasive artifacts, the role of pet-like agents, canine-inspired communication, affective learning, and the development of emotionally intelligent, multimodal systems.

2.1 Emotional Expression in Persuasive Artifacts

Persuasive technology, defined by Fogg (2002), aims to influence attitudes and behaviors through digital systems. While early research focused on text, images, or humanoid robots, newer approaches highlight the role of emotion in fostering trust, empathy, and compliance (Batson, 1991; Davis, 1994; Breazeal, 2003; Picard, 1997). Humanoid robots express emotion through facial expressions, tone, and gestures but these can create social pressure or discomfort. Non-verbal emotional communication, using motion, posture, and vocalizations, offers subtle persuasion that encourages voluntary action.

This study emphasizes the term artifact over "robot" to highlight flexibility. Its dog-like virtual object leverages intuitive, emotionally expressive behaviors like head tilts and gaze direction, expanding applications to mixed-reality agents, mobile systems, and ambient technologies.

2.2 Pet-Like Artifacts and Emotional Influence

Prior research highlights the emotional and persuasive capabilities of pet-like robotic systems, often used for emotional support in eldercare and therapy (e.g., AIBO, Fujita 2000; Paro, Wada & Shibata 2007; LOVOT, Robinson et al. 2014). These systems leverage animal-like cues, tail movement, ear positioning, and gaze, for emotionally resonant experiences.

Recent studies have explored their persuasive potential. Okada's "Weak Robot" (2012) showed how emotional vulnerability evokes empathy to inspire action. Yamaji et al. (2011) designed a context-aware trash bin using social cues to elicit help. Building on this, our work examines how pet-like expressions, such as sadness or confusion, combined with movement patterns, can motivate voluntary user actions, positioning such artifacts as persuasive companions in daily tasks.

2.3 Canine-Inspired Communication as a Design Model

Dogs excel in nonverbal communication, using cues like gaze alternation (shifting eye contact between a person and an object), body posture (such as sitting, bowing, or leaning), tail motion (like wagging to show excitement or lowering to indicate submission), and vocal sounds (such as whining, barking, or growling to express needs or emotions) (Miklósi et al., 2000; Lakatos et al., 2012).

These signals are not only rich in emotional content but are also easily interpreted by humans, making dogs especially well-suited for intuitive, cross-species interaction without the need for language or complex facial expressions.

Research has shown that such dog behaviors can significantly enhance human comfort, reduce ambiguity, and support smoother communication in human–robot interaction. For instance, Maginnity and Grace (2014) found that dogs are capable of adjusting their gaze behavior depending on the human's line of sight, demonstrating an understanding of human attention and perspective, which is key for joint attention and social bonding.

Similarly, Heerink et al. (2010) investigated socially assistive robots and concluded that non-verbal behaviors like posture, movement, and timing significantly increase users' willingness to accept and interact with the robot, especially in elderly care or therapeutic contexts. These findings support the idea that dog-like cues, when replicated in artificial agents, can foster natural, low-pressure interactions. Our design incorporates canine-inspired cues, head tilting, tail posture and hesitant movements, to evoke emotions like sadness or joy. These signals serve as abstract emotional expressions, ensuring intuitive interaction without relying on speech or humanoid features, promoting empathetic engagement over obligation.

2.4 Emotional Persuasion and Affective Learning

This work introduces affective learning, where emotionally expressive artifacts enhance motivation, attention, and social engagement. Instead of direct instruction, these systems use emotional cues, like concern for missed tasks or joy for achievements, to create personalized, socially intuitive interactions. This approach expands persuasive design, positioning artifacts as emotionally intelligent learning partners. Through non-verbal emotional cues, these agents guide attention, encourage effort, and foster deeper engagement. Such effects are supported by research in affective computing and educational psychology, which demonstrates that emotional feedback during learning enhances engagement and cognitive outcomes (D'Mello & Graesser, 2012).

2.5 Toward Emotionally Intelligent, Versatile Artifacts

Our dog-shaped, emotionally expressive artifact is designed to be impactful and adaptable across platforms, including physical robots, MR agents, mobile apps, and ambient interfaces, as it avoids dependence on specific forms or verbal dialogue.

The strength of these artifacts lies in their ability to blend emotional resonance with intuitive communication. As they integrate into daily life, their impact depends on effectively conveying needs and intentions while respecting user autonomy and emotional sensitivity.

This work advances emotionally intelligent design, highlighting how subtle, animal-inspired behaviors enhance human-artifact interaction in education, therapy, domestic assistance, and public spaces.

3. Methods of Persuasion via Movement and Emotional Expression

This study examined how emotional and behavioral cues in a dog-like artifact influenced decision-making. Using a three-dimensional Mixed Reality (MR) model with expressive motion and sound, the artifact aimed to persuade users to dispose of trash through emotional movement-based signals, without verbal instructions.

Research in HRI highlights the importance of emotional intelligence for persuasive agents,with humanoid robots using facial expressions, tone, and gestures to convey intent (Breazeal, 2003; Picard, 1997). Pet-like agents, however, rely on strategies like posture, motion, and vocalizations. This chapter details the design of the artifact's emotional expressions, the creation of animated stimuli, and their deployment in an MR-based experimental setup.

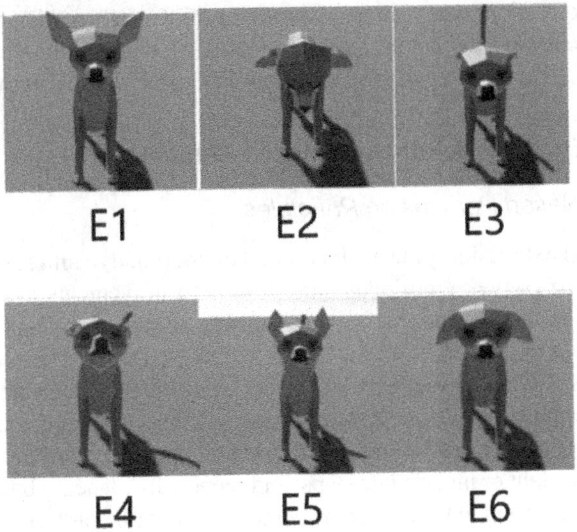

Fig. 1 Emotional Expressions of the Dog Model. The six designed emotional expressions (Neutral (E1), Sadness (E2), Anger (E3), Joy (E4), Surprise (E5), and Confusion (E6)) demonstrated through dynamic animations of the dog's neck, head, ears, tail, vocalizations, and movement speed. These animations were developed to investigate their persuasive potential in influencing human behavior.

3.1 Emotional Design of the Artifact

Importance of Emotion in Persuasion

Emotions are pivotal in persuasive interactions, enabling influence without direct commands. Based on research in affective computing and social robotics, we designed emotional expressions for the artifact using body movements, postures, and sounds to elicit engagement and empathy, prompting actions like trash disposal. Inspired by canine non-verbal communication, tail wagging, head tilts, ear positions, gaze, and movement speed (Miklósi et al., 2000; Lakatos et al., 2012), these cues form the artifact's expressive range.

Emotion Categories and Expression Mapping

The artifact displayed six emotional states, Neutral, Sadness, Anger, Joy, Surprise, and Confusion, through a blend of posture, motion, and sound. For instance:

- Neutral: Steady movement with a calm gaze.
- Sadness: Slow, drooping motions, lowered ears, and soft whimpers.
- Anger: Tense posture, rigid movements, raised tail, and sharp sounds.
- Joy: Tail wagging, bouncing motions, and happy vocalizations.
- Surprise: Quick pauses, head turns, and slight backward steps.
- Confusion: Head tilts, alternating gaze, and hesitant movements.

These expressions were validated through a study where participants confirmed their alignment with intended emotional labels. Dynamic animation parameters like tail speed, neck angle, and vocalization were used to convey each emotion.

3.2 Constructing Persuasive Motion Sequences

Movement-Based Persuasion Principles

Without facial expressions, the artifact relied on motion dynamics, speed, fluidity, and rhythm, to convey emotional intent. Smooth movements are perceived as friendly, while abrupt motions suggest urgency or agitation (Shibata & Wada, 2011). Inspired by Okada's "Weak Robot" concept (2012), which demonstrated that robots displaying emotional vulnerability could elicit empathy and cooperative behavior from humans, we integrated a range of subtle, empathetic behaviors into our virtual artifact. These behaviors included shifting body weight from side to side, taking hesitant or incomplete steps, and repeatedly glancing between the user and an object, all designed to mimic the demeanor of a vulnerable, uncertain animal seeking help. This strategy aimed to evoke emotional concern rather than apply explicit commands, thereby encouraging voluntary assistance and engagement through empathic resonance rather than obligation.

Levels of Movement Complexity

We explored motion complexity's impact on persuasion using two levels:

- **Low-complexity (M1):** Minimal gestures like slight turns, brief glances, and soft whimpers conveyed intent subtly.
- **High-complexity (M2):** Richer actions, including head tilts, gaze alternation, movement back-and-forth, and frequent vocalizations like whining or squealing, offered more expressive cues.

Combining Emotions and Movement

We combined six emotional expressions (E1–E6) with two movement levels (M1, M2), creating 12 animations (A1–A12) to examine emotional valence and behavioral richness. Comparable pairs like A1 (Neutral + M1) vs. A7 (Neutral + M2) allowed systematic analysis of how emotional tones and animation complexity influenced user perception and behavior.

3.3 Mixed Reality Deployment and Interaction Design

Rationale for Using Mixed Reality

Conventional persuasive robotics rely on physical robots, but face challenges like mechanical reliability and limited expressiveness. To overcome this, we used Mixed Reality (MR) to embed a virtual agent into the participant's physical space seamlessly. Using MR provided three key benefits: precise animation control, immersive interaction with the artifact integrated into real space, and a cost-effective, realistic alternative to hardware prototyping.

System Implementation

We utilized Microsoft HoloLens 2, a head-mounted MR display, to create an interactive experience with a Unity3D-developed artifact. Integrated spatial mapping ensured alignment with real-world objects like the trash and trash can. Participants triggered animations via a hand-tracked virtual menu, while the virtual dog moved autonomously, enhancing presence and reinforcing the illusion of shared space.

Participant Experience

The MR interface allowed participants to interact with the artifact naturally, allowing movement and viewpoint changes unlike screen-based interactions. Many felt emotionally connected, noting its behaviors, like "looking at them" or "asking for something," effectively supported persuasive communication in non-verbal agents.

4. Experiment

This study used Mixed Reality (MR) to explore how a four-legged expressive artifact influences behavior through emotional and movement cues. The virtual dog, designed to display varied emotions and motions, aimed to prompt trash disposal without verbal instructions. Participants evaluated its emotional state, intent, and their motivation to act, with details on setup, procedures, and challenges outlined in this chapter.

4.1 Experimental Setup

Participants and Recruitment

The study included ten computer science students (ages 20–23) to ensure familiarity with MR technology and enable controlled comparisons. This participant group aligns with prior research showing that technically proficient users are particularly suited for evaluating persuasive systems in experimental settings (Xu & Chen, 2020). Consistent with prior work, small participant groups, like those used in this study, are often ideal for generating in-depth behavioral insights and observing nuanced responses (Breazeal, 2003; Okada, 2012).

Environment and Apparatus

The experiment took place in a quiet lab to minimize distractions, with a real trash item positioned on a desk and a trash can 1.5 meters away. This setup required participants to physically act to discard the item. Using Microsoft HoloLens 2, participants viewed a life-sized virtual dog seamlessly integrated into their physical space. The artifact's movements, rendered in Unity3D, were synchronized with spatial mapping to ensure alignment with real objects. Participants interacted via hand-tracked gestures, selecting animations from a floating menu for a controlled, immersive experience.

Experimental Procedure

Each 30–40 minute session followed a standardized flow. Participants were briefed on the experiment's purpose, signed consent forms, and trained to use the HoloLens 2 and hand-tracking menu. After calibration to position the virtual artifact, they observed 12 animations (10–15 seconds each) combining emotional expressions (e.g., Sadness, Anger) with movement complexity. Participants completed questionnaires after each animation, evaluating emotions, intent, and their willingness to act, followed by open-ended feedback and debriefing.

4.2 Questionnaire and Data Collection

To assess the persuasive impact of each animation, participants completed a three-part questionnaire (emotional recognition, intent clarity, and behavioral influence) 12 times using a 5-point Likert scale. Emotional perception targeted categories like sadness and confusion. Intent clarity evaluated if participants understood the artifact's cues. Behavioral influence measured willingness to act, such as trash disposal. Open-ended questions gathered insights on motivating behaviors and overall impressions, identifying themes in compelling elements.

4.3 Anticipated Challenges and Mitigation Strategies

Challenges were anticipated and mitigated for this experiment. To reduce participant bias, animation sequences were randomized, addressing familiarity with MR and virtual agents. Immersion issues, like spatial misalignment, were countered through pre-session alignment tests, ensuring the artifact integrated seamlessly into the physical environment. Lastly, a preliminary validation study confirmed the clarity of emotional expressions, accounting for subjective and cultural differences in emotion interpretation.

5. Results

This chapter details the user study findings, analyzing how emotional expressions and movement complexity in a four-legged virtual artifact shaped participant impressions and behavior. Using quantitative data and qualitative feedback, we assessed the clarity of emotional communication, intent, and the artifact's success in motivating action.

5.1 Emotional Impressions

A key goal was to evaluate how well participants recognized the artifact's emotional expressions. While some emotions were clearly understood, others faced ambiguity or misinterpretation.

Recognition of Emotional Expressions

Participants rated emotional perceptions on a 5-point Likert scale, with Sadness (E2) and Confusion (E6) scoring 4.3 and 4.1, respectively, as the most recognizable states. Anger (E3) evoked mixed responses, ranging from frustration to intimidation, shifting focus from persuasion to avoidance. Joy (E4) was seen as playful, often conflicting with its intended goal. Surprise (E5) led to varied interpretations, from genuine emotion to curiosity, highlighting inconsistent recognition.

Misinterpretation of Emotional Cues

While most expressions were fairly recognizable, some emotional cues proved ambiguous due to the artifact's non-humanoid nature. Tail wagging in Joy (E4) was often seen as playful rather than persuasive. Anger (E3) appeared threatening, discouraging engagement and Surprise (E5) lacked distinctiveness, causing confusion.

These findings highlight the need for precise calibration of non-verbal, animal-like behaviors to ensure clear communication.

5.2 Behavioral Impact

This study explored whether the artifact's emotional expressions could prompt trash disposal as a measure of persuasive success. Findings show that certain emotions were more effective in motivating action than others.

Effectiveness of Different Emotions in Persuasion

Participants rated their motivation to dispose of trash after each animation. Sadness (E2) and Confusion (E6) were most persuasive, scoring 4.4 and 4.2, as they evoked empathy and responsibility. Neutral (E1) and Surprise (E5) had moderate impact, averaging 3.7, lacking strong emotional force. Anger (E3) and Joy (E4) were least effective, with scores of 2.9 and 3.1, either causing discomfort or failing to clearly signal assistance. Empathy-driving emotions proved most effective for persuasion.

Participant Reflections on Persuasive Mechanisms

Participants' open-ended feedback highlighted empathy as a key driver of persuasion. Many felt the artifact "needed help" or "seemed troubled," especially in Sadness and Confusion states, which inspired personal responsibility. Anger, however, often triggered avoidance due to its perceived aggression, creating disengagement. Joy appeared playful but lacked goal clarity, while Surprise felt ambiguous, leaving participants unsure of intent. These findings emphasize the importance of emotional clarity in persuasive non-verbal artifacts to encourage meaningful responses.

5.3 *Influence of Movement Complexity*

We analyzed how movement complexity influenced participants' engagement and motivation alongside emotional expressions.

Persuasion and Movement Complexity

Statistical analysis (Wilcoxon signed-rank test) showed no significant difference in persuasive effectiveness between low (M1) and high-complexity (M2) movements ($p > 0.05$). However, dynamic movements amplified the emotional impact of Sadness (E2) and Confusion (E6), enhancing connection or urgency. Anger (E3) and Joy (E4), however, saw no benefit, as complexity failed to resolve their inherent ambiguity.

Participant Observations on Movement

Participants noted that high-complexity animations made the dog appear "more alive" and interactive, enhancing its ability to convey the need for help in empathetic conditions. However, excessive movement was sometimes perceived as chaotic or indecisive, highlighting the importance of calibrating motion dynamics to align with emotional tone for effective persuasion.

5.4 *Correlations Between Emotional Interpretation, Intent, and Action*

We analyzed correlations between emotional recognition, intent comprehension, and behavioral motivation.

Emotion perception ($r = 0.78$, $p < 0.01$) and intent recognition strongly correlated, as did intent recognition and behavioral influence ($r = 0.82$, $p < 0.01$), showing clear understanding drives action. Movement complexity had a weaker correlation with behavior ($r = 0.29$, $p > 0.05$), emphasizing the importance of clear emotional expression over motion alone for persuasion.

6. Discussion

6.1 *Summary of Findings and Key Insights*

This study examined how a dog-shaped virtual artifact, presented in a Mixed Reality (MR) environment influenced trash disposal through emotional and movement cues. Sadness and confusion were the most persuasive, evoking empathy and action, while anger discouraged engagement and joy caused intent confusion. Movement complexity had minimal impact compared to the clarity of emotional expressions, highlighting the importance of precise, intuitive communication in designing persuasive human-artifact interactions.

6.2 Theoretical Implications: Why Certain Emotions Were More Persuasive

Empathy is a strong motivator for prosocial behavior, as individuals tend to assist others perceived as vulnerable or distressed. In this study, sadness and confusion effectively triggered empathy, prompting action, consistent with Okada's (2012) findings on "weak robots." Conversely, anger proved counterproductive, interpreted as hostility and discouraging engagement. Joy enhanced likeability but lacked urgency, being seen as playful rather than goal-directed. These results emphasize aligning emotional expression with the interaction's context and goals for effective persuasion.

6.3 Implications for Behavioral Design in Human-Robot Interaction

This study provides key design insights for emotionally persuasive agents. Emotional expressions like sadness and confusion effectively elicit empathy, while anger may hinder persuasion unless contextually justified. Joy, although engaging, requires clarity to avoid obscuring intent. The research also challenges the notion that complex animations alone enhance persuasion, emphasizing that clarity in emotional gestures is more impactful. Designers should focus on simple, targeted movements, such as alternating gaze, for effective communication over elaborate yet ambiguous animations.

6.4 Limitations of the Study

This study has notable limitations. The small sample of ten computer science students aged 20–23 limits generalizability; future research should include diverse demographics. Mixed Reality constraints, like HoloLens 2's field of view, impacted artifact realism and engagement levels, highlighting the need for comparisons with physical robots. Lastly, short-term interaction assessments missed insights into long-term persuasion effects, warranting studies on repeated or extended engagements.

6.5 Future Directions for Research and Applications

This study highlights future directions for emotionally expressive agents. In education, pet-like companions could enhance motivation by offering emotional feedback, such as expressing confusion for errors or joy for progress. Assistive technologies may use virtual pets to promote healthy habits and eco-friendly behaviors through emotional cues. Interdisciplinary research is crucial, as psychologists, AI researchers, educators, and ethicists can refine these systems to ensure they are adaptive, impactful, and prioritize user well-being.

6.6 Toward Emotionally Intelligent Pet-Like Artifacts

This study highlights how pet-like artifacts can influence behavior through non-verbal emotional cues. It emphasizes the effectiveness of sadness and confusion in evoking empathy, the value of emotional clarity in design, and the potential applications of emotionally intelligent artifacts in education and assistive technologies. As robotic companions become more integrated into daily life, future research should explore diverse use cases, long-term interactions, and adaptive emotional models to create intuitive and supportive systems across various domains.

7. Conclusion

This study explored how a dog-shaped virtual artifact in a Mixed Reality (MR) setting influences human behavior through non-verbal, emotionally expressive interactions. By emphasizing emotional clarity and intuitive engagement, the research revealed sadness and confusion as the most effective expressions for evoking empathy and action. Anger and joy were less effective due to misinterpretation, and movement complexity added little to persuasion compared to clear emotional signals. These findings suggest pet-like robotic agents could foster motivation in education, healthcare, and sustainability, acting as non-intrusive, empathic companions that enhance human-centered interaction.

Further Reading

For a detailed analysis, refer to the original study: [DOI=10.1007/978-3-031-58226-4_12].

Column: Emotional Robotics and the Future of Human-Companion Interaction

Incorporating emotional expression into pet-like robotic systems advances human-computer interaction by prioritizing empathy and engagement over mere efficiency. This study showed that emotional cues, like sadness and confusion, effectively prompt actions, such as trash disposal, without relying on verbal commands.

The Role of Emotion in Human-Machine Relationships

Emotion is key to human interaction, and embedding it into robotics bridges functionality with intuitive engagement. Pet-like robots excel in emotional communication through non-verbal cues like posture and gaze, offering advantages over humanoid designs. This study highlights the importance of emotional clarity, sadness and confusion evoked empathy and action, while anger discouraged interaction, and joy was seen as playful. Designing clear, context-sensitive emotional behaviors is crucial for effective interaction.

Opportunities and Challenges

Emotionally expressive pet-like robots have versatile applications, such as encouraging recycling, promoting activity, or supporting resilience. However, their design must ensure emotional cues avoid misinterpretation across cultures and address ethical concerns about over-dependence and authenticity, prioritizing complementary social interactions over replacement.

Looking Ahead

Emotionally intelligent robots are set to transform human-machine relationships. Adaptive AI-driven emotional responses could enable personalized, evolving interactions, with longitudinal studies crucial for exploring impacts on behavior, trust, and motivation. This study showcases pet-like artifacts as early examples of persuasive technology, paving the way for assistive robotics and affective learning. These robots are envisioned not just as tools but as companions that foster connection and support.

5 | Affective Learning in Human-Robot Interaction

1. Introduction

Technology has revolutionized education, making information more accessible and classrooms more interactive. AI and robotics have expanded possibilities, enabling personalized learning experiences and redefining traditional teaching methods with dynamic approaches tailored to diverse student needs (Salem & Sumi, 2024). As they evolved from industrial tools to versatile companions, robots became increasingly present in households, and by 2015, one in 25 U.S. households had one, a figure projected to reach one in 10 by 2020. Initially focused on cleaning and entertainment, advancements now position robots in healthcare, hospitality, and education, tailored for meaningful human interaction, especially with children.

Robots in classrooms represent a transformative step in education. They offer personalized support, foster engagement, and address gaps in traditional teaching. By providing real-time feedback, adapting to learning styles, and maintaining patience, robots cater to diverse needs, serving as teaching assistants, mediators, and companions to create a more inclusive environment.

Despite their potential, robots in education face skepticism about their limitations, risk of replacing teachers, and ethical concerns over their role in child learning (Sharkey, 2016). Perceptions of robots vary, ranging from helpful tools to potentially disruptive and autonomous agents, especially among younger users (Brink & Wellman, 2020; Reich-Stiebert & Eyssel, 2016). Balancing excitement with evidence-based approaches is crucial for their integration into classrooms, as highlighted in studies on affective AI and educational deception (Salem & Sumi, 2024). Researchers, educators, and policymakers are collaborating to optimize robots for education. Roboticists focus on intuitive design, educators align capabilities with curricula, and psychologists study trust, engagement, and emotional connection in student-robot interactions. The potential of robots in education extends to Human-robot interaction (HRI), emphasizing emotional intelligence. By recognizing and responding to emotions, robots can enhance learning by boosting motivation, attention, and retention. For example, a robot detecting frustration in a student can adapt its teaching style to provide clearer explanations or encouragement, fostering a more empathetic environment.

This chapter delves into the concept of affective learning through HRI, a domain that combines technological innovation with psychological insights. It explores the significance of emotions in HRI, examining how robots can support educational objectives by fostering emotional connections with students. Additionally, the chapter addresses the ethical, technical, and cultural challenges associated with

DOI: 10.1201/9781003782735-7

implementing robots in classrooms. These challenges include ensuring data privacy, avoiding cultural biases in robot design (Howard & Borenstein, 2017), and addressing concerns about equity and accessibility.

To provide a comprehensive understanding of the opportunities and challenges of using robots in education, this chapter also presents real-world case studies and examines the role of generative AI in educational contexts. For example, while generative AI systems like ChatGPT have shown promise in facilitating inquiry-based learning, they also present risks such as the dissemination of inaccurate information. By integrating insights from case studies, research findings, and theoretical perspectives, the chapter aims to offer practical recommendations for leveraging robots and AI in education responsibly and effectively.

Ultimately, integrating robots and AI in education transcends technology, reimagining and enhancing the learning experience. By bridging the gap between human empathy and machine efficiency, robots have the potential to make education more inclusive, personalized, and engaging. However, achieving this vision requires a thoughtful and collaborative approach, one that prioritizes the needs and well-being of students while addressing the ethical and practical considerations of using advanced technologies in classrooms. As we stand on the cusp of this transformative era, the lessons learned from current research and implementation efforts will shape the future of education for generations to come.

2. The Role of Emotions in HRI

To understand how emotions enhance human-robot interaction, this chapter explores their role in shaping communication, learning outcomes, and behavioral engagement. By examining both the benefits and challenges of emotional integration in educational robotics, we highlight why emotion-aware systems are essential for building effective and empathetic learning environments.

2.1 Why Emotions Matter in HRI

Emotions play a fundamental role in human communication, decision-making, and social interactions. In the context of Human-Robot Interaction (HRI), the ability of robots to recognize and express emotions is crucial for fostering natural and effective engagement, particularly in educational settings. Traditional educational technology, such as online learning platforms or intelligent tutoring systems, primarily focuses on delivering content efficiently. However, these systems often lack the ability to adapt to students' emotional states, which can significantly impact motivation, attention, and learning outcomes.

When interacting with a teacher, students respond not only to the information being provided but also to nonverbal cues such as facial expressions, tone of voice, and body language. These emotional signals help establish rapport, build trust, and enhance comprehension. Without the ability to interpret and respond to emotions, robots risk being perceived not as supportive companions but as intrusive or impersonal entities, a concern raised by Brink & Wellman (2020) regarding public perceptions of educational robots.

Robots designed for educational environments must go beyond simple programmed responses and incorporate affective computing principles—technologies that allow machines to detect, interpret, and respond to human emotions. For instance, if a student struggles with a difficult math problem, a robot equipped with emotion recognition can detect signs of frustration through facial expressions, body language, or speech patterns. Instead of continuing with the same explanation, the robot could adapt its approach, offering simpler explanations, encouragement, or even humor to ease the student's anxiety.

This approach aligns with findings from affective tutoring research, which show that systems capable of recognizing and responding to student emotions can enhance learning by improving engagement and reducing frustration (Woolf et al., 2009; Tiam-Lee & Sumi, 2019; Moise et al., 2024).

Furthermore, emotions in HRI are not just about responding to students' needs but also about guiding behavior. A robot expressing enthusiasm when a student succeeds can reinforce positive behaviors and encourage continued effort. Conversely, a subtle expression of disappointment when a student disregards instructions can serve as an implicit corrective signal without needing direct reprimand.

Emotional intelligence in robots thus serves a dual function:

1. Recognizing user emotions, enabling adaptive responses that personalize and optimize learning experiences.
2. Expressing emotions appropriately, reinforcing positive behaviors, maintaining engagement, and creating a sense of companionship and motivation. The way a robot communicates—including its speech rhythm and narrative backstory—can significantly shape how students perceive its personality and emotional depth (Kory-Westlund & Breazeal, 2019b).

Without these emotional capabilities, robots in education risk being seen merely as digital assistants rather than interactive, engaging learning companions.

2.2 Benefits of Emotional Interaction

The integration of emotional capabilities in educational robots yields numerous benefits, transforming both the learning experience and the effectiveness of instructional methods.

Increased Engagement and Motivation

Emotions drive motivation, and motivation fuels learning. Students, especially younger ones, tend to engage more with content that is dynamic and interactive. Robots with emotional expressions, such as smiling, nodding, or adjusting their voice tone, can create a sense of presence and attentiveness that keeps students interested.

Studies on social robots in classrooms have shown that emotionally expressive robots can significantly enhance student engagement (Kory-Westlund & Breazeal, 2019a; Belpaeme et al., 2018). The emotional feedback these robots provide helps students feel acknowledged, fostering continued participation.

Personalized and Adaptive Learning

Students learn at their own pace, with emotions often indicating their understanding or struggles with a concept. Affective computing allows robots to personalize interactions based on real-time emotional feedback. For instance:

- If a student exhibits frustration, the robot can slow down and provide additional explanations.
- If a student appears confident and excited, the robot can challenge them with more complex problems.
- If a student seems disengaged or tired, the robot might suggest a short break or introduce a more interactive activity.

Such adaptability creates a tailored learning experience that mirrors the flexibility of human tutors.

Strengthening Social and Emotional Skills

Emotional robots can foster social and emotional intelligence by modeling empathy, self-regulation, and interaction skills essential for personal and professional growth. This is particularly beneficial in educational and therapeutic contexts where learners may require structured, low-pressure environments to develop these abilities.

For example, children with autism spectrum disorder (ASD) benefit from social robots' consistent cues, aiding in the development of communication skills (Scassellati et al., 2012).

Children with ASD often face challenges in interpreting complex social signals such as facial expressions, gestures, and tone of voice, making typical human interactions stressful or overwhelming. Social robots, by contrast, can provide predictable, simplified, and repeatable social behaviors, such as steady eye gaze, controlled vocalizations, and clear body orientation, which help children engage without anxiety. These robots act as stable, nonjudgmental partners that offer structured opportunities to practice fundamental social behaviors such as joint attention, turn-taking, and affective reciprocity.

Over time, this consistent interaction helps reinforce core communication patterns and can even facilitate the transfer of learned behaviors to real human interactions. Thus, emotional robots not only serve as learning tools but also as therapeutic agents that scaffold the development of vital interpersonal competencies in populations with unique learning needs.

Reinforcing Positive Learning Behaviors

Feedback in learning involves more than simply indicating whether an answer is right or wrong—it also depends heavily on emotional reinforcement. Positive emotional cues, such as praise and encouragement, play a crucial role in motivating learners to continue their efforts and persist through challenges.

Robots capable of expressing supportive emotions, such as smiling, nodding, using an enthusiastic tone, or offering virtual rewards, can enhance students' sense of achievement and reinforce their confidence (Kory-Westlund & Breazeal, 2019a; Saerbeck et al., 2010). These emotional signals are especially powerful for younger learners, who often respond more strongly to affective feedback than to abstract performance scores or verbal corrections.

Moreover, robots can subtly guide students through nonverbal cues that signal areas for improvement. For instance, expressing mild concern or displaying a puzzled reaction when a student makes a mistake can prompt the learner to reflect and self-correct, without invoking fear or embarrassment. This method promotes a growth mindset, in which errors are viewed as part of the learning process rather than as failures.

These emotionally nuanced responses help build a psychologically safe learning environment, one where students feel supported, motivated, and willing to take intellectual risks. In this way, emotionally expressive robots do not merely deliver instruction; they actively shape learner behavior by embedding social-emotional learning into the educational experience.

2.3 Challenges in Implementing Emotions in Robots

While emotional interactions in HRI offer clear benefits, challenges remain in ensuring these systems are reliable, effective, and ethically sound.

Accuracy of Emotion Recognition

A key challenge in affective robotics is accurately detecting human emotions, which relies on various inputs, such as:

- **Facial recognition** (analyzing expressions) **Speech analysis** (tone and patterns).
- **Physiological sensors** (heart rate, skin conductance, pupil dilation)

Human emotions are intricate and context-dependent. A smile may express nervousness, politeness, or sarcasm rather than happiness (Cowie et al., 2000). Minimal facial expressions in some individuals further complicate interpretation, with inaccuracies potentially causing unhelpful or frustrating robotic responses.

Cultural and Individual Differences

Emotional expressions differ across cultures, and direct eye contact signals confidence in some cultures but disrespect in others (Howard & Borenstein, 2017).

This highlights the importance of culturally sensitive design in educational robots, as misinterpreted emotional signals can hinder communication or create discomfort.

Robots with Western-centric emotional models may face challenges with non-Western students (Howard & Borenstein, 2017).

This underscores the need for emotion recognition systems to be trained on diverse datasets to ensure inclusivity and equity across cultural contexts.

To overcome this, emotional AI must adapt culturally, leveraging diverse datasets and refining responses through user interactions.

Ethical Concerns in Emotional Manipulation

Robots designed to influence emotions must balance support and manipulation. Excessive excitement or disappointment may unintentionally pressure students, hindering genuine learning (Bartneck & Saerbeck, 2010). As noted by Salem & Sumi (2024), educators and designers must be especially cautious when introducing affective AI into classrooms, as emotionally persuasive systems may unintentionally mislead or manipulate students without transparent intent.

This suggests that strong emotional cues from robots, while intended to motivate, can sometimes create anxiety or reduce intrinsic motivation if not used judiciously.

Excessive reliance on robotic tutors may foster emotional bonds, leading to over-dependence on artificial companionship and decreased human-human interactions if not carefully managed.

Thus, emotional AI in education should support human connection rather than replace it, promoting healthy interpersonal development.

Cost and Accessibility

Developing emotionally intelligent robots demands sophisticated AI, sensors, and processing, resulting in high costs. Budget-constrained schools may face limited access, posing a challenge to ensure widespread adoption without deepening educational inequalities.

3. Integrating Generative AI in Education: Opportunities and Risks

As generative AI becomes increasingly integrated into education, it is essential to consider both its transformative potential and the risks it introduces. This chapter explores how tools like ChatGPT can personalize learning, increase accessibility, and enhance engagement, while also examining the challenges of misinformation, critical thinking, and responsible use in the classroom.

3.1 The Promise of Generative AI

Generative AI, like ChatGPT, is transforming education by offering dynamic, personalized learning experiences. Unlike fixed curricula, it adapts in real-time to students' queries and learning paces. Research highlights its potential for individual learning while noting concerns about reliability and oversight (Luckin et al., 2016; Zawacki-Richter et al., 2019; Xie et al., 2019).

Personalized and Adaptive Learning

Generative AI excels in personalized education, using AI-powered tools to assess understanding, identify knowledge gaps, and tailor explanations to diverse learning styles. For example, a student struggling with algebra may get step-by-step problem breakdowns, while an advanced learner is offered real-world applications, ensuring tailored support that builds on strengths and addresses weaknesses.

Accessibility and Inclusivity in Education

Generative AI democratizes education by offering instant feedback, explanations, and tutoring, ensuring high-quality learning for students without access to experienced teachers or specialized resources.

AI-driven education acts as a virtual tutor for students in remote or underprivileged areas, offering subject guidance where human instruction is scarce. It also supports students with disabilities through tools like text-to-speech, speech-to-text, and adaptive learning interfaces tailored to their needs.

Enhancing Engagement Through Interactivity

Generative AI boosts engagement by offering interactive, conversational learning experiences, making education more dynamic compared to traditional textbooks and lectures.

AI can simulate historical figures from various cultural backgrounds, turning passive learning into active exploration by making historical events, scientific discoveries, and literary themes more relatable and memorable.

AI-generated content like quizzes, prompts, and challenges gamifies learning by offering adaptive difficulty, instant rewards, and feedback loops, boosting engagement and reinforcing positive learning behaviors.

Reducing the Workload of Educators

Teachers often juggle heavy workloads including planning, grading, and student support. Generative AI assists by automating tasks such as:

- Grading assignments based on predefined rubrics.
- Generating personalized study plans for students.

- Providing instant explanations to commonly asked questions, allowing teachers to focus on higher-order instructional tasks.

By handling administrative tasks, AI allows teachers to focus on student interactions, critical thinking exercises, and emotional engagement, which are irreplaceable aspects of education.

While generative AI offers many benefits, its widespread adoption in education requires addressing key challenges to ensure its ethical and effective implementation.

3.2 The Risk of Hallucinations in AI

Generative AI's exciting potential is tempered by risks like "hallucinations," where systems produce false or misleading information. Studies on large language models (LLMs) reveal that these errors stem from structural generation methods, posing challenges in education where accuracy is crucial (Bender et al., 2021; Ji et al., 2023).

Understanding AI Hallucinations

AI hallucinations occur because generative models rely on statistical probabilities from large datasets, unlike human instructors who use verified facts and experience. Since AI lacks human-like understanding, it may confidently provide plausible yet incorrect answers, posing risks when students rely on these without verifying with reliable sources.

Case Study: Hallucinations in AI-Powered History Lessons

A real-world classroom case in Japan illustrates how generative AI can create plausible but inaccurate historical narratives. During an elementary school lesson on Tokugawa Ieyasu, a major historical figure who unified Japan in the early 17th century, students used AI to learn about his early life. When they asked what Ieyasu did at specific ages, the AI confidently returned inconsistent and randomly generated ages. In another case, the AI fabricated detailed stories about his childhood based on estimated timelines, even though such specifics are not historically documented. These invented yet believable stories risk misleading young learners if there is no proper supervision or source verification.

Why This Matters: The Consequences of AI Hallucinations in Learning

AI hallucinations matter because:

- Misinformation disrupts learning, leading to persistent false knowledge. Students may overly rely on AI, trusting responses without critical evaluation.
- Teachers face challenges in verifying AI content, as hallucinations occur even in advanced systems.

To mitigate these risks, schools must adopt strategies to teach students how to critically engage with AI-generated information, rather than passively accept it.

3.3 Educating Students About AI Limitations

To make AI a valuable educational tool, students must learn its limitations and practice critical thinking when using generative models. AI literacy has become vital, with scholars advocating for curricula and policies to guide responsible AI use (Ng et al., 2021; Smuha, 2021).

Teaching Verification Techniques

Educators should integrate fact-checking into AI-assisted learning, encouraging students to:

- Cross-reference AI responses with reliable academic sources, textbooks, and expert opinions.
- Utilize multiple AI tools or knowledge bases to compare responses for accuracy.
- Employ critical reading strategies to identify inconsistencies or ambiguous statements in AI outputs.

Promoting Critical Thinking and Inquiry-Based Learning

AI literacy should encompass critical engagement with AI-generated content. Students should learn to:

- Evaluate the source and credibility of AI-provided information.
- Identify instances where AI expresses uncertainty or provides speculative answers.
- Distinguish factual data from AI-derived assumptions.

Understanding AI's Probabilistic Nature

Unlike human educators who rely on expertise, reasoning, and judgment, AI generates responses through pattern recognition and probabilities. Students should grasp that:

- AI predicts answers using statistical models, not by "knowing" facts. AI-generated content can lack context, which may cause misinterpretations or overlook nuances
- AI cannot assess ethical or moral considerations as human educators do.

Promoting AI literacy empowers students to use AI as a tool to complement human learning, while preserving critical thinking and reliance on human expertise.

4. Case Studies: Applications of Affective HRI

This chapter presents real-world case studies that illustrate how affective HRI (Human-Robot Interaction) can enhance educational experiences. By focusing on emotional engagement, adaptive support, and inclusive applications, these examples demonstrate the practical value of emotionally intelligent robots in diverse learning environments.

4.1 Enhancing Engagement through Emotional Robots

The Role of Emotions in Sustaining Student Engagement

- **Emotionally expressive** robots enhance classroom engagement by addressing motivational challenges in traditional learning. They create interactive experiences, connecting lessons to students' emotions and personal interests. A study with elementary students revealed that emotional robots enhanced classroom engagement by dynamically responding to student progress and fostering interaction through supportive feedback. Kennedy et al. (2015), who investigated emotionally expressive robots in classrooms, found that such robots maintained long-term student engagement through dynamic, personalized responses. Similarly, Belpaeme et al. (2018) demonstrated that robots equipped with emotion recognition could adjust feedback in real time, helping students stay attentive and involved. Unlike static materials, these systems adapted to student progress, enhancing engagement through dynamic feedback loops.
- Emotionally expressive robots boosted participation by offering supportive facial expressions, nods, and phrases like "Give it another try!" when students hesitated, fostering engagement. Kanda et al. (2004) showed that children responded positively to robot gestures and speech patterns, viewing them as friendly and approachable classroom partners.
- Interactive emotional responses enhanced classroom dynamics, with research demonstrating that emotionally expressive robots positively impact classroom behavior (Kennedy et al., 2015; Gordon et al., 2015).

Gamification and Emotional Feedback in Education

Affective robots transform routine learning into immersive experiences by combining gamification with emotional intelligence. They can:

- Simulate animated "emotion badges" to reward persistence, creativity, or teamwork. Leyzberg et al. (2014) explored how visual emotional rewards from robots can reinforce desirable student behaviors without using verbal commands.
- Display concerned expressions when students err, encouraging reflection rather than discouragement (Kennedy et al., 2015).
- Adjust tone and interaction style based on engagement levels, using enthusiastic speech to re-engage students. Gordon et al. (2015) demonstrated that emotionally adaptive robots could maintain classroom attention by dynamically shifting communication strategies, while Kory-Westlund &

Breazeal (2019a) emphasized how vocal enthusiasm and timely feedback enhance students' emotional connection and sustained motivation.

In a third-grade spelling game, an emotional robot responded in real-time through two key strategies:

- **Supporting Struggles:** Provided hints with patience and encouragement when students struggled.
- **Celebrating Success:** Mirrored students' enthusiasm after correct answers, making learning feel rewarding and personal.

Students felt more connected to the process, viewing the robot as a responsive learning companion rather than a passive instructor (Kory-Westlund & Breazeal, 2019a).

These findings underscore the transformative impact of emotional engagement strategies on student interaction with educational content.

4.2 Supporting Struggling Students

Adaptive Teaching Through Emotion Recognition

Affective robots can detect signs of frustration and adjust teaching styles in real time. This capability is particularly beneficial for struggling learners, who may need personalized guidance that adapts to their needs.

In a junior high school math classroom, an AI-powered robot was programmed to:

- Detect frustration through behavioral indicators such as pauses, repeated errors, or confused expressions, as highlighted by Leite et al. (2013), who emphasized the value of real-time behavioral tracking in detecting emotional states during learning.
- Modify its instructional style by breaking complex problems into smaller steps or switching explanation methods. Leyzberg et al. (2018) demonstrated that such adaptive strategies lead to greater learning gains, while Gordon et al. (2015) showed improvements in engagement when emotional feedback was integrated into teaching.
- Provide encouragement with supportive phrases like "You're really close! Let's try another angle," a method found by Leyzberg et al. (2018) to increase persistence in difficult tasks.

Reducing Learning Anxiety and Building Confidence

Fear of failure often creates anxiety for struggling students, leading to avoidance behaviors that hinder learning (FitzGerald et al., 2018).

Building Confidence with Emotionally Aware Robots

Emotionally aware robots can boost students' confidence in their abilities. In a study on robot-assisted foreign language learning, students who initially felt nervous reported:

- Lower anxiety when practicing with robots, as they offered non-judgmental feedback (Kennedy et al., 2015), showing that emotional neutrality in robots helps ease performance pressure.
- Greater willingness to experiment with language, encouraged by the robots' supportive expressions and low-pressure environment (Leyzberg et al., 2018), which proved especially effective in language acquisition contexts.
- Improved retention and performance through frequent practice supported by adaptive, encouraging guidance (Leyzberg et al., 2018; Belpaeme et al., 2018), with both studies noting the benefits of repeated emotional support over time.

Long-Term Impacts of Emotionally Intelligent Tutoring

Researchers conducted a six-month study with middle school students to assess the long-term effects of emotionally aware tutoring robots on learning science and math (Leyzberg et al., 2018; Gordon et al., 2015).

Findings from this study highlighted that:

- Students with emotionally adaptive tutoring demonstrated greater test score improvements compared to peers who received neutral, text-based instruction, which Leyzberg et al. (2018) linked this to deeper engagement and tailored support.
- Motivation levels stayed consistently high throughout the study, with Gordon et al. (2015) emphasizing the role of affective feedback in sustaining learning interest.

Students who initially struggled with self-confidence in learning tasks showed the greatest improvements, suggesting that affective HRI can foster the development of self-efficacy in learners (Rosenthal-von der Pütten & Bock, 2018; Leite et al., 2014), particularly through emotionally responsive scaffolding and encouragement.

4.3 Expanding the Use of Emotional Robots: Future Applications

Supporting Students with Special Educational Needs (SEN)

Emotional robots show great potential in supporting students with autism spectrum disorder (ASD) and special educational needs (SEN), addressing challenges in interpreting social cues and verbal communication. Affective robots can support these students by:

- Structured, predictable interactions enable students to practice social communication in a controlled setting. Cabibihan et al. (2013) demonstrated that routine-based robot interactions can improve comfort and communication for children with ASD.
- Using clear verbal cues and exaggerated facial expressions, robots help students recognize emotions in conversations. Bekele et al. (2014) showed that

enhanced visual-emotional expressions by robots aid emotional recognition in autistic children.

- Acting as social mediators, robots assist students in learning how to participate effectively in group activities with peers. A study by Pennisi et al. (2015) found that children with ASD were more responsive to robots displaying expressive, consistent behaviors than to human instructors, due to reduced unpredictability and pressure.

Emotional Robots in Higher Education and Professional Training

Though much research has centered on primary and secondary education, emotional robots are now being explored in higher education and professional training contexts such as medical education, engineering, and law. These applications focus on helping students develop not only technical expertise but also emotional intelligence and decision-making skills.

- Simulated emotional responses in robotic patients help medical students develop better bedside manners and empathy skills. Cramer et al. (2009) introduced robotic patient simulators with emotional feedback, which improved humanistic skills in clinical education.
- AI-powered virtual mentors utilize affective computing to guide students through complex decision-making scenarios, such as patient diagnosis. Davenport & Kalakota (2019) emphasized the importance of emotional and cognitive reasoning in high-stakes learning environments.
- Emotionally responsive tutoring robots are being studied in fields like engineering and law to assist students with high-pressure problem-solving tasks, where emotional regulation and stress management are critical for decision quality.

5. Discussion

This chapter synthesizes findings from prior experiments and theoretical discussions to reflect on the implications of emotionally intelligent robots in education, especially regarding engagement, motivation, and ethical challenges.

5.1 Bridging the Emotional Gap in HRI

A key challenge in human-robot interaction (HRI) is the emotional gap between robots and users. While educational robots excel at delivering factual content, their inability to address emotional cues can lead to less engaging and, at times, frustrating interactions. This disconnect is critical, as learning involves both cognitive and emotional processes. When a student struggles with a problem, a robot that overlooks frustration risks discouragement. An emotionally intelligent robot, however, can detect signs like pauses or errors, adapting its approach by offering encouragement, simplifying explanations, or breaking problems into steps, emulating the adaptive strategies of human educators (Kory-Westlund & Breazeal, 2019b; Gordon et al., 2015).

The Role of Emotional Intelligence in Human-Robot Interaction

For robots to serve as effective learning companions, they must detect and respond to students' emotional cues. Emotional intelligence in HRI builds rapport, sustains engagement, and enhances motivation.

Emotionally neutral robots risk appearing cold, reducing motivation, particularly for younger learners who need emotional reinforcement. For instance, a robot acknowledging frustration with supportive feedback, such as "Let's break it down together," can restore confidence and re-engage students.

Empirical Evidence: Emotional Robots in Education

Studies affirm the effectiveness of emotionally intelligent robots. Leite et al. (2013) found that empathetic behaviors like facial expressions and verbal affirmations increase student engagement. Robots displaying enthusiasm and curiosity also enhance students' attitudes toward learning (Kory-Westlund & Breazeal, 2019b; Gordon et al., 2015). While emotional robots boost engagement, a study by Saerbeck et al. (2010) showed they can foster reliance on robotic feedback, reducing independent problem-solving. This underscores the need to balance support with encouraging self-motivation.

Challenges in Bridging the Emotional Gap

Despite the promising research, several challenges remain in the development of emotionally intelligent robots:

1. Accuracy in Emotion Recognition
AI-driven robots face challenges in accurately interpreting emotions, particularly in diverse classrooms where cultural differences influence emotional expression. Pre-programmed systems often struggle to respond effectively.

2. Over-Reliance on Robots for Emotional Support
Over-reliance on robotic encouragement can hinder self-motivation and resilience. Future designs should prioritize fostering human-to-human collaboration over solely providing emotional reinforcement.

3. Cultural Variability in Emotional Expression
Emotional expression varies widely across cultures, as a smile might be encouraging in one but insincere in another. Robots need adaptive emotional models to adjust responses based on cultural context.

Future Directions in Emotional HRI

Advancements in affective computing and deep learning are essential to tackle these challenges. Emotionally intelligent robots must be trained on diverse datasets for cultural adaptability, while adaptive algorithms can enable personalized interactions, complementing rather than replacing human emotional intelligence in education.

Integrating emotion recognition with adaptive responses enables HRI to deliver personalized, engaging education while preserving students' emotional agency and independence.

5.2 The Intersection of Generative AI and Emotional Interaction

Generative AI advancements, including large language models like ChatGPT, have revolutionized robot-student interactions by enabling adaptive, real-time responses. Unlike static pre-programmed systems, AI-driven robots dynamically adjust their language, tone, and emotional expressions to meet students' needs.

The integration of Generative AI with emotional intelligence advances HRI by enabling personalized, engaging learning experiences. However, it also poses risks like hallucinations, emotional manipulation, and ethical challenges.

How Generative AI Enhances Emotional HRI

Generative AI: Key enhancements in emotional HRI:

1. **Personalized Emotional Responses**
   AI-powered robots analyze students' learning behaviors and emotional cues to deliver supportive, tailored responses in real time.
2. **Dynamic Conversation Flow**
   Generative AI enables fluid, intuitive interactions, making student communication feel less robotic and more engaging.
3. **Adaptive Teaching Strategies**
   AI-driven robots adjust teaching methods using real-time feedback to keep students engaged and prevent overwhelm.

Example: An AI-integrated robot teaching math could detect frustration in a student's voice and respond with encouragement, saying: "This problem is tricky, but you're making great progress! Let's go step by step, I know you can do this!"

Emotionally adaptive AI fosters resilience, motivation, and a growth mindset, helping students persist through challenges.

The Risks of AI-Generated Emotional Interaction

Despite its benefits, the combination of generative AI and emotional intelligence raises significant challenges, particularly concerning accuracy, trust, and ethics.

Risk of Hallucination in Educational AI

One of the biggest dangers in AI-driven education is hallucination, when AI fabricates false or misleading information. This is particularly problematic because students, especially younger ones, tend to trust AI-generated content without questioning it.

Example: In our recent classroom study, an AI educational assistant engaged students with responses about historical figures but occasionally provided inaccurate or speculative information, risking misconceptions if unchecked. This issue reflects broader concerns about the spread of false information by AI, a risk highlighted in other domains as well, for instance, on social media, where false news is known to spread faster than truthful content (Vosoughi et al., 2018).

Ethical Manipulation of Emotions

AI-driven emotional robots can shape student behavior, requiring careful regulation. Excessive praise may lead to overconfidence, while overly critical feedback might demotivate struggling students. Corporations could also misuse emotional AI to promote products or embed ideological biases in educational content (Calo, 2014).

Loss of Human Judgment in Emotional Support

Although AI can mimic empathy, it lacks true emotional comprehension. Excessive reliance on AI for emotional support may hinder students' development of real-world emotional intelligence and social skills.

5.3 *Ethical Considerations in Affective HRI*

The integration of generative AI into affective HRI marks a major advancement in educational technology. Models like ChatGPT and Bard enhance adaptive tutoring and emotionally expressive robots, creating personalized learning opportunities. However, this evolution also raises ethical concerns, including issues of accuracy, bias, emotional manipulation, and reliance on AI-driven emotional interactions. AI-powered robots offer real-time emotional feedback but require careful deployment. Without ethical safeguards, they risk spreading misinformation and unintentionally impacting students' cognitive and emotional development.

1. *The Hallucination Problem: Can We Trust Emotionally Persuasive AI?*

AI-generated hallucinations, where incorrect or misleading information is fabricated, pose ethical concerns, especially with emotionally expressive systems that encourage blind trust. In an experiment with primary students, an AI chatbot role-playing historical figures delivered engaging but inaccurate responses, such as fabricated events or misattributed opinions. Its emotional nuance and confidence led students to accept the misinformation without questioning it, embedding false understanding more deeply.

Mitigation Strategy: Educational robots should include real-time fact-checking systems and promote AI literacy, teaching students to critically assess AI-generated responses.

2. *The Risk of Emotional Manipulation in AI-Driven Education*

AI can unintentionally influence student emotions during learning, requiring balanced engagement. A review found that subtle strategies like exaggeration or omission can affect trust, decisions, and credibility in unexpected ways (Esposito,

Rossi, & Rossi, 2024). This highlights how even subtle emotional cues in AI can unintentionally manipulate learner perception.

a. Over-Expressing Sympathy
Excessive reassurance can lead to dependency and hinder resilience. For instance, an AI repeatedly saying, "This is hard for everyone," may encourage helplessness rather than problem-solving.

b. Over-Authoritative Responses
Conversely, if AI tutors adopt a rigid tone, e.g., "No, that answer is incorrect", students may stop questioning content and rely uncritically on the AI.

Mitigation Strategy: AI should balance encouragement and challenge. Its tone and language should support confidence and curiosity while promoting independent thinking.

3. Over-Reliance on Emotional Robots

Emotionally responsive AI reduces stress and boosts engagement but may deter interaction with teachers. Students often favor robots in high-stress situations for their non-judgmental nature (Sharkey, 2016). This suggests that emotionally neutral AI can become preferable to human teachers under pressure. However, long-term reliance on emotional AI may hinder development of:

- Communication and collaboration skills
- Emotional intelligence and empathy
- Real-world resilience

Mitigation Strategy: Educational policy should define AI use boundaries. Robots should supplement, not replace, human interaction.

4. Bias in AI-Generated Emotional Interactions

AI reflects the biases in its training data. In educational settings, this can perpetuate inequality.

Representative examples of such biases include:

- **Cultural bias:** Favoring students with assertive communication styles over those from more modest cultures (Howard & Borenstein, 2017). This reflects how AI can unintentionally privilege dominant cultural norms in communication.
- **Gender bias:** Encouraging boys more than girls toward STEM-related content (Buolamwini & Gebru, 2018). This highlights the risk of AI systems reinforcing gender stereotypes through biased training data.

To mitigate these risks, the following strategies are recommended:

- Train AI on diverse datasets
- Perform regular bias audits
- Maintain human oversight to ensure equitable emotional engagement

5. *Best Practices for Ethical AI in Affective HRI*

To ensure responsible use of emotional AI, institutions should adopt the following:

- **Transparency:** Robots must disclose their limitations and clarify that AI emotions are simulated.
- **Mandatory AI Literacy:** Teach students to evaluate AI-generated responses critically.
- **Fact Verification:** Cross-check all output with trusted sources.
- **Interaction Boundaries:** Set emotional engagement limits to prevent over-dependence.
- **Ethical Oversight:** Conduct regular audits for bias, misinformation, and over-reliance.

Balancing Innovation and Ethics in Affective HRI

Affective AI in education holds tremendous potential to create engaging, adaptive, and personalized learning experiences. However, without ethical safeguards, the same technology could lead to misinformation, emotional dependency, and bias reinforcement.

By implementing transparency, AI literacy, and human oversight, educators can ensure that AI-powered robots support, not replace, human learning and development. The real challenge is not just making robots emotionally intelligent, but ethically responsible.

6. Conclusion

Affective learning through human-robot interaction (HRI) presents a transformative shift in education, offering new ways to engage, support, and motivate students. Robots that can recognize and express emotions foster personalized learning experiences, making education more interactive and adaptive. These capabilities have the potential to enhance engagement, encourage perseverance, and provide tailored assistance, particularly for students who struggle with conventional learning methods. However, to fully harness these benefits, several critical challenges must be addressed.

One of the most pressing concerns is cultural variability in emotional expression. Emotions are deeply tied to social and cultural norms, meaning that a robot designed with a fixed set of emotional responses may not resonate universally with all students. Future advancements in adaptive emotional AI models will be necessary to ensure that robots can effectively interpret and respond to diverse student emotions in a culturally sensitive manner.

Additionally, ethical considerations in affective HRI cannot be overlooked. The ability of robots to influence students' emotions carries inherent risks, including over-dependence on AI-driven emotional support, bias in AI training models, and the potential manipulation of student behavior. To mitigate these risks, clear ethical guidelines must be established, ensuring that AI-driven robots enhance human learning rather than replace essential social and emotional development.

Transparency in how these systems operate, human oversight in AI-driven interactions, and ongoing ethical audits should be central to the development and implementation of affective educational robots.

The integration of generative AI further magnifies both the opportunities and challenges of affective HRI. AI-powered educational assistants can personalize learning content, provide real-time feedback, and foster interactive conversations, making education more accessible and engaging. However, as seen in recent educational trials, generative AI is prone to hallucinations, producing incorrect or misleading information. This highlights the urgent need to educate students about AI limitations, teaching them critical thinking skills and fact-verification techniques to navigate AI-generated content responsibly.

To ensure the responsible and effective implementation of affective robots in education, collaboration between educators, technologists, psychologists, and policymakers is crucial. By fostering interdisciplinary cooperation, we can design emotionally intelligent robots that support, rather than hinder, student development. Furthermore, longitudinal studies are needed to assess the long-term impact of emotional AI on learning outcomes and social-emotional development.

Ultimately, the future of AI-driven emotional robots in education depends on our ability to balance technological advancements with ethical integrity. If developed and implemented thoughtfully, these systems can revolutionize education, making learning more engaging, accessible, and emotionally intelligent. However, without proper oversight and ethical considerations, they risk becoming tools that inadvertently misguide, manipulate, or diminish essential human interactions. By maintaining a human-centered approach, we can ensure that AI-driven affective learning enhances, rather than replaces, the emotional and cognitive richness of education.

Further Reading

For an in-depth analysis, refer to the original study: [DOI=10.3389/frai.2024.1493348].

Column 1: Risks and Precautions When Using Robots in Education

The integration of robots and generative AI brings opportunities for personalized learning but also risks, like AI-generated misinformation, which can cause lasting misconceptions in education. A study with Japanese middle school students revealed that AI-powered robots using deceptive tactics like lying and pandering were highly convincing. Most students failed to detect misinformation, emphasizing the need for safeguards in deploying such tools (Salem & Sumi, 2024).

Key Precautions to Mitigate Risks

Verification of Information

Educational robots should use fact-verified content, with educators regularly reviewing responses and ensuring students understand that AI-generated information might not always be accurate.

Teaching AI Literacy

Schools should integrate lessons that:

- Teach fact-checking strategies using trusted sources
- Develop students' critical thinking so they question AI outputs
- Explain how generative AI predicts responses rather than "knows" facts

Transparency in AI Usage

Educators and students should be informed about AI usage, including its capabilities and limits. Predefined scripts help minimize reliance on unpredictable AI responses.

Managing Social Influence

Human-like AI robots can significantly impact students psychologically. Educators should present AI as an assistant, not an authority, while fostering independent verification of information. By adopting these measures, schools can enhance AI benefits while reducing risks such as misinformation and over-dependence.

Column 2: The Impact of Robot Facial Design on Education

The facial design of educational robots significantly impacts student engagement, trust, and information retention. Human-like and anime-style/cartoon faces have unique psychological effects on learners. A study found that anime-style faces increased engagement, while human-like faces enhanced perceived authority and trust but encouraged greater belief in false information (Salem & Sumi, 2024), highlighting the strategic importance of facial design.

Design Considerations for Educational Robots

1. *Anime-Style Faces*

- **Higher engagement:** Students enjoy engaging with playful, cartoon-like robots due to their fun and approachable nature.
- **Healthy skepticism:** Lower authority perception encourages students to question content rather than accept it unquestioningly.
- **Cultural fit:** Particularly effective in Japan, where anime is deeply ingrained in youth culture.

2. *Human-Like Faces*

- **Greater trust and rapport:** These robots are perceived as intelligent and highly expressive emotionally.
- **Risk of over-trust:** Students are prone to trusting robot responses, even if they're inaccurate.
- **Cultural and Contextual Fit:** Cultural preferences affect responses to robot faces, with minimalistic or mechanical designs being more suitable in certain regions. Robot design should align with educational goals.

6 Observation of Students' Behavior for Affective Learning

1. Introduction and Background

Human behavior reveals hidden insights, especially emotions expressed unintentionally during actions. These emotions can be analyzed for applications like marketing, security, user experience in human-robot interaction, and affective learning—this chapter's focus.

Affective learning improves education by analyzing students' emotions, such as confusion or interest, through their behaviors. Instructors can adapt teaching styles in real-time to enhance learning. For example, they may simplify lessons or add engaging content if students seem bored or assign challenging tasks to boost engagement.

Personalized learning is essential, as students have varied abilities. Quick learners can be supported to advance further, while slower learners may benefit from tutoring or parental collaboration.

Instructors often assign group learning tasks, emphasizing equal participation for fairness and effectiveness. Monitoring teamwork and resolving conflicts is vital. Automatic emotion prediction can aid instructors and improve collaboration, enhancing overall learning efficiency.

2. Technologies for Emotion Detection from Movement

Emotion prediction for affective learning uses cues like facial expressions, speech tone, and body language. This chapter explores methods to extract such emotional data to enhance learning and engagement.

Studies show emotions can be predicted from walking styles. Observing students' posture before and after class helps assess emotional states, identify those needing support, and gauge engagement with class activities.

Walking posture reveals emotions, requiring skeletal data from motion-capturing equipment. Marker-based devices like Vicon and OptiTrack offer high accuracy but need suits, complex setups, and significant investment.

Markerless motion capture, using computer vision, tracks skeletal data from a distance without requiring suits or markers. While less accurate than marker-based systems, it monitors movement unobtrusively, often unnoticed.

These devices use RGB and infrared cameras to capture depth images, processed by machine learning to predict joint positions like hands and hips. Microsoft's Kinect, Intel RealSense, and Orbbec Femto offer similar motion capture capabilities without requiring suits or markers.

DOI: 10.1201/9781003782735-8

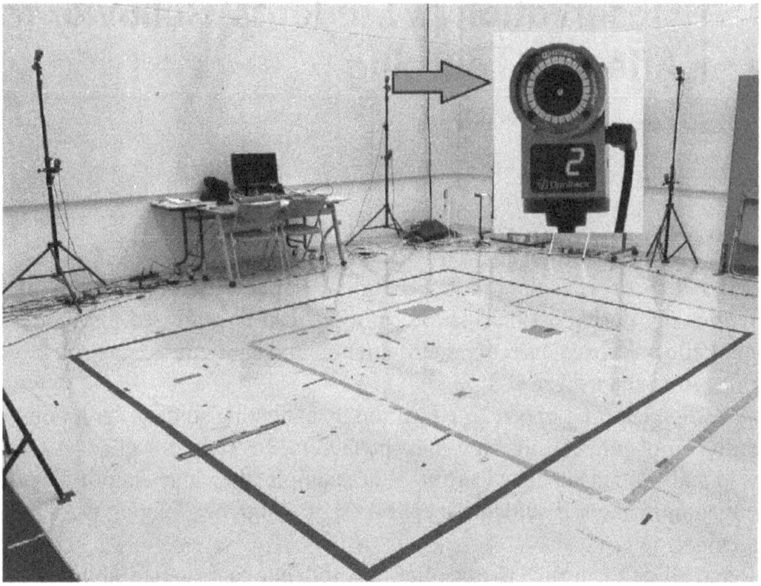

Fig. 1 Sample Environment Setup for Marker-based Motion Capturing System (Equipment: OptiTrack Flex 3, two devices per pole, 14 devices in total)

Fig. 2 Specialized Suits with Multiple Markers are Essential for Marker-Based Motion Capture

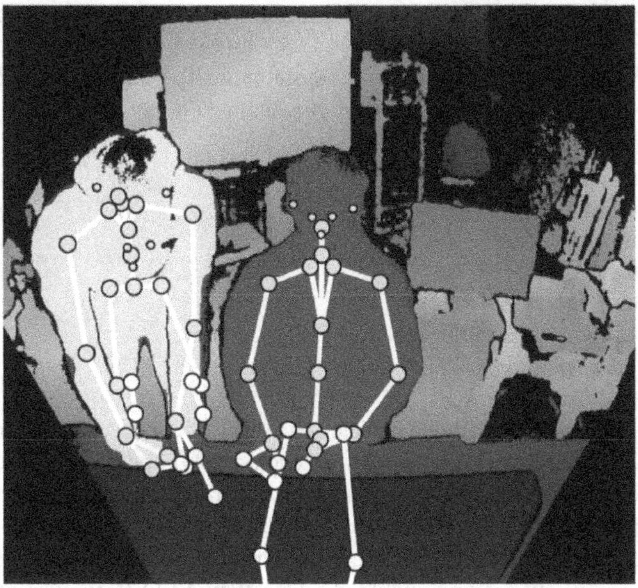

Fig. 3 Human Skeletal Data from Kinect Body Tracking SDK (Markerless System). Missing Joints are Inferred When Some Parts of the Body are Occluded.

When motion tracking equipment isn't feasible, videos or still images offer a cost-effective, flexible alternative, though less accurate. Sources like CCTV, webcams, or phone cameras can be used for skeleton tracking. OpenPose, a tool by Carnegie Mellon University, extracts 2D joint coordinates from standard videos or images using regular cameras. While less accurate than specialized devices, it offers an affordable, accessible solution for emotion prediction without needing complex setups.

To detect emotions from skeletal data, analyzing angles between connected body joints is effective. For instance, angles between ankle-to-knee and knee-to-hip reveal leg movement, pelvis-to-chest and chest-to-neck show body bending, chest-to-neck and neck-to-head indicate head tilting, while wrist-to-elbow and elbow-to-shoulder assess arm swing.

3. Experimental Design and Findings

Capturing walking data without participants' awareness brings challenges, like varied walking paths. In studies, participants walked freely while viewing emotional videos on Microsoft HoloLens 2, blending stimuli with their environment. Data from 49 individuals showed body movement differences between happiness and sadness. Most walked in circular patterns, with 146 trials categorized by direction and trajectory types, including counterclockwise, clockwise, and mixed paths.

In previous studies (Jianwattanapaisarn et al., 2022 and Jianwattanapaisarn, 2022), variations in walking straightness (curvature) and walking direction were found to influence body movements. To systematically analyze these effects, each frame of walking data was categorized into distinct curvature groups, as follows:

- Clockwise Direction
  - Small Curved Walking (–15° to –5°)
  - Moderate Curved Walking (–25° to –15°)
  - Large Curved Walking (–35° to –25°)
- Straight Walking (–5° to 5°)
- Counter-Clockwise Direction
  - Small Curved Walking (5° to 15°)
  - Moderate Curved Walking (15° to 25°)
  - Large Curved Walking (25° to 35°)

For further analysis, angles between each pair of connected body joints were computed. Subsequently, the standard deviation (SD) and mean values of each angle were calculated across the entire walking trial. As a result, each trial was characterized by a set of gait features, represented by the mean and SD values of these joint angles, effectively capturing the participant's walking posture.

Analyses of gait features included a One-Way ANOVA to examine if mean and SD values of angles varied across emotions—happiness, sadness, or neutral. Significant differences were further analyzed using a Tukey HSD test, focusing on happiness vs. sadness.

Results show that within each curvature group, at least one gait feature significantly differed between happiness and sadness. The most consistent feature across groups is the SD of the angle representing left arm swing, which reflects arm movement magnitude. Left arm swing exhibited significant differences between happy and sad walking across all curvature groups, whereas the right arm swing did not. This asymmetry was analyzed further, revealing that outside arms in circular walking (left during clockwise, right during counterclockwise) had larger movements than inside arms.

Figures 7 and 8 analyze arm swing differences under emotional states. Figure 7 shows that with high curvature, the left arm swing's magnitude differs significantly between happiness and sadness when positioned outside. As curvature decreases, the difference lessens but remains detectable. Inside positioning results in smaller differences compared to outside positioning. Figure 8 shows that differences in right arm swing magnitude between happiness and sadness are smaller compared to the left arm across all curvature levels. When the right arm is outside with high curvature, the difference is more noticeable than with small curvature or inside positioning. Overall, arm swing magnitude on either side is consistently greater during happy walking than sad walking, regardless of position or curvature.

A Multi-Factor ANOVA analyzed factors influencing arm swing magnitude across all curvature levels. Significant factors included emotion, walking curvature, arm side-emotion interaction, and curvature-arm side interaction. A Tukey HSD test confirmed a notable impact of emotion, revealing significant differences in

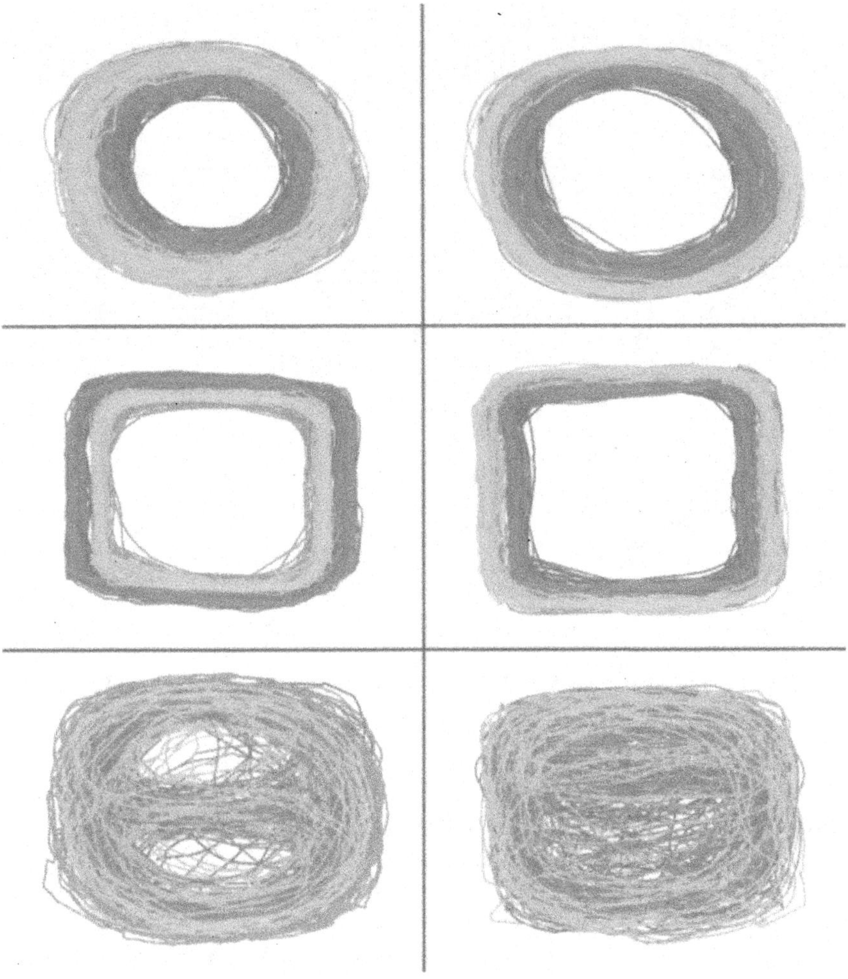

Fig. 4 Example of Walking Trajectories showing Different Walking Patterns.

arm swing magnitude between happiness and sadness. To further examine left and right arm swings, linear regression analyses compared their regression slopes. The left arm swing magnitude showed a significant difference between happy and sad walking, while the right arm did not exhibit statistically significant differences. These results align with previous findings, highlighting that arm swing magnitude during sad walking differs significantly from happy walking, specifically in the left arm. The reason for this asymmetry remains uncertain, warranting further investigation. Certain questions remain unresolved, including whether gender influences emotional expression and if arm movement asymmetry is linked to dominant hand side. The initial dataset lacked dominant hand data and had an uneven male-to-female ratio, complicating gender analysis. To address these gaps,

Fig. 5 A Participant walking in the Recording Area in a Direction-Free Pattern.

a subsequent study (Jianwattanapaisarn, 2022) recruited more participants for a similar experiment as in (Jianwattanapaisarn et al., 2022). This time, dominant hand preferences were recorded, hypothesized to affect arm swing differences, and the dataset was balanced in the number of male and female participants.

The new dataset consists of 13 female and 10 male participants. Dominant hand preference was recorded using a questionnaire-based dominant hand score evaluation. Additionally, dominant foot and dominant brain side data were recorded, as these factors might be related to asymmetries in arm movements. In total, 69 walking trials were collected. The data collection method was identical to that used for the first dataset in (Jianwattanapaisarn et al., 2022). Figure 9 presents examples of walking trajectories from this dataset, which are comparable to those in the first dataset.

However, since the dataset size is relatively small, analyzing it separately may not yield statistically robust results. To enhance the reliability of the analysis, the dataset was combined with the first dataset, resulting in a total of 72 participants (51 male and 21 female). The average age was 19.76 years, with a standard deviation of 2.05 years.

A similar analysis to that conducted on the first dataset was performed. The results of One-Way ANOVA indicate that walking with sadness and happiness emotions also produces differences in walking postures. However, statistically significant differences were not observed across all curvature levels, as was the

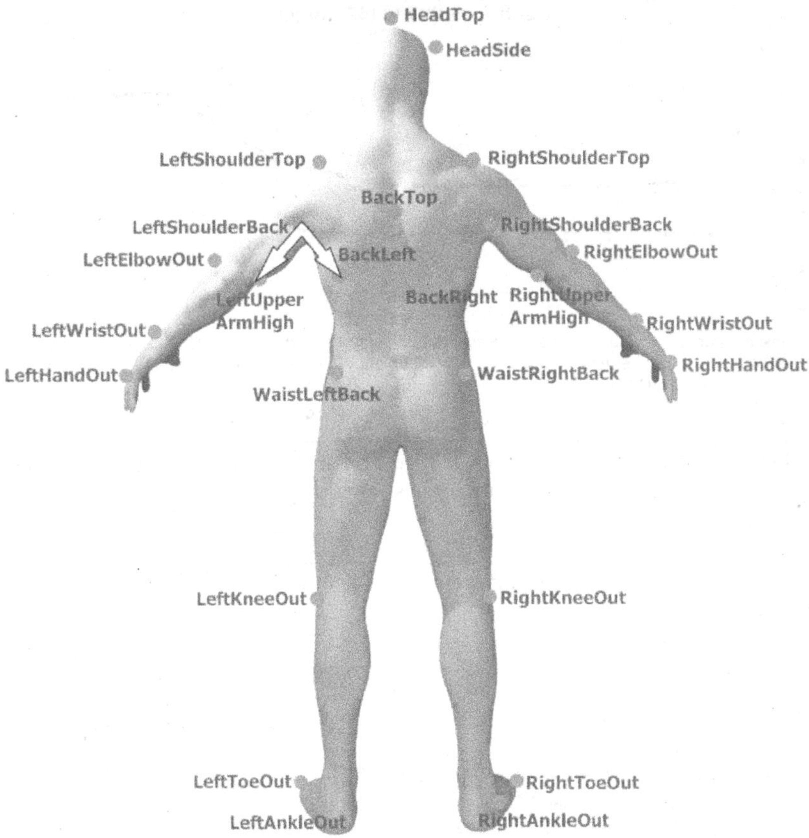

Fig. 6 The angle representing Left Arm Swing Magnitude.

case in the first dataset. In the combined dataset, curvature levels were categorized in the same manner as in the first dataset, but statistically significant differences in arm swing magnitudes were only found in moderate curved walking (–25° to -15°) and large curved walking (25° to 35°). In contrast, the first dataset exhibited significant differences across all curvature levels.

Despite the lack of statistical significance across all curvature levels, the trends in arm swing magnitudes in the combined dataset align with those observed in the first dataset, particularly in curvature levels that demonstrated significant differences.

To further validate the differences between sad and happy walks, arm swing magnitudes were plotted for each curvature level, distinguishing between when each arm was inside versus outside. This visualization was conducted in the same manner as in the first dataset analysis. Figures 10 and 11 illustrate these differences.

Figure 10 demonstrates that the left arm's swing magnitude shows minimal variation when positioned inside, regardless of curvature level. However, when

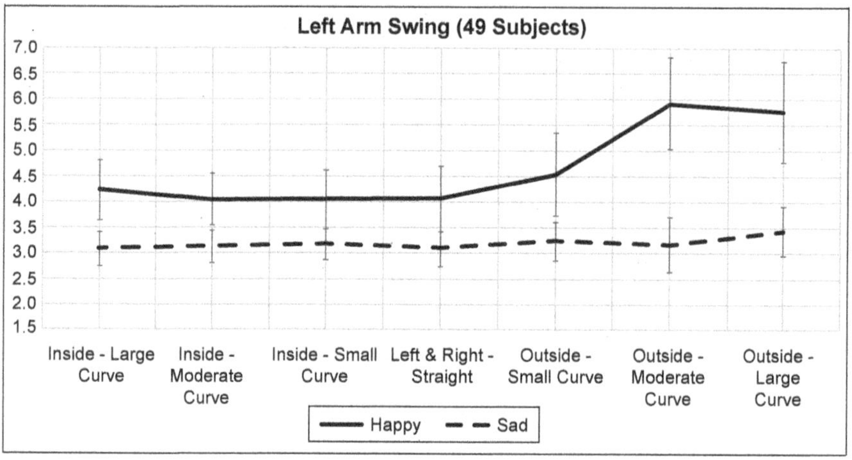

Fig. 7 Plot of Arm Swing Magnitude when the Left Arm is Inside and Outside with Different Curvatures (49 participants).

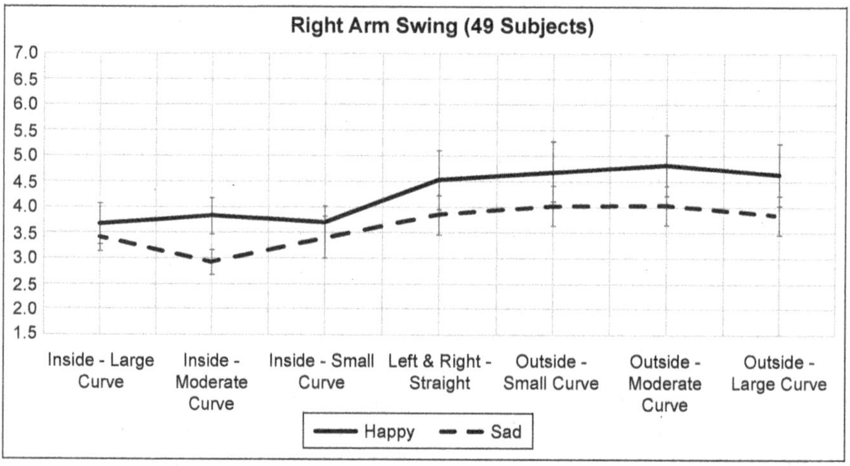

Fig. 8 Plot of Arm Swing Magnitude when the Right Arm is Inside and Outside with Different Curvatures (49 participants).

positioned outside, the magnitude consistently increases with higher curvature. Differences in swing magnitude between sadness and happiness are generally small across conditions but become more distinguishable at large curvature levels.

Figure 11 highlights the differences in right arm swing magnitudes between happiness and sadness across various curvature levels and positions (inside or outside). These differences are less pronounced than those in the left arm but show a similar behavioral pattern. The plots show that the arm swing magnitude increases when positioned outside and decreases when positioned inside for both

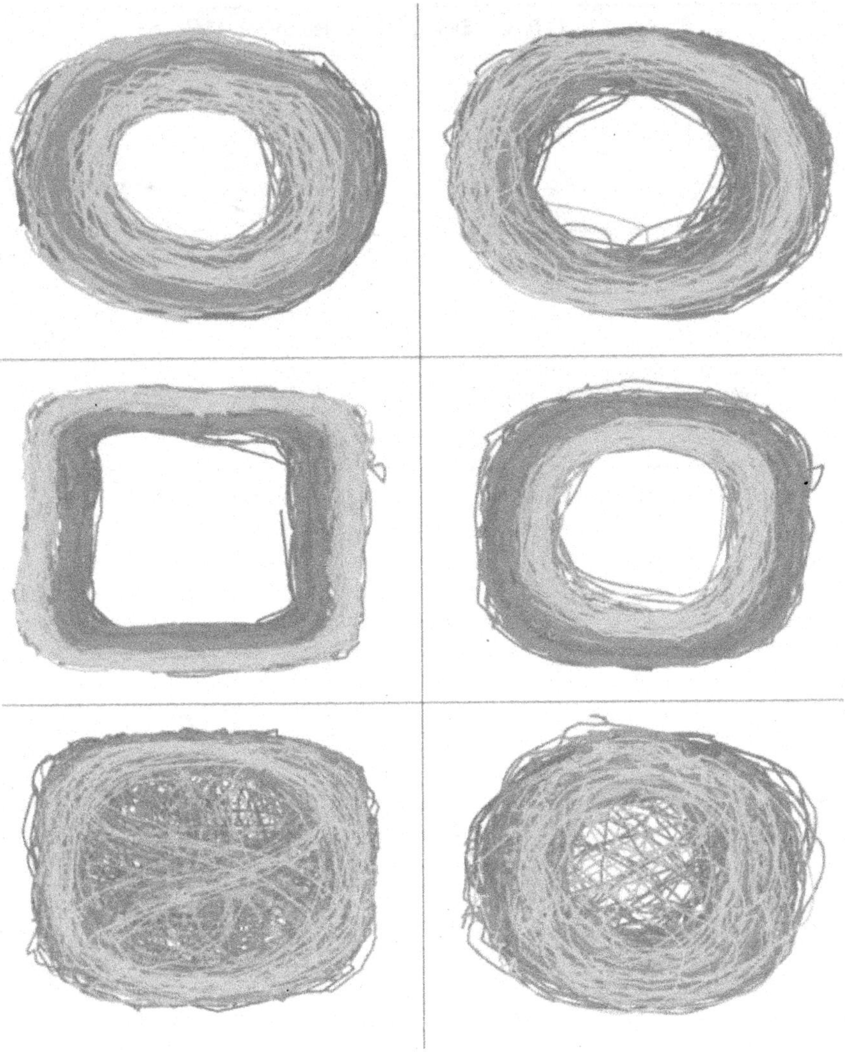

Fig. 9 Examples of Walking Trajectories in the Second Dataset.

arms. Emotional differences between happiness and sadness are minimal during straight walking but more noticeable during high-curvature walking, especially in the left arm. These results align with findings from the first dataset, indicating that left arm swing magnitude better reflects emotional states, particularly when positioned outside during large curvature walking. Using the combined dataset, Multi-Factor ANOVA analyzed left and right arm swing magnitudes along with dominant hand, dominant foot, and dominant brain side. Key factors influencing arm swing magnitudes include emotion (happiness or sadness), walking curvature

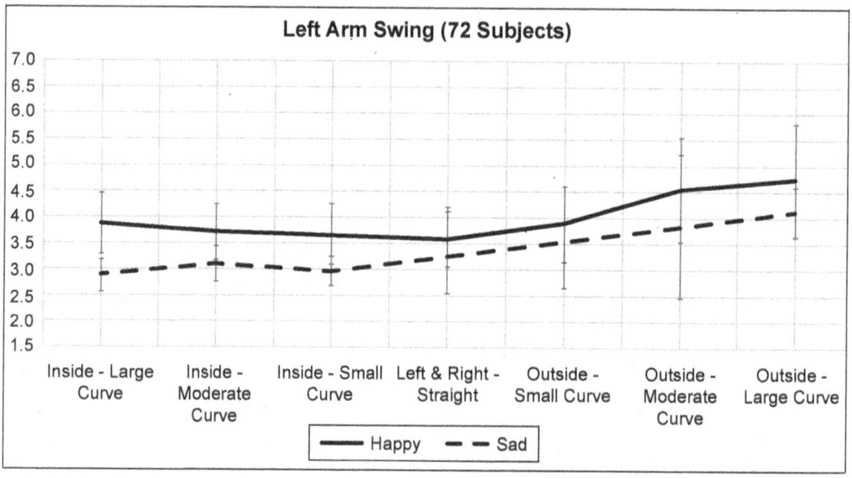

Fig. 10 Plot of Arm Swing Magnitude when the Left Arm is Inside and Outside with Different Curvatures (72 participants).

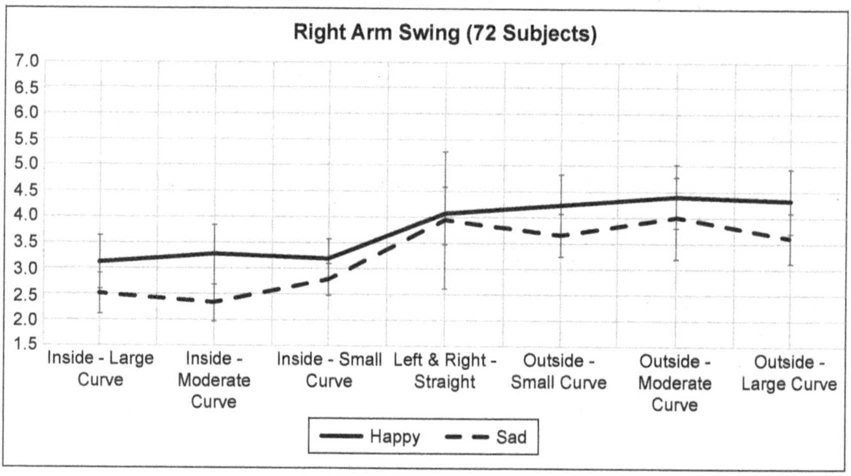

Fig. 11 Plot of Arm Swing Magnitude when the Right Arm is Inside and Outside with Different Curvatures (72 participants).

(level and arm positioning), and gender. Interactions were observed between arm side, emotion, and gender, as well as between walking curvature and gender. Dominant brain side and gender showed significant effects, with an interaction between gender and dominant hand side. Tukey HSD tests confirmed emotional state and gender significantly impact arm swing magnitudes, highlighting differences between male and female participants across all conditions.

4. Summary and Educational Implications

Summary of Findings

In the first dataset, emotional states influenced body movements, with left arm swing magnitude consistently differing across all curvature levels. Prior studies (Kuhtz-Buschbeck et al., 2008 and Killeen et al., 2018) highlight common asymmetry between left and right arm swings. Similarly, the combined dataset shows the left arm swing magnitude reliably reflecting emotions, aligning with earlier findings. This suggests that including arm-side data and considering walking curvature, especially high-curvature patterns, enhances emotion prediction accuracy. With a balanced number of male and female participants in the second dataset, findings indicate that gender significantly influences arm swing magnitudes, with distinct behaviors observed between genders across all conditions. However, due to the small sample size within each gender group, results may vary with larger datasets. Dominant brain side also showed a significant effect on arm swing magnitude, but limited participant numbers in each category prevent definitive conclusions.

Implications for Affective Learning and Education

This study highlights that left arm swing magnitude is a strong indicator for distinguishing between happiness and sadness during walking, while the right arm shows weaker emotional cues. Walking curvature also plays a key role, with high-curvature patterns offering clearer emotional distinctions. Incorporating arm-side data and walking curvature enhances emotion prediction accuracy through movement analysis.

These findings have practical implications for affective learning in education. By analyzing students' walking posture before and after class, their emotional states and responses can be assessed. This enables evaluation of students' learning experiences and instructors' teaching effectiveness, supporting timely adjustments and improvements.

The findings suggest that arm swing magnitude during walking is an effective indicator for distinguishing between happiness and sadness. Students' arm swing patterns can therefore help identify challenges in their learning experiences. A monitoring system using standard CCTV cameras or markerless motion capture devices, such as Microsoft Kinect, can be developed to track emotional states in common school areas. This affordable and simple setup enables instructors to detect signs of severe sadness or depression and offer timely support.

Further Reading

For a detailed exploration of this research, we encourage readers to refer to the original study: [DOI=10.3389/frai.2022.989860].

Acknowledgement

This work was supported by the JST Moonshot R&D program (Grant Number JPMJMS2011).

7 Cross-Cultural Perspectives on Persuasive Affective Learning through Information Media

1. Introduction and Research Background

In affective learning and serious games, information is crucial in persuasive technology. With platforms like YouTube, social network services, and metaverse communities, optimizing presentation strategies for marketing becomes essential.

This chapter builds on studies about emotional content's influence on purchase decisions, delving into modern marketing and persuasive technology. It analyzes virtual avatars' effectiveness in metaverse environments and explores cultural dimensions of media dissemination, identifying culturally preferred content.

This chapter explores the impact of avatars' persuasive expressions in metaverse interactions, the role of personality traits, and emotional or culturally influenced content in health marketing. It also examines emotions and culture in metaverse persuasion and highlights the need to uncover effective marketing techniques from a Japanese cultural perspective.

2. Persuasive Facial Expressions of Avatars

2.1 Persuasive Facial Expressions of Avatars in Metaverse Interaction

Persuasive technology leverages computing to influence and motivate individuals by integrating elements of persuasion and social influence (Fogg, 2002). Its effectiveness is measured by its ability to alter opinions and attitudes, steering cognitive dispositions toward a defined state. Sumi and Nagata (2010) analyzed 96 content patterns, including emotional scenarios, facial expressions, and avatar communication, revealing that avatars projecting positive impressions were more persuasive. Additionally, animation's movement enhanced intuitive understanding (Sumi, 2010).

Building on prior research, Anggia and Sumi (2023) explored the persuasive effectiveness of avatars using positive and negative expressions and storytelling techniques in a culturally diverse metaverse setting to influence Japanese audiences.

In an experimental study, 37 Japanese students (aged 18–24) were divided into three groups: Group 1 [Up] (11 participants with smiling agents at a low camera angle), Group 2 [W] (11 participants with smiling agents at a standard angle), and Group 3 [none] (16 participants with non-smiling agents at a standard angle). Random assignment ensured equal distribution without duplicate interactions. The experimental system, built with Unreal Engine, showcased agents' movements,

DOI: 10.1201/9781003782735-9

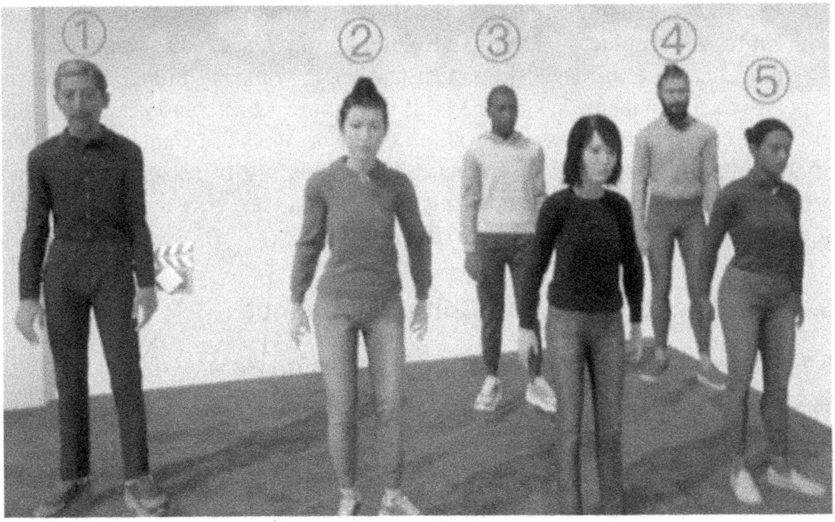

Fig. 1 The six virtual agents, named as (1) Stephan, (2) Pia, (3) Kellan, (middle) Danielle, (4) Aoi, and (5) Kendra.

facial expressions, and verbal communication using Japanese speech synthesis. Persuasion impact was analyzed via two-way ANOVA without replication, while Big Five personality traits were assessed using one-way ANOVA. The experiment's procedural sequence is outlined as follows:

1. Using Unreal Engine 4.27, a system was created to display virtual agents, mapping speech and facial expressions to keyboard inputs. This keyboard allowed voice activation, camera angle adjustments, facial expression alterations, and avatar actions, all controlled by the experimenter during participants' interactions with the agents.
2. Before interacting with the virtual agents, participants were briefed on the study's purpose and signed consent forms. They then completed a pre-questionnaire assessing their knowledge of Royal Jelly's health benefits and drawbacks, chosen to illustrate persuasive factors in nutritional topics.
3. Participants wore headphones, faced a computer display, and interacted with virtual agents. The session began with the virtual agent Danielle, followed by interactions with Stephan, Pia, Kellan, Aoi, and Kendra with dialogue presented through synthesized voice recordings. The six virtual agents featured in the experiment are shown in Figure 1.
4. The experimenter used the keyboard to guide participants in interacting with virtual via a headset microphone. While true interactive dialogue was not supported, participants were instructed to engage as though in conversation with the virtual agent.
5. After the interaction phase, participants completed a post-questionnaire to evaluate the agents' persuasiveness and were asked to explain the reasoning behind their responses.

The study highlighted a clear contrast between Group 1 [Up], featuring agents with smiles and laughter viewed from a close, upward angle, and Group 3 [none], where agents were displayed from a distant angle without smiling or laughing expressions. Participants in Group 1 [Up] were more receptive to persuasion due to the perceived friendliness and warmth of the avatars. The camera angles and affable impressions positively influenced susceptibility to persuasion. Avatars projecting positive traits, like body language and attitudes, were more persuasive, supporting Sumi and Nagata's (2010) findings.

3. Personality Traits and Cultural Influence

3.1 User's Personality Traits and Persuasion Potential

The Big Five model defines personality across five dimensions: openness, conscientiousness, extraversion, agreeableness, and neuroticism (Barrick and Mount, 1991). These traits significantly shape receptiveness to persuasive messages (Gerber et al., 2013) and are effectively integrated into character design (Thomas et al., 2022). Research confirms the success of personalized persuasion techniques based on the Big Five personality traits (Xu et al., 2022). This study examines how these traits influence subjects' susceptibility to agents' persuasion.

In Anggia and Sumi's 2023 experiment, most participants characterized their personality as follows:

- *"I perceive myself as being disorganized and careless"* (72.9%).
- *"I consider myself compassionate individual and prioritize the well-being of others"* (48.6%).
- *"I see myself as energetic and outgoing"* (43.24%).

These responses suggest a tendency toward extraversion. Individuals characterized by high levels of extraversion are marked by a strong focus on social interaction but potential carelessness in other areas (Bawack et al., 2021). Extroverted individuals demonstrate a keen concern for the well-being and opinions of others. The shared trait of extraversion between virtual agents and participants contributed to smoother persuasion.

The individuals who shifted from negative to positive opinions exhibited openness, conscientiousness, and extraversion, reflecting strong external engagement. When asked about their opinion change, they emphasized valuing social harmony and avoiding conflict, making them more susceptible to the agents' persuasion.

Participants who shifted from positive to negative opinions displayed low conscientiousness and high neuroticism. These traits are linked to a focus on personal achievement, critical evaluation, and reduced susceptibility to persuasion by the agents.

4. Cross-Cultural Persuasion through Media

4.1 Affective Computing and Cross-Culture Communications

Affective computing develops systems to interpret and simulate human emotions, integrating computer science, psychology, and cognitive science. As cultures differ in values, communication, and emotional influence, tailoring persuasion strategies boosts the impact of systems, marketing campaigns, and scholarly research in a globalized world. Meyer's Culture Map (2014) outlines eight dimensions of cultural differences, such as trust-building and decision-making, aiding professionals in global contexts. Integrating these dimensions into affective computing enhances system design by incorporating cultural nuances. The following country pairs highlight contrasting cultural tendencies across dimensions, showcasing their application in affective computing:

Communicating Dimension

This scale evaluates the extent to which communication is explicit or high-context in a culture. High-context cultures rely on implicit cues and non-verbal communication, while low-context cultures favor direct, explicit exchanges. Example: The U.S. vs. Japan – Americans tend to communicate explicitly, whereas Japanese communication heavily depends on context and non-verbal signals. Application: Affective computing systems should support both explicit and implicit communication styles. In high-context cultures, systems may need to focus on interpreting subtle behavioral cues.

Evaluating Dimension

This scale assesses how cultures give feedback—whether direct or indirect.

- **Example:** Germany vs. Japan – Germans tend to provide blunt and direct criticism, while Japanese feedback is typically indirect and diplomatic to maintain harmony.
- **Application:** Feedback mechanisms in affective computing systems should adapt to cultural preferences. For indirect feedback cultures, nuanced and softened responses may be more effective.

Persuading Dimension

This dimension differentiates between principles-first (deductive) and applications-first (inductive) persuasion.

- **Example:** Germany vs. the U.S. – Germans often use deductive reasoning (starting with a principle, then applying logic), while Americans prefer inductive reasoning (beginning with facts or stories, then drawing a conclusion).
- **Application:** The way persuasive content is structured in affective computing systems should align with cultural preferences for deductive or inductive reasoning.

Leading Dimension

This scale measures the degree of hierarchical vs. egalitarian leadership structures.

- **Example:** China vs. Denmark – Chinese leadership tends to be hierarchical, whereas Danish leadership is egalitarian.
- **Application:** Systems in hierarchical cultures should emphasize respect and deference to authority, while those in egalitarian cultures should treat all users equally.

Deciding Dimension

This scale differentiates between consensus-based and top-down decision-making.

- **Example:** Japan vs. the U.S. – Japanese decision-making is typically consensus-driven, while American decision-making values speed and efficiency.
- **Application:** Affective computing systems should facilitate group discussions for cultures favoring consensus, while allowing for individual decision-making where efficiency is prioritized.

Trusting Dimension

This scale differentiates between task-based and relationship-based trust.

- **Example:** The U.S. vs. China – In the U.S., trust is built through work reliability, whereas in China, India, and Indonesia, trust is cultivated through social interactions and shared experiences.
- **Application:** Systems in relationship-based cultures should focus on fostering interpersonal connections, while those in task-based cultures should emphasize reliability and consistency.

Disagreeing Dimension

This dimension measures how cultures handle disagreement and debate.

- **Example:** Germany vs. Japan – Germans view open debate as a means to reach the best outcome, while Japanese culture considers disagreement disruptive to harmony.
- **Application:** In cultures that value open disagreement, systems should facilitate debate and discussion, while in harmony-oriented cultures, they should prioritize conflict avoidance.

Scheduling Dimension

This scale contrasts linear-time vs. flexible-time cultures.

- **Example:** Germany vs. India – Germans prioritize punctuality, while Indian culture embraces fluid scheduling.
- **Application:** Systems in linear-time cultures should emphasize strict time management, while those in flexible-time cultures should accommodate adaptability–flexibility might be prioritized.

Applying Meyer's Culture Map to Affective Computing

The correlation between Meyer's Culture Map and affective computing in information media can be observed in the following ways:

Understanding Cultural Context

- Affective computing systems can interpret emotional cues based on cultural norms.
- What is perceived as a positive emotional expression in one culture may be neutral or negative in another.

Designing Culturally Aware Systems

- Culture-aware design improves user experience and fosters more natural interactions.
- For instance, systems targeting direct-communication cultures can provide straightforward feedback, while those for indirect-communication cultures should incorporate more nuanced responses.

Improving User Experience

Aligning system responses with cultural expectations increases user satisfaction and engagement.

Enhancing Communication

- Affective computing can adapt content dynamically based on the user's cultural background.
- For example, persuasive content can be tailored to cultural reasoning preferences (deductive vs. inductive).

5. Emotional Influence in Metaverse Advertising

5.1 Persuasion in Metaverse: The Roles of Emotions and Culture

Previous research has demonstrated that emotional content plays a significant role in influencing customer purchase decisions (Guo et al., 2020). Both traditional and contemporary marketing strategies share the common objective of persuading their target audiences. However, a fundamental question arises: What is the impact of emotional content on customer persuasion?

Despite varied findings—where both positive and negative emotional content can effectively shape consumer perspectives—understanding the underlying determinants can help marketers refine audience targeting strategies. In the realm of persuasive technology, modern marketing practices leverage conversational agents or dialogue systems to present interactive product advertisements. These may take the form of:

- Virtual avatars
- Robots
- Embedded characters within digital platforms
- Animated content with human-like traits, including facial expressions, emotions, and cultural nuances

The prevalence of emotions in marketing is well-established in the literature (Bagozzi et al., 1999). The interaction between consumption experiences and product usage can evoke emotional responses in customers, both during and after consumption, thereby influencing purchase decisions and post-purchase behaviors (Babin et al., 2000).

Previous studies have demonstrated that customers' emotional reactions to various stimuli—including:

- Store environments (Dennis et al., 2010)
- E-commerce platform designs (Floh et al., 2013)
- Advertisements (Ha et al., 2010)

As a result, the experiment conducted in this study was designed to identify the specific emotional content most closely associated with customer purchasing decisions.

Experimental Design

Experiments were conducted to investigate whether the efficacy of persuasion varies based on emotional and cultural backgrounds, utilizing video advertisements.

In recent years, commercials—including those on platforms such as YouTube—have adopted diverse formats. This study employs videos inspired by YouTube content and explores potential distinctions in emotional response and persuasion efficacy, which may be influenced by the viewer's cultural background.

The objective is to validate assertions suggesting that certain cultural contexts are more conducive to specific persuasion strategies.

In the experiment conducted by Anggia and Sumi (2024), subjects were recruited to evaluate the persuasiveness of videos, examining potential correlations between persuasion, emotional content, and cultural background, as illustrated in Figure 2.

Experimental Design and Findings

The study specifically examined whether Japanese subjects were more inclined to align with a group purportedly susceptible to persuasion by other Japanese individuals. A minority of participants expressed interest in utilizing health supplements, whereas the majority reported no prior experience with such products.

Fig. 2 Emotional and Cultural Induced Health Marketing Content.

Notably, the participant pool exhibited diversity in religious affiliations, with some individuals not adhering to any particular faith, despite the homogeneous nature of their country of origin and ethnicity.

Procedural Sequence of the Experiment

1. Stimuli Design

The study utilized six animated videos incorporating emotional content to persuade Japanese participants to consider purchasing a health supplement. These videos were created using Vyond, a cloud-based animated video creation tool featuring AI-generated expressive facial expressions and AI-text-to-speech narration. Each video depicted one of six primary emotions, as outlined in previous research (Anggia and Sumi, 2023):

- Anger
- Happiness
- Fear
- Sadness
- Surprise
- Disgust

2. Cultural Context and Narrative Strategy

The narratives were crafted to resonate with Japanese viewers by employing the "sinking boat joke" method, a persuasion technique based on the concept that "everyone else has already jumped". Participants were subtly influenced by the notion that others had already begun consuming the supplements and had been convinced of their efficacy.

Additionally, efforts were made to:

- Design characters resembling typical Japanese representations
- Utilize a female voice, aligning with common marketing practices in Japan

3. Experimental Procedure

Each video was paired with a 15-second neutral video and followed by questions presented via Google Forms. Six different forms were distributed to students in a random order, employing a counterbalánced presentation of the content.

The experiment involved recruiting 17 Japanese students from a Japanese university, all of whom engaged with the content presented in the Google Forms. The study sought to:

- Explore cultural variations in persuasion
- Identify the most persuasive emotion among Japanese participants
- Assess the effectiveness of the content

Findings and Discussion

The analysis of the animated videos revealed that emotions such as anger, happiness, and positive surprise elicited the most assertive responses from participants. Among these emotions:

- Disgust was perceived as the most authentic
- Positive surprise conveyed the friendliest impression

Participants displayed a notable inclination to follow the narratives closely, occasionally expressing visceral reactions and sensations evoked by the content.

Motivated by a desire to safeguard their health and mitigate potential health concerns depicted in the videos, participants felt compelled to alter their behavior, ultimately leading them to consider purchasing the supplement.

In summary, disgust emerged as the sole emotion among the six animated video narratives that significantly influenced Japanese participants to consider purchasing the health supplement.

6. Conclusion and Implications

6.1 Conclusion

The integration of computing technologies into daily tasks has led to the emergence of persuasive technology, a field that explores how technology can effectively change opinions and attitudes. This study has emphasized the importance of positive persuasion, distinguishing it from coercion, and highlighting its role in enhancing user engagement and decision-making.

This chapter concludes by acknowledging the study's limitations, particularly the need for a larger sample size and greater uniformity across subgroups to enhance the generalizability of the findings. Additionally, it underscores the importance of precision in developing dialogue agents, taking into account the alignment between avatars' and users' cultural backgrounds and personality traits to achieve effective persuasion.

Ensuring that narratives, animated facial expressions, and other persuasive elements align with the characteristics of the target audience is crucial. Prior research (Anggia and Sumi, 2023a) suggests that congruence between an individual's personality and an agent's facial expressions significantly enhances persuasive effectiveness. This study provides empirical recommendations for marketing-related content that integrates technology, emotional perspectives, and cultural context. It presents a novel perspective aimed at advancing discussions on persuasive technology and its applications.

In conclusion, this chapter highlights the intricate relationship between emotional content, agent design, and cultural nuances in persuasive technology. The findings serve as a foundation for future research, particularly in the creation of effective and culturally sensitive virtual agents for affective learning and serious games. Ultimately, this chapter provides valuable insights into the interplay between affective learning, persuasive technology, and virtual agent design, offering contributions to both academic research and practical applications.

Further Reading

For readers interested in a comprehensive analysis of this research, we recommend consulting the original study: [DOI=10.57417/jrnal.10.3_226] and [DOI=10.1109/COMPSAC61105.2024.00336]

Part 3
Serious Games

Play is a powerful driver of learning, capable of transforming abstract concepts into tangible experiences. Serious games go beyond entertainment by harnessing the mechanics of gameplay to address real-world challenges, encourage behavioral change, and support knowledge acquisition through interactive, experiential environments.

This part presents research exploring the educational potential of serious games across a wide range of applications. The chapters delve into systems that promote social awareness, such as etiquette training for social media and anti-bullying education, as well as platforms for learning English vocabulary through animation and etymology. Further, this part introduces a novel approach to knowledge acquisition through gameplay in which players help build a visual effect dictionary—demonstrating how play can be used not only to learn, but to construct new knowledge. It also explores immersive training systems for athletic performance and spatial cognition, highlighting how serious games can enhance physical and cognitive skills in sports education.

By engaging learners emotionally, visually, and cognitively, these chapters illustrate how serious games can create impactful educational experiences that are both meaningful and enjoyable.

8 Serious Games for Teaching Social Media Etiquette Through Simulated Experience

1. Introduction

With the growing influence of social networking services (SNS) like Twitter (X), Instagram, and TikTok, digital communication, education, and interaction have been transformed. While these platforms enable information sharing and identity building, they also pose challenges such as cyberbullying, misinformation, privacy breaches, and online conflicts. Scholars such as Gillmor (2010) emphasize the participatory nature of modern media, while Boyd (2014) documents the social complexities of teenage digital life. Duggan's (2014) Pew Research Center report provides detailed insights into the prevalence and impact of online harassment.

Digital literacy education is vital for preparing students to navigate online spaces responsibly. However, traditional methods often fall short in addressing the risks and ethical dimensions of SNS use, particularly for young learners. Interactive and experiential learning approaches can help students safely explore social media dynamics before facing real-world consequences.

This study examines the educational potential of serious games for teaching SNS etiquette. Through a simulated Twitter-like platform, students make decisions and observe outcomes, offering a more engaging and impactful learning experience compared to passive methods like lectures or videos. The study highlights the importance of social media literacy, experiential learning, and the design motivations behind developing a serious game to foster digital responsibility.

1.1 The Growing Importance of Social Media Literacy in Education

In today's world, where social media is pervasive, children are exposed to digital environments long before they acquire the skills to navigate them responsibly. Even without actively posting content, they often witness online interactions through family devices, YouTube comments, or gaming chat features. This early exposure can normalize harmful behaviors, such as public shaming, misinformation, or privacy violations, without offering a framework for critical evaluation.

Therefore, implementing social media literacy education before children begin independently using SNS is crucial. Many digital citizenship programs target middle or high school students, based on the assumption that firsthand SNS experience is needed for reflection. However, developmental neuroscience research by Immordino-Yang and Damasio (2007) shows that foundational social

DOI: 10.1201/9781003782735-11

and empathetic habits begin forming in late childhood, suggesting that waiting until adolescence may allow uncritical behaviors to become entrenched.

Buckingham (2007) stresses that media education should cultivate ethical judgment and critical reflection. Likewise, Nesi and Prinstein (2015) find that peer dynamics and feedback-seeking via social media can significantly affect adolescents' mental health and self-concept, highlighting the need for early guidance.

Research also supports active learning models. Alfieri et al. (2011) demonstrate that guided discovery-based instruction enhances deep learning by enabling students to understand cause-and-effect relationships. Meanwhile, the OECD (2021) underscores the importance of early digital literacy initiatives, particularly those that promote critical thinking, respectful communication, and ethical awareness. Introducing such education at the upper elementary level is developmentally appropriate and timely.

1.2 The Need for Experiential Learning in Digital Literacy

Experiential learning theories suggest that active engagement enhances knowledge retention (Kolb, 1984). Passive methods like reading or watching videos often fail to drive behavioral change because they lack emotional involvement and decision-making opportunities (Kirschner et al., 2006; Mayer, 2004).

Serious games provide a safe, interactive way to promote active learning and reflection. They enable students to explore behaviors, experience consequences, and reflect on choices. Educator involvement, such as posing reflective questions or facilitating post-game discussions, can further enhance understanding and retention (de Freitas, 2006; Connolly et al., 2012; Schrier & Gibson, 2011).

This method replicates real-world SNS use, enabling students to make mistakes and learn from them in a safe environment. This is essential for developing digital responsibility, which depends heavily on emotional and social context (Immordino-Yang & Damasio, 2007).

This study employs serious games to bridge theoretical knowledge and practical application in digital literacy education, aligning with frameworks by Reeves and Leighton (2003) and supporting evidence from gamified learning outcomes in other domains (Gentry et al., 2019).

1.3 Targeting Students Before Their First SNS Experience

This study focuses on upper elementary students, aiming to build responsible digital habits before they fully engage with SNS. Many existing programs are reactive, addressing problems only after they arise. In contrast, this study advocates a proactive model that uses simulated SNS environments to instill lasting behaviors in advance.

This approach aligns with Sousa's (2022) neuroscience-based educational framework, which emphasizes the importance of age-appropriate interventions during critical learning windows. As adolescents increasingly engage with digital platforms, early preparation becomes vital for both skill development, and the protection of their rights as digital citizens (Boyd, 2014; Livingstone & Third, 2017).

Controlled SNS interactions within serious games allow students to practice and internalize concepts such as online safety, digital footprints, and ethical communication before encountering real-world risks.

1.4 The Social Context: Real-World Consequences of SNS Flaming

Real-world incidents underscore the urgency of SNS education. Inappropriate online behavior has led to serious social, financial, and legal repercussions, especially among youth. Duggan (2014) documents numerous high-profile cases illustrating these dangers.

For instance:

- Convenience store workers posted images of themselves barefoot on food counters, violating hygiene standards.
- Fast-food employees uploaded photos of food tampering, sparking public backlash, job losses, and legal actions.
- Some participated in viral challenges by entering industrial freezers, resulting in store closures and lawsuits.

A single reckless post can provoke widespread controversy and tangible damage to individuals, businesses, and communities. Teaching children about the permanence and reach of online content is essential to prevent such incidents.

1.5 Developing a Serious Game for Social Media Etiquette

This study proposes a serious game that simulates a Twitter-like environment to enhance SNS literacy. Unlike traditional methods, this interactive approach allows students to:

- Engage with a simulated SNS platform, post content, and observe real-time outcomes.
- Experience "flaming" scenarios, and recognize the potential impact of inappropriate behavior.
- Reflect on digital citizenship, and responsible online actions within a safe, controlled setting.

Studies have shown the efficacy of serious games in education, especially when they include immersive elements and clear learning objectives (de Freitas, 2006; Connolly et al., 2012). Gentry et al. (2019) further show that gamified systems significantly enhance motivation and knowledge retention in health education, suggesting similar benefits for digital literacy.

Ethical game design is critical for behavior change. Schrier and Gibson (2011) argue that embedding moral reasoning into gameplay fosters critical thinking and reflection. The game developed in this study follows this approach, encouraging learners to make age-appropriate ethical decisions through simulated SNS experiences.

1.6 Objectives of This Study

This study has two primary objectives:

- To evaluate the effectiveness of serious games in teaching SNS etiquette, and compare them with traditional instructional methods in terms of their impact on students' understanding of online safety.
- To investigate how simulated "flaming" influences learning and memory retention, particularly whether experiencing online backlash increases students' awareness of digital responsibility.

Through controlled experimentation, the study examines whether serious gaming offers a more engaging and effective educational experience compared to passive, conventional methods.

2. A Serious Game for Teaching SNS Etiquette Through Simulated Experience

The rise of SNS highlights the need for engaging digital literacy education. Traditional methods often fall short for young learners new to SNS. This study introduces a serious game, offering a safe, immersive way for students to explore social media behavior and its consequences. This chapter outlines the game's design, mechanics, and learning principles, showcasing how a simulated Twitter-like environment fosters experiential learning. By combining interactive features, real-world case studies, and guided reflection, it helps upper elementary students improve SNS etiquette.

2.1 Overview of the System

The serious game simulates real-world SNS mechanics and interactions while integrating educational elements to teach responsible online behavior. Players explore, post messages, and face the consequences of their actions in a controlled virtual environment.

The system targets students new to SNS, offering a safe simulation to build digital literacy, fostering awareness and caution before real-world use.

The game offers an exploratory role-playing experience, where players interact with pre-scripted SNS events, exposing them to both positive engagement and risks to understand the consequences of their online actions.

Previous studies on immersive game-based learning validate this approach, emphasizing how simulated experiences enable learners to explore consequences in a risk-free environment (de Freitas, 2006).

The system comprises three key components:

1. Virtual World, a navigable environment where players explore interactive locations triggering SNS-related events.
2. Simulated SNS Interface, a dynamic Twitter-like timeline that updates posts and reactions based on player decisions.
3. Real-Time Learning Navigator, an AI-driven character offering feedback, guidance, and explanations, to ensure students grasp SNS dynamics and etiquette effectively.

Integrating these components allows students to actively engage, reflect, and internalize key lessons on social media etiquette through firsthand experience.

2.2 Game Interface and Interactive Components

The game interface is designed to mirror real-world SNS platforms while maintaining an educational and age-appropriate environment. As shown in Figure 1, the interface consists of two primary sections:

1. A Simulated Twitter-Like Interface (left side of the screen)
   - Displays the player's timeline, including their tweets, and reactions from virtual users.
   - Updates dynamically based on the player's choices, reflecting either positive engagement, or negative consequences (flaming).
   - Features a red-screen effect, and an influx of critical comments when a flaming event occurs, simulating real SNS backlash.
2. A Virtual World (right side of the screen)
   - Allows free navigation within a semi-open digital environment.
   - Includes interactive elements (sparkling spots) that trigger tweetable events.
   - Presents various in-game scenarios, some leading to positive engagement, while others risk negative social consequences.
   - Prevents players from progressing without making posts, ensuring that they actively engage with SNS experiences, rather than avoiding them.

2.2.1 The Role of the "Navigator" Character

To facilitate learning, the system incorporates a Navigator character, prominently displayed in the upper-right corner of the interface. Acting as an educational guide, the Navigator helps players not only engage with SNS interactions but also grasp the lessons embedded within their actions. The Navigator:

- Explains SNS features such as likes, retweets, and comments.
- Providing contextual feedback based on the player's choices.
- Intervening during flaming events,offering guidance on the social consequences of such situations.
- Encouraging critical reflection, prompting players to thoughtfully evaluate their decisions.

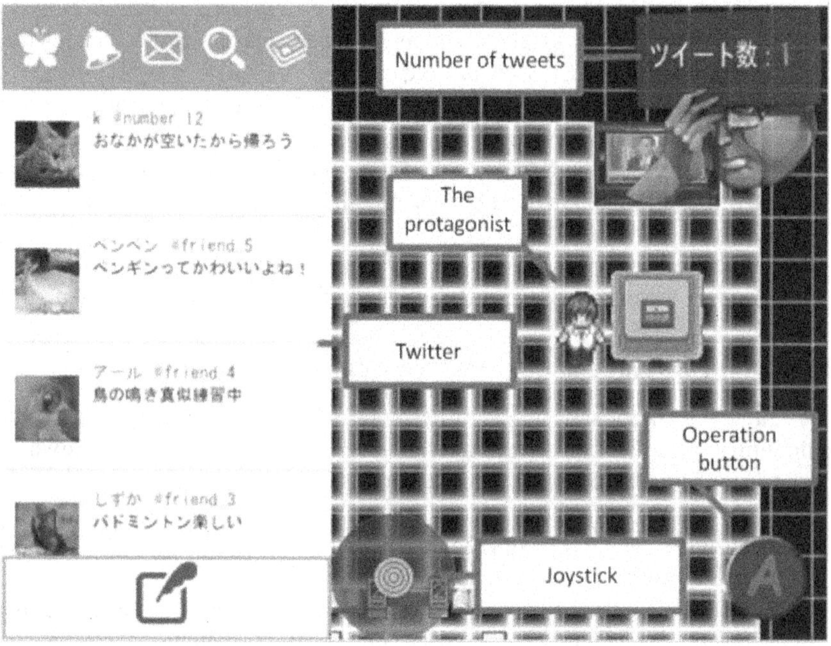

Fig. 1 Overview of the Serious Game Interface for Simulated SNS Education. The game interface consists of two main sections: on the left, a simulated Twitter (X) interface displaying the user's timeline and reactions to their posts; on the right, a virtual 3D world where the user navigates and interacts with events. The main character, identifiable by a cat thumbnail icon, posts tweets triggered by events discovered in the virtual environment. A "Navigator" character in the upper right corner provides real-time guidance, explanations of Twitter functionality, and feedback on the player's actions. Interactive elements include sparkling spots within the 3D world that prompt tweetable events, a total of 15 tweet opportunities (4 of which are inappropriate), and visual feedback mechanisms, such as a red-screen effect and timeline inundation during flaming incidents. The system combines touch-based controls and immersive feedback to facilitate experiential learning about the dynamics and risks of social networking sites.

This real-time guidance system ensures that students actively participate in the SNS simulation, while gaining a deeper understanding of the ethical implications tied to their online behavior.

2.3 Key Game Mechanics and Learning Design

The serious game emphasizes interactive decision-making and consequence-based learning to actively teach students SNS etiquette. Grounded in psychological principles like the Zeigarnik effect, where unresolved tasks enhance memory retention (Zeigarnik, 1927; Kellogg, 2007), the game fosters cognitive engagement by requiring students to act, receive immediate feedback, and reflect on their choices, rather than passively learning about social media risks. By incorporating open-ended scenarios, such as damaged reputations or lost followers, the game fosters deeper reflection and enhances memory retention, turning gameplay into a meaningful and impactful learning experience.

2.3.1 Posting Mechanism and Decision-Making

A key feature of the game is its structured posting system, designed to engage students in simulated SNS interactions while encouraging thoughtful decisions about their online behavior. Within the virtual world, players encounter "tweetable events" that require them to decide whether and how to respond.

To ensure active participation, the system prevents students from entirely avoiding social media interactions. Certain areas of the game are gated, requiring players to post a tweet to proceed. However, multiple posting options are provided, allowing students to exercise choice in their SNS interactions:

- Appropriate and responsible posts generate positive feedback from virtual SNS users, reinforcing healthy digital habits.
- Neutral posts elicit moderate responses, mirroring typical online interactions.
- Problematic or inappropriate posts trigger flaming events, demonstrating the risks of social media misuse.

This structured yet adaptable system facilitates student engagement with SNS dynamics, while supporting autonomous decision-making.

2.3.2 Flaming Event Simulation and Consequences

A standout feature of the game is its flaming event simulation, which mirrors real-world social media backlash. Triggered by inappropriate posts, it vividly demonstrates the consequences of irresponsible SNS behavior through immediate visual and emotional feedback.

How Flaming Events are Triggered:
These occur when a player engages in inappropriate or risky online behavior.

For example, a flaming event may involve posting a photo inside a freezer, based on real-world incidents widely reported in Japanese media.

Other scenarios include:

- Sharing personal information carelessly, illustrating the risks associated with online privacy violations.
- Participating in harmful social media trends, such as standing on train tracks to take a photo, demonstrating how dangerous challenges spread through SNS.

These pre-scripted scenarios are designed to reflect actual social media incidents, making the consequences relatable and impactful for students.

Effects of a Flaming Event

Once a flaming event is triggered, the game initiates an immediate and immersive response to simulate real-world backlash:

- The screen turns red, visually signaling the severity of the situation.
- The SNS timeline floods with negative comments, showing how quickly online criticism spreads.
- NPCs (non-playable characters) react differently, with some warning the player and others avoiding interaction.
- In extreme cases, the player's SNS account may be temporarily suspended or locked, simulating real-world consequences such as bans or loss of access due to online misconduct.

These mechanics reinforce the social and emotional impact of digital missteps, helping students develop a heightened awareness of online responsibility.

2.4 Real-World Reflection and Case Studies

To ensure that students connect their in-game experiences with real-world digital literacy, the system incorporates a post-flaming reflection phase. This component is designed to reinforce learning by drawing parallels between gameplay and actual social media incidents, such as viral backlash or reputational harm due to thoughtless posting.

Case studies include examples of employees facing professional consequences for inappropriate posts, or businesses suffering reputational loss due to viral social media incidents. These examples provide context for students to understand how digital behavior carries real-world implications. After experiencing a flaming event in the game, students are guided to analyze and revise their choices, promoting metacognitive engagement and digital self-awareness.

In this way, the game not only simulates online behavior but also helps students transfer their insights to future decision-making. Educators are encouraged to facilitate group discussion and reflection, ensuring that students process these events as learning experiences rather than personal failure.

2.4.1 Real-World Examples of SNS Consequences

After experiencing a flaming event, students are presented with case studies of real-world SNS incidents that mirror the in-game situations. These examples include:

- Employees fired or sued for inappropriate social media posts.
- Businesses suffering financial damage due to viral scandals caused by employee misconduct.
- Individuals facing legal or reputational consequences after engaging in harmful online behavior, such as spreading misinformation, cyberbullying, or privacy violations.

By seeing the real-life impact of SNS misuse, students gain a deeper understanding of why digital literacy and responsible posting are critical skills.

2.4.2 Learning Reinforcement and Post-Game Discussion

At the end of the game, students participate in a structured reflection phase to analyze their choices and learn from their experiences. The game guides them through a series of self-reflective questions, such as:

- Why did this post lead to a flaming event?
- How could this situation have been avoided?
- What would have been a more responsible post?

To reinforce these lessons, the system allows players to revise and rewrite their posts. For example, if a student originally posted an insensitive joke that led to a flaming event, they can rephrase it in a more neutral or thoughtful manner, demonstrating how slight changes in wording and content can dramatically alter public perception and response.

Educators are encouraged to facilitate classroom discussions following gameplay, helping students process their experiences and apply their newly acquired digital literacy skills to real-life social media use.

2.5 Summary

This chapter details the design, mechanics, and educational framework of the serious game, emphasizing its role in teaching social media etiquette through simulated experiences. The game is structured to provide a controlled yet engaging learning environment, integrating multiple interactive elements to enhance student engagement, decision-making, and digital responsibility.

The core features of the game include:

- A virtual world, where students navigate and engage with SNS-like interactions.
- A simulated Twitter-like interface, that updates dynamically based on player actions.
- A guided learning assistant (Navigator character), providing real-time feedback and educational guidance.
- A structured posting system that encourages students to make critical decisions about their social media behavior.
- A realistic flaming event simulation, to demonstrate the risks and consequences of irresponsible SNS use.
- Post-game reflection and real-world case studies to reinforce digital literacy and critical thinking in online interactions.

The system blends experiential learning, interactive SNS simulation, and real-world relevance to provide a compelling alternative to traditional digital literacy education.Through active participation and firsthand experience of social media interactions and consequences, students gain deeper insights into responsible online behavior. Immediate feedback, social consequences, and guided reflection help students internalize SNS etiquette effectively. The next chapter explores the experimental methodology used to assess the game's impact, covering study design, participant selection, and evaluation metrics for understanding and retention.

3. Experimental Evaluation: Challenges, Methodology, and Results

Assessing the serious game's effectiveness in teaching SNS etiquette required a structured experiment. With SNS use rising among younger users, early digital literacy is crucial to help students at an impressionable age form responsible online habits. Classroom experiments in elementary schools provided a practical setting to evaluate the game's impact in a controlled environment. This chapter outlines the challenges of creating an age-appropriate SNS simulation for young students, details the experimental methodology, covering participant selection, study design, and assessment procedures, and presents key findings on knowledge retention, engagement, and the effects of simulated flaming experiences.

3.1 Challenges in Designing an Age-Appropriate SNS Simulation

Developing the serious game required balancing realism and developmental appropriateness for elementary students unfamiliar with SNS. Young learners lack the technical skills and social awareness of older users, necessitating a design that ensured meaningful exploration of SNS behavior without overwhelming content. The upcoming subsections highlight three major challenges in this process.

3.1.1 Designing a Meaningful Experience Without Real SNS Exposure

Since fifth and sixth graders, the study's primary audience, had limited or no SNS exposure, designing a relevant and educational simulation was challenging. To tackle this, SNS mechanics were gradually introduced, mirroring real-world interactions without overwhelming complexity. Tutorials and features were embedded within gameplay, employing a context-based, real-time learning approach. The Navigator character, a virtual mentor, offered context-sensitive guidance throughout the game. It explained SNS functions like likes, comments, and retweets, while providing feedback on students' actions. This design encouraged exploration and reflection, creating an engaging and accessible learning experience for those new to social media.

3.1.2 Balancing Realism and Emotional Impact

A key challenge was balancing realism with emotional intensity. The game simulated social consequences like "flaming" or public backlash for inappropriate posts, aiming to reflect these outcomes accurately while ensuring the experience remained constructive and not overwhelming for young players.

To balance engagement with emotional safety, flaming events used attention-grabbing yet non-anxiety-inducing effects, like a red screen overlay and critical comments. The Navigator character provided guidance, while teachers were encouraged to hold debriefing sessions to help students reflect on and understand the educational purpose of these experiences. Although some students initially found flaming events emotionally intense, feedback revealed that this discomfort enhanced memory retention, consistent with the Zeigarnik effect (Kellogg, 2007). This aligns with Immordino-Yang and Damasio's (2007) assertion that emotional engagement is integral to cognition and long-term learning.

3.1.3 Encouraging Player Engagement Without Encouraging SNS Misuse

The game ensured student engagement while avoiding the promotion of reckless SNS behavior by requiring players to post content to progress. Multiple posting options, from responsible to risky, allowed students to make meaningful choices and experience the consequences of their actions. The game emphasized reflective thinking through in-game feedback and post-session discussions, encouraging students to evaluate their actions and explore alternative approaches. Inappropriate behavior, such as posts leading to flaming or backlash, provided no in-game rewards, ensuring students associated responsible SNS use with positive outcomes. These strategies created an educational yet emotionally safe environment for practicing digital citizenship before engaging with real-world platforms.

3.2 Experimental Methodology

A comparative classroom experiment assessed the serious game's effectiveness in teaching SNS etiquette. It aimed to determine if interactive learning through simulated SNS experiences improved understanding and retention better than traditional methods like videos or lectures. The design enabled a structured comparison of active and passive learning in an elementary school setting.

3.2.1 Participants and Study Design

The study involved 90 elementary students aged 10 to 12 from fifth and sixth grade classrooms, randomly assigned to one of three instructional method groups. The game-based learning group engaged with the serious game, making SNS-related decisions and experiencing simulated flaming events and feedback. The video-based learning group watched an instructional video on SNS risks and etiquette, followed by a teacher-led discussion. The Control Group received a traditional lecture-style lesson on online safety using textbook examples and verbal explanations. This design allowed researchers to compare the effectiveness of interactive, visual, and didactic teaching methods in fostering SNS responsibility.

3.2.2 Experiment Structure

Each 45-minute session began with a pre-test of multiple-choice questions to assess students' baseline knowledge of SNS etiquette and online risks, establishing a benchmark for comparison. Following the pre-test, students engaged in 20-minute learning sessions tailored to their group. The game-based group explored a simulated SNS environment with tweetable events, flaming incidents, and case studies. The video-based group watched an instructional video on SNS risks, followed by a teacher-led discussion. The control group received a traditional lecture, with the teacher explaining SNS concepts through examples. After the instructional period, students completed a post-test with self-reflection questions on online responsibility. A survey and discussion followed, gathering qualitative feedback on engagement, comprehension, and relevance. This structure captured both quantitative and qualitative data on the impact of different teaching methods on knowledge, emotional engagement, and readiness for real-world digital citizenship.

3.3 Experimental Results

The study revealed significant differences in learning outcomes across the game-based, video-based, and lecture-based groups, highlighting how the type of learning experience influenced students' knowledge, engagement, and reflection.

3.3.1 Improvement in SNS Knowledge

Post-test results showed measurable gains across all groups, with the game-based group achieving the highest improvement at 31.2%, excelling in identifying risky SNS behaviors. The video-based group improved by 18.6%, though struggled with applying concepts to new contexts. The lecture-based control group saw an 11.4% increase, facing challenges in real-world application. These findings highlight the superiority of active, experiential learning for internalizing digital responsibility.

3.3.2 The Impact of Flaming Experiences

A secondary analysis showed that students who experienced in-game flaming incidents scored higher on post-test items about online responsibility and decision-making. Those receiving only passive warnings via videos or lectures had a less nuanced grasp of emotional and reputational consequences, highlighting how firsthand, emotionally charged experiences drive deeper understanding and behavioral change.

3.3.3 Engagement and Student Feedback

To evaluate motivational impact, students completed questionnaires on engagement and willingness to reuse the system. The game-based group reported the highest engagement (89%) and interest in reuse (91%), followed by the video-based group with moderate engagement (63%) and reuse interest (35%). The lecture-based group ranked lowest, with 42% engagement and 18% reuse interest. Researchers observed that game-based students actively participated in discussions,often referencing in-game events and consequences. They stayed focused throughout, unlike lecture-group students, who showed signs of disengagement. Game-based learners also demonstrated better recall of lessons, connecting their in-game choices to broader digital responsibility concepts. These findings highlight serious games as an engaging, sustainable tool for digital literacy, offering immersive, impactful learning experiences applicable to real-world online behavior.

3.4 Key Findings and Insights

Active Learning is More Effective Than Passive Learning

The results show that serious games significantly outperform passive teaching methods in knowledge retention. Students in the game-based group, who made real-time decisions and faced their consequences, improved test scores by 31.2%, compared to 18.6% for the video-based group and 11.4% for the lecture group. This demonstrates that immersive SNS scenarios, paired with immediate feedback and reflection, foster deeper learning and long-term memory. These findings align with Mayer's (2004) view that guided, interactive learning enhances understanding, especially in abstract or ethical areas like digital citizenship.

Experiencing Flaming Events Leads to Stronger Understanding

Flaming incidents effectively reinforced responsible online behavior, with students demonstrating a deeper understanding of SNS risks and scoring higher on digital responsibility questions. These findings align with Kolb's (1984) experiential learning theory, which highlights how emotionally relevant experiences enhance engagement and memory retention. Simulated backlash fostered personal involvement and critical evaluation of online behavior, surpassing the impact of passive warnings through lectures or videos.

Engagement and Motivation Drive Learning Outcomes

Student engagement greatly influenced learning outcomes. The game-based group reported the highest engagement (89%) and reuse interest (91%), outperforming the video-based group (63% engagement, 35% reuse interest) and the control group (42% engagement, 18% reuse interest). Observational data revealed that game-based students actively participated in discussions, referenced in-game events, and demonstrated stronger motivation to grasp the impact of their actions. As Buckingham (2007) highlights, digital literacy extends beyond technical skills to foster critical thinking, ethical reasoning, and interpretive understanding, qualities nurtured through immersive, interactive experiences.

Emotional Impact Needs to Be Managed

While emotional engagement enhanced learning, some students felt discomfort from harsh in-game criticism during flaming events. Teachers provided reassurance and follow-up discussions to help them process these experiences. To balance emotional intensity with safety, future versions could include adaptive features like gradual exposure to flaming scenarios or a "safe mode" with milder consequences, ensuring educational value while supporting emotional well-being.

Synthesis and Implications

The study highlights serious games as effective tools for combining active learning, emotional engagement, and real-time feedback. Simulated flaming events proved impactful in promoting understanding and behavioral change, supported by reflection phases and educator facilitation. These findings emphasize the need for emotionally intelligent design in digital literacy education and lay the groundwork for further exploration. The next chapter examines broader implications for digital citizenship training, along with study limitations and future research directions.

4. Discussion

This study demonstrates the effectiveness of serious games as immersive tools for teaching digital literacy and social media etiquette. Unlike passive methods like lectures or videos, interactive simulations offer experiential learning through realistic SNS scenarios in a controlled environment. By exposing students to both positive and negative interactions, the study emphasizes experiential learning as a key driver of digital literacy. It explores contributions, early intervention, implications for digital citizenship, psychological theories like the Zeigarnik effect, interdisciplinary collaborations, limitations, and future research directions.

4.1 Key Contributions of This Study

Experiential Learning Reinforces Digital Etiquette

The serious game's interactive design excelled in boosting knowledge retention and engagement. Students who faced consequences for inappropriate SNS behavior gained a deeper understanding of social media risks and ethics. This aligns with Kolb's (1984) experiential learning theory, which highlights the value of concrete experiences and reflection in fostering lasting understanding.

Early Intervention Before SNS Usage Is Critical

Targeting upper elementary school students without SNS experience, the study shows that early exposure to simulated interactions fosters responsible online behavior. Guided opportunities to navigate positive and negative online scenarios in a safe setting benefited these learners, preparing them for real-world social media challenges.

Flaming Experiences Enhance Learning Outcomes

Students who experienced simulated flaming events scored higher on online responsibility questions than those who only received warnings, showing better understanding of social media dynamics and consequences. This supports Immordino-Yang and Damasio's (2007) view that emotions drive memory formation and decision-making, as emotional engagement through backlash fosters deeper reflection and cognitive processing. Pekrun's (2006) control-value theory highlights that emotionally significant, relevant situations enhance meaningful engagement. Flaming events were crafted to reflect plausible SNS scenarios, fostering relevance. These findings show that well-designed simulated consequences effectively teach responsible social media behavior, boosting understanding and long-term retention.

The Zeigarnik Effect Strengthens Digital Learning

The game design leveraged the Zeigarnik effect (Kellogg, 2007), which highlights the tendency to remember unresolved tasks. Flaming events created emotional and cognitive tension, prompting deeper reflection and extending learning. By applying this cognitive principle, the game enhanced the impact and retention of digital literacy education through emotionally resonant, open-ended scenarios.

4.2 The Importance of Early Digital Citizenship Education

The study highlights the urgency of early digital literacy education as smartphone use rises among children. With SNS becoming common at younger ages, proactive teaching is essential to equip elementary students with responsible online behavior skills. By integrating serious games into digital literacy curricula, educators can:

- Prevent negative SNS behaviors before they occur.
- Teach students to critically evaluate their online actions.
- Reduce future cases of online flaming, cyberbullying, and reputational damage.
- Encourage students to "think before they post" and develop a sense of online responsibility.

Serious games provide a practical, engaging, and effective method for teaching complex digital ethics concepts in a way that young learners can easily grasp and retain.

As Buckingham (2007) suggests, effective media literacy should help students not only access and use technology but critically interpret its social and cultural dimensions.

4.3 Interdisciplinary Collaboration and Practical Applications

Given the rapid evolution of social media, interdisciplinary collaboration is essential to developing effective, scalable, and psychologically sound digital literacy programs.

Educational Technology and Game-Based Learning Researchers

Collaboration with educational institutions and game developers can help refine serious games to suit different age groups and educational settings. By incorporating adaptive difficulty settings and personalized content delivery, these partnerships can further improve learning outcomes and ensure that the games remain both relevant and engaging across diverse contexts.

Cognitive and Behavioral Psychologists

Insights from cognitive psychology can optimize game mechanics by leveraging well-established principles such as the Zeigarnik effect and strategies for enhancing memory retention. Additionally, continued research into emotionally engaging learning experiences can contribute to more effective educational game design, ensuring that emotional triggers are used responsibly and pedagogically.

Cybersecurity and Digital Safety Organizations

Partnerships with government agencies and NGOs can help ensure that educational content aligns with current and emerging cyber risks. These collaborations also promote the cultural relevance of the material, helping students better understand the practical applications of digital literacy in their own online environments.

Policymakers and School Administrators

Integrating serious games into national or regional curricula could provide a structured and standardized approach to teaching digital citizenship. Policymakers may also consider the implementation of mandatory SNS training programs at the elementary and middle school levels, ensuring that digital literacy becomes a foundational component of early education.

Taken together, these collaborative efforts have the potential to extend the impact of serious games well beyond experimental contexts, transforming them into widely accepted and effective tools for digital education.

4.4 Limitations of the Study

While this study provides valuable insights into the effectiveness of serious games in digital literacy education, several limitations must be acknowledged. One of the primary constraints of this research is the relatively limited sample size and demographic scope. The study was conducted with upper elementary school students, which restricts its generalizability to younger children, teenagers, or older age groups. Since digital literacy needs vary across different age ranges, future research should extend its focus to middle school, high school, and even adult learners to determine whether similar engagement and learning benefits occur at different developmental stages.

Another limitation is the short-term nature of the learning assessment. The study primarily measured immediate knowledge retention following the gameplay experience. However, it remains unclear whether students retain their learning over an extended period or whether the knowledge gained through the game influences their actual social media behavior in the long run. Future studies should incorporate longitudinal assessments, tracking students' knowledge retention and online behavior over weeks, months, or even years to evaluate the sustained impact of the educational intervention.

Despite these limitations, the findings of this study provide a strong foundation for understanding how serious games can enhance digital literacy education. Addressing these challenges in future research will further refine the approach, ensuring that serious games continue to be an effective and scalable method for teaching responsible SNS behavior.

4.5 Future Research Directions

Building on the findings of this study, future research should explore ways to refine and expand the effectiveness of serious games for digital literacy education. An area for improvement is the adaptive difficulty of the game experience. Since students have different levels of digital literacy, AI-driven content adaptation could be implemented to tailor the learning experience to individual needs. For example, AI could dynamically adjust the intensity of flaming events, providing mild social consequences for beginners while allowing more realistic challenges for advanced learners. This personalized approach could enhance engagement while ensuring that the emotional impact remains appropriate for each student.

Additionally, further exploration of long-term learning effects is necessary. Future research should investigate whether the knowledge gained through serious game-based learning is retained over time, and whether it influences students' actual SNS behavior. Longitudinal studies that assess behavioral changes in digital citizenship beyond the immediate post-experiment phase would provide valuable insights into the lasting impact of experiential learning in this context.

Another promising direction is the integration of hybrid models that combine serious games with real-world SNS interactions in a controlled setting. While this study effectively simulated a social media experience, students did not interact with actual online users. A future version of the game could include a moderated real-world posting experience, allowing students to apply their learning in an authentic but safe environment. This could be done in collaboration with educational institutions and digital literacy organizations to ensure proper supervision and ethical considerations.

Expanding the applicability of serious games to a broader demographic range is also a key research area. While this study targeted upper elementary school students, similar educational interventions could be developed for middle school, high school, and even adults who may benefit from structured SNS etiquette training. Age-specific modifications, such as more advanced privacy settings exploration for older students or workplace SNS training for young professionals, could extend the reach of this educational approach.

Future research should also examine cultural and regional differences in SNS behavior and digital literacy. Social media norms and online risks vary across countries and cultures, meaning that serious games should be tailored to reflect the specific challenges faced by different populations. Cross-cultural studies could help identify universal principles of SNS etiquette while allowing for localized adaptations based on cultural context.

By addressing these future directions, serious games can continue to evolve as a scalable, adaptable, and effective tool for teaching responsible social media behavior across diverse learning environments.

5. Conclusion

This study demonstrates the effectiveness of serious games as an engaging, scalable, and immersive method for teaching SNS etiquette and digital responsibility. By simulating real-world social media interactions, the game provides a safe space for students to explore the consequences of their online actions.

The findings confirm that experiential learning methods significantly outperform passive instruction in the context of digital literacy education. Specifically, students who actively participated in game-based scenarios demonstrated stronger retention and a deeper understanding of online safety compared to those in more traditional learning environments. Flaming events within the game created lasting cognitive impressions, compelling students to reflect on their behavior and reinforcing the importance of responsible SNS usage.

Furthermore, the results suggest that serious games hold strong potential as an effective and scalable solution for digital citizenship training. Their ability to provide immersive, emotionally resonant learning experiences makes them particularly suited to teaching complex, behavior-based concepts such as social media etiquette.

As social media continues to evolve, digital literacy education must also adapt, embracing interactive tools like serious games to ensure that future generations are equipped to navigate the online world with awareness, empathy, and responsibility.

Further Reading

For readers interested in a comprehensive analysis of this research, we recommend consulting the original study: [DOI=10.1007/978-3-319-49616-0_3].

Column 1: The Zeigarnik Effect in Learning

Subtitle: How Unfinished Tasks Enhance Memory Retention

The Zeigarnik effect, named after Russian psychologist Bluma Zeigarnik, describes the tendency to remember incomplete or unresolved tasks better than completed ones. This phenomenon is at the core of the serious game described in this chapter.

In the game, unresolved flaming events, where players face criticism for inappropriate posts, leave a lasting impression. The experience of seeing a virtual timeline flood with negative comments triggers the cognitive discomfort associated with incomplete resolution. This discomfort reinforces the lessons learned, making players more likely to remember the consequences of inappropriate online behavior.

Using the Zeigarnik effect in educational games like this transforms potentially abstract concepts into memorable, impactful experiences that resonate with young learners.

Column 2: Real-World Lessons from Simulated Flaming Events

Subtitle: Bridging the Gap Between Virtual Experiences and Reality

The simulated flaming events in the game are not just fictional scenarios, they are modeled on real-life incidents, such as posting photos of dangerous stunts or inappropriate behavior in public places. By presenting these incidents in a controlled environment, the game allows students to explore the potential consequences without actual harm.

For example, players might see their avatar face virtual arrest or account hijacking, mirroring real-world outcomes of careless online behavior. This connection between the virtual and real world bridges the gap between theoretical knowledge and practical application, making the lessons more relatable and impactful.

Teachers can further enhance this learning by discussing real-life cases after gameplay, encouraging students to draw parallels and think critically about their online actions.

Column 3: Preparing Students for the Digital Age

Subtitle: Teaching Information Literacy Through Play

Digital literacy has become an essential life skill in the 21st century. However, traditional methods of teaching online etiquette often fail to resonate with young learners who lack firsthand experience with social media.

Serious games like this SNS simulation fill that gap by providing a safe, hands-on introduction to the challenges of digital life. By letting students experiment with online interactions in a controlled environment, these games prepare them for the complexities of the real digital world.

This approach aligns with the principle of "learning by doing," empowering students to navigate the online landscape responsibly and confidently.

Column 4: When Serious Games Become Too Serious

Subtitle: Balancing Intensity and Accessibility in Digital Literacy Education

While serious games are a powerful tool for teaching digital literacy, their immersive nature can sometimes make learning experiences emotionally intense. In this study, some students reported feelings of anxiety or discomfort when experiencing in-game flaming events. Although this emotional impact reinforced the seriousness of social media risks, it also highlighted the need for careful management of students' psychological responses.

To ensure that serious games remain effective without causing undue stress, two key strategies should be considered: educator-guided debriefing sessions and adaptive difficulty settings. Educators play a crucial role in helping students process their in-game experiences. By facilitating structured discussions after gameplay, teachers can guide students in interpreting the simulated backlash, addressing misconceptions, and reinforcing constructive online behavior. These discussions help shift the focus from emotional distress to critical reflection, ensuring that students internalize the lessons in a positive manner.

On the game development side, adaptive difficulty settings can help tailor the experience to individual students' comfort levels. For instance, the game could introduce a progressive flaming intensity system, where early scenarios involve mild feedback, gradually escalating in severity as players demonstrate greater understanding. This would allow students to build resilience and digital literacy skills in a step-by-step manner. Another approach could be the implementation of a "Safe Mode" option, in which players can choose a version of the game with softer social consequences while still learning the principles of responsible SNS usage.

Ultimately, balancing emotional intensity with accessibility ensures that serious games remain both engaging and educational. When properly managed, emotionally impactful experiences can be powerful tools for long-term retention, reinforcing key lessons about digital responsibility while keeping students motivated and confident in their online interactions.

9 Learning English Through Etymology and Animation: A New Approach for Elementary Students

1. Introduction

In an era of increasing globalization, proficiency in English has become an essential skill for young learners, not only for academic advancement but also for future participation in international society. As English language education becomes increasingly prominent in Japan's elementary curriculum, the challenge remains: how can we foster meaningful, long-term language acquisition in children with limited exposure and minimal contextual need for English?

This study explores an innovative solution to this challenge by integrating etymology-based instruction and animated visualizations in a digital learning environment tailored for Japanese elementary school students. It aims to enhance vocabulary learning and sentence construction by making abstract linguistic structures clear and memorable. The following sections outline the theoretical and practical foundations of this approach.

1.1 The Growing Importance of English Education in Japanese Primary Schools

The Japanese Ministry of Education (MEXT) has reformed the curriculum to make English a core subject from Grade 5, emphasizing communicative competence alongside vocabulary and grammar development (MEXT, 2017). However, studies have revealed persistent challenges in vocabulary retention and communicative application among Japanese students. Butler (2005), through comparative surveys of elementary school teachers in East Asia, found that Japanese learners often face difficulties in retaining vocabulary due to limited opportunities for authentic communicative practice.

Furthermore, Nakata (2011) reported that even Japanese high school EFL teachers frequently lacked the pedagogical readiness to promote learner autonomy, possibly reflecting foundational weaknesses in early-stage English instruction.

Traditional approaches centered on rote memorization and teacher-led explanations often fail to consider the cognitive developmental stages and intrinsic curiosity of young learners. Cameron (2001) argues that children benefit more from exploratory and interactive learning methods, given their emerging metalinguistic awareness and need for contextualized language input. This underscores the

DOI: 10.1201/9781003782735-12

importance of engaging, developmentally appropriate instructional strategies that support meaningful learning experiences for younger students.

1.2 The Cognitive Benefits of Etymology in Language Learning

Understanding the etymological structure of words, such as their roots, prefixes, and suffixes, aids vocabulary acquisition by fostering morphological awareness, enhancing reading comprehension, spelling, and vocabulary growth (Bowers & Kirby, 2010; Carlisle, 2003). For instance, learning that "transport" derives from Latin trans- (across) and portare (to carry) helps students grasp meanings of related terms like "export" and "import." Semantic transparency enhances lexical inferencing, enabling learners to deduce unfamiliar word meanings through morphology analysis (Kieffer & Lesaux, 2007). Children's pattern-seeking instincts help them organize and recall vocabulary, promoting deep learning in early language education.

Etymology is often taught at higher education levels, but studies suggest young learners can benefit from age-appropriate, visually supported morphological instruction (Devonshire et al., 2013). However, this approach remains underutilized in L2 English education for Japanese elementary students.

1.3 Visualization and Animation as Memory Enhancers in Language Learning

Visualization in education is well-supported by cognitive psychology and instructional design. According to dual coding theory (Paivio, 1986), learning is enhanced when verbal and visual information are processed simultaneously through separate cognitive channels. In the context of language acquisition, combining word definitions with corresponding images or animations strengthens memory by activating multiple encoding pathways (Mayer, 2009; Plass et al., 1998). In particular, Plass et al. (1998) found that learners in second language environments benefit significantly from multimedia instruction that supports both visual and verbal learning preferences, thus reinforcing the efficacy of dual-channel processing.

Abstract vocabulary is harder for young learners to grasp without sensory aids. For example, explaining that "spectator" derives from Latin spectare (to watch) becomes clearer when paired with an animation of someone watching a soccer match. Animations enhance understanding by illustrating action, causality, and sequencing, boosting retention (Clark & Mayer, 2016).

Visual storytelling and animated metaphors engage students' imagination and emotions, essential for long-term memory encoding (Immordino-Yang & Damasio, 2007). Animation acts as a cognitive tool, improving comprehension, recall, and language application beyond mere decoration.

1.4 Research Gap and Contributions of This Study

Previous studies highlight the benefits of morphological instruction and multimedia learning, yet few combine these approaches into a unified, developmentally appropriate system for young language learners. Most tools prioritize vocabulary drills or isolated grammar, overlooking structured word formation through visualized etymology. This study contributes to the field in three primary ways:

1. Pedagogical integration: It presents a novel instructional design that combines etymological principles with animated storytelling, grounded in cognitive theories of learning.
2. Learner appropriateness: It adapts complex linguistic concepts into a format that is accessible and engaging for elementary-aged L2 learners.
3. Empirical evaluation: It empirically tests the effectiveness of this system in improving vocabulary retention and sentence production in real classroom settings.

Thus, this research not only proposes an innovative teaching methodology but also contributes to the theoretical discourse on visual-supported morphological learning in early second-language education.

2. System Design and Rationale

To support early vocabulary development in young English learners, this chapter introduces the design of an interactive learning system that combines etymology-based instruction with animated visualization. The following sections explain the educational rationale, system components, and interaction flow.

2.1 Overview of the Educational Goal and Target Learners

This study focuses on helping upper elementary students learn English vocabulary through an interactive system combining etymological decomposition and animated visualization. It targets fifth and sixth graders, whose cognitive abilities allow abstract reasoning but still benefit from multimodal stimuli. As Piaget (1969) explains, children at this stage are transitioning from the concrete operational stage to the formal operational stage, making them capable of understanding abstract linguistic patterns when supported by visual and interactive input (Mayer, 2009). The system aims to enhance vocabulary retention and teach word structure by analyzing prefixes, roots, and suffixes. Traditional vocabulary teaching often relies on memorizing word lists without exploring their structure or origins, leading to poor retention and limited application in tasks. In contrast, this system promotes meaningful learning by guiding students to analyze word components and reconstruct meanings, creating easier-to-recall mental representations.

2.2 Why Etymology?

This system's core principle is etymological analysis, breaking words into components (e.g., tele + scope → telescope). Morphological awareness enhances vocabulary development, especially in L2 learners, by offering strategies to decode unfamiliar words and encouraging generative learning (Carlisle, 2000; Nagy et al., 2006). Nation (2001) emphasizes that understanding the morphological composition of words not only aids in vocabulary acquisition but also fosters learners' ability to infer meanings of unfamiliar words in reading and listening contexts, which is particularly valuable in early L2 education. For instance, understanding that bio- means "life" helps learners infer meanings of terms like biology or biography. Teaching word formation logic fosters morphological inferencing, supporting long-term vocabulary growth.

2.3 Why Animation? Educational Justification for Visual Dynamic Representation

The system innovatively uses animated visual metaphors to represent etymological meaning. Unlike static images, animations depict temporal, causal, and transformational relationships, effectively showcasing the dynamic process of etymological composition.

Cognitive theories of multimedia learning (Mayer, 2009) highlight that dual-channel processing, combining verbal and visual inputs—boosts memory and understanding. According to Paivio's dual coding theory (1986), the brain processes verbal and visual information through distinct but interconnected systems, enhancing recall when both are activated. The Multimedia Principle states that learning improves with words and pictures, while the Modality Principle suggests animated visuals with narration are especially effective for younger learners developing reading fluency. Plass et al. (1998) further demonstrated that learners in second-language multimedia environments benefit when instructional design supports both visual and verbal preferences, reinforcing the effectiveness of dual-channel processing in L2 vocabulary retention.

The system uses animations to illustrate both word meanings and their construction. For instance, "transport" is broken into trans- ("across") with an object crossing a bridge, and port ("carry") with a character lifting it, combining these to depict "to carry across." This approach helps students recall and reconstruct words by grounding abstract linguistic elements in concrete, memorable visuals.

2.4 System Structure and Functional Components

The system is a tablet-based application tailored for young learners using iPads. It enhances vocabulary learning through an interactive interface that integrates animation, sound, and touch-based features, combining multimodal elements for effective engagement. The main screen displays ten icons representing compound nouns, all derived from familiar animal-related words (e.g., firefly, starfish, ladybug). This thematic consistency helps maintain learner interest and connects vocabulary acquisition to prior knowledge. When a student selects an icon, such as "firefly," the application transitions to a dedicated learning screen for that word.

2.5 Pedagogical Flow and Interaction Design

The learning experience follows a scaffolded flow aligned with constructivist principles and gradual release of responsibility (Pearson & Gallagher, 1983), this instructional model emphasizes a transition from teacher-led guidance to learner independence, where responsibility for task completion is gradually shifted from the educator to the student, supporting autonomy and deeper engagement.

1. Guided Discovery: Students begin by exploring the meaning of word parts via short, engaging animations.
2. Conceptual Integration: They then observe how parts combine to form a word with new meaning.
3. Active Output: Students create sentences using the word, either orally or in writing.
4. Review and Reinforcement: Through game-like quizzes, students revisit the words over spaced intervals.

Importantly, each word can be "replayed" at any time, supporting self-paced learning. Teachers can use the system in whole-class instruction or assign individual exploration as part of homework or learning centers.

3. Experimental Design and Evaluation

This chapter evaluates the English vocabulary learning system from Chapter 2, comparing animated etymological explanations to still images and text-based definitions. The study analyzed learning outcomes, user experiences, and pedagogical implications through experiments with elementary students.

3.1 Objectives of the Evaluation

The evaluation aimed to determine if etymology-based animations improved vocabulary acquisition in elementary school students, focusing on key research questions regarding effectiveness, engagement, and retention:

1. Does learning compound nouns with etymological animations enhance recall and understanding better than using still images or text-based methods? How do young learners emotionally and cognitively react to animated versus static educational materials?
2. Does the animation-based approach create an engaging, memorable learning experience that aids long-term retention?

These questions were explored through quantitative and qualitative analyses of learners' performance and feedback.

3.2 Methodology

3.2.1 Participants

Thirty-six elementary students (Grades 4–6) from two public schools with varying English exposure were randomly assigned to three groups to assess different learning modalities.

- Animation Group: Learned compound nouns through etymology-based animations.
- Image Group: Studied the same vocabulary through still images derived from the animations.
- Text Group: Studied the definitions and example sentences without visual aids.

3.2.2 Materials and Procedure

Ten English compound nouns were selected for the study, each representing a combination of two familiar words (e.g., "firefly" = fire + fly, "starfish" = star + fish). These words were chosen based on their concreteness, visual representability, and relevance to elementary-level learners.

Each participant used an iPad application specifically designed for this experiment. The learning interface and features were as described in the Figure 1. Depending on the group, the participants either viewed the animation, a still image of the final compound noun, or only text descriptions. The learning session was followed by a brief break and a vocabulary test.

3.2.3 Assessment

Three main forms of assessment were conducted:

1. Immediate Recall Test: Participants were asked to write the English word corresponding to a Japanese meaning.
2. Recognition Test: Participants matched compound words with their meanings from a list.
3. Delayed Post-Test: A similar test was administered after one week to measure retention.
4. Qualitative Feedback: Participants provided feedback on their enjoyment, ease of understanding, and perceived usefulness.

3.3 Results

3.3.1 Quantitative Analysis

The immediate and delayed post-test results were analyzed using ANOVA and post hoc comparisons.

- The Animation Group scored significantly higher on immediate and delayed tests ($p < 0.01$), suggesting that the use of animated etymology enhanced both encoding and retention.
- The Image Group showed moderate performance but did not significantly outperform the Text Group, indicating that static images alone may not sufficiently support cognitive processing for young learners.
- The Text Group had the lowest scores overall, although they did show some understanding of the definitions.

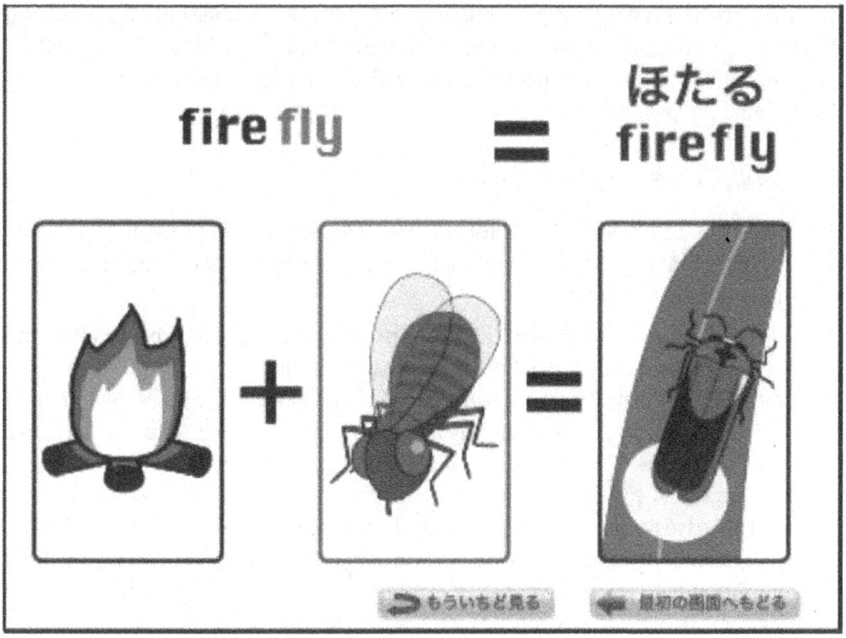

Fig. 1 Interface and Features of the English Vocabulary Application for Learning Compound Nouns (Example: "fire + fly"). The application interface showcases ten compound noun icons on the main screen, each representing an animal (e.g., "firefly," "starfish"). When the user selects the "firefly" icon, the screen transitions to a detailed learning interface for this compound noun. Key features include:
Animation Playback: Touching the "?" button activates an animation illustrating the etymology of *firefly*. The animation begins by visually separating *fire* and *fly*, with their respective meanings represented (e.g., flames for *fire* and a flying insect for *fly*). The components then merge dynamically to form *firefly*, accompanied by the English pronunciation of each part and the whole word. This visual narrative reinforces the meaning of each component and how they combine to create the compound noun.
Whole Word Visualization: The "=" button displays an animation or static picture of a *firefly* (or the Japanese characters "ほたる" in the Japanese mode), reinforcing the learner's understanding of the full word in both languages.
Replay Functionality: Users can replay the animations and sounds at any time, allowing for repeated exposure and review, a principle consistent with spaced repetition theory in vocabulary retention (Nation, 2001).

3.3.2 *Qualitative Feedback*

Feedback collected via post-experiment surveys revealed the following trends:

- 92% of students in the Animation Group reported that the animations helped them "imagine the word" and "remember the parts."
- Students in the Image Group found the still visuals "helpful but less engaging."
- Text Group participants expressed that it was "hard to remember the English words without a picture."

Students in the Animation Group also demonstrated greater engagement and motivation, with many eager to reuse the system. Comments like "The fire and fly came together, and then I remembered it easily," highlight how animations aided mental imagery construction.

3.4 Interpretation and Analysis

These findings indicate that etymology-based animations significantly enhance English vocabulary comprehension and retention in elementary students, driven by various cognitive factors:

- **Dual coding theory (Paivio, 1986):** The animations provide both verbal and visual representations, enhancing memory encoding.
- **Cognitive load reduction:** Animations demonstrate parts and meanings in motion, scaffolding understanding and minimizing extraneous cognitive load.
- **Zeigarnik effect:** The animation's unfolding narrative structure leverages the Zeigarnik effect, a psychological phenomenon where incomplete or interrupted tasks are better remembered than completed ones (Kellogg, 2007). By visualizing each component of a word incrementally and delaying the final combination (e.g., combining "trans" and "port" at the end), the animation maintains cognitive tension and enhances retention.

Animations effectively clarify the semantic logic of compound nouns, fostering deeper learning and enabling learners to deduce meanings of unfamiliar words with similar structures.

3.5 Summary and Key Insights

The evaluation highlights the pedagogical benefits of animated etymological visualizations for young English learners, showing that animations, compared to text or static images, led to:

- Higher immediate and delayed recall of vocabulary.
- Greater student engagement and satisfaction.
- Enhanced conceptual understanding of word formation.

These findings advocate for incorporating animated tools into English vocabulary curricula, particularly in early language learning. The next chapter examines implications for instructional design, interdisciplinary collaboration, and personalized learning development.

4. Discussion

This study examined how etymology-based animations improve English vocabulary acquisition in elementary students enhancing retention, comprehension, and engagement over traditional methods. This chapter discusses broader implications, theoretical foundations, interdisciplinary applications, study limitations, and future research directions.

4.1 Key Findings and Implications for Language Learning

The experiment's results highlight the effectiveness of etymology-based animations as a powerful tool for vocabulary learning, particularly for young learners. Key findings from the study include:

1. Etymology Enhances Word Retention and Understanding

Understanding word etymology, particularly for compound nouns enhances retention of meaning and spelling. Breaking words into components helps form cognitive connections, making learning more intuitive. Carlisle (2000) demonstrated that morphological awareness, recognizing and understanding the structure of complex words, supports early reading and vocabulary development, especially in young learners. Nagy et al. (2006) further found that such awareness contributes significantly to literacy outcomes beyond phonological knowledge. These findings align with the benefits of etymology-based instruction in this study.

Visual Learning Strengthens Memory and Conceptualization
Animations improved recall and recognition of English words over static images and text-based methods. Aligning with Paivio's (1971) dual coding theory, animations combine verbal and visual inputs, enhancing memory and making abstract vocabulary more tangible for young learners.

Multimodal Interaction Increases Engagement
Students in the animation-based learning group demonstrated higher engagement levels than those using text or static images. The interactive iPad app and dynamic visuals captured their attention and curiosity, supporting Mayer's (2009) theory that meaningful multimedia boosts learning efficiency.

2. Sequential Processing Supports the Zeigarnik Effect

Animated sequences showing compound word formation may utilize the Zeigarnik effect where incomplete tasks are better remembered (Zeigarnik, 1927; Kellogg, 2007). This likely sparked curiosity and mental engagement, enhancing retention.

These findings collectively suggest that integrating etymological analysis with animations offers an effective, engaging method for vocabulary acquisition, particularly for young learners beginning second-language studies.

4.2 The Role of Etymology and Animation in Vocabulary Acquisition

The study highlights the value of etymology-based instruction, where analyzing roots, prefixes, and suffixes deepens understanding of lexical structures and word families. This approach fosters metalinguistic awareness, enabling students to infer unfamiliar word meanings. According to Bowers and Kirby (2010), structured morphological instruction improves vocabulary acquisition by helping learners recognize meaningful word parts, facilitating the inference of related words and promoting generative vocabulary learning. Animations illustrating word etymology improve comprehension by dynamically showing semantic relationships and compound word formation. This mirrors conceptual blending theory (Fauconnier & Turner, 2002), which posits that the mind combines elements from different mental spaces to generate novel meaning. In this context, animations visually guide learners to blend form and meaning, creating a more engaging and memorable learning experience. The blend of animation and etymology enhances dual-channel processing, engaging visual and verbal pathways (Mayer, 2009). This approach benefits elementary students who struggle with abstract vocabulary taught through text alone.

4.3 Pedagogical and Interdisciplinary Applications

The study's findings have several pedagogical and interdisciplinary implications:

1. Educational Technology and Digital Learning Platforms

Integrating animated etymology into digital learning offers promising educational potential. Adaptive platforms could use AI to create personalized, dynamic vocabulary lessons based on student progress.

2. Second Language Acquisition Research

This study advances second language acquisition (SLA) by highlighting the impact of morphological instruction and visual learning on vocabulary retention. Future studies could examine responses across age groups and proficiency levels to etymology-based animation.

Cognitive and Developmental Psychology
The findings correspond with cognitive development theories, including conceptual metaphor theory and schema theory. Lakoff and Johnson (1980) argued that abstract thought is largely shaped by metaphorical mappings based on concrete experiences; in this case, animations help map abstract word meanings onto concrete visual experiences, facilitating understanding. Similarly, schema theory (Rumelhart, 1980), which views comprehension as the activation and modification of existing mental frameworks or "schemas," suggests that vivid and structured visual input can help learners integrate new vocabulary into their pre-existing knowledge structures more effectively. This supports the idea that animation-based vocabulary learning could enhance instructional design.

Cross-Linguistic Applications
The approach could be adapted for languages with complex morphological structures like Chinese, Arabic, and German, benefiting from their rich etymological histories and compound words.

4.4 Limitations of the Study

While the study shows strong evidence for the benefits of etymology-based animations, several limitations exist:

- Sample Size and Demographics: Conducted with Japanese elementary students, findings may not apply universally. Further research should explore diverse educational settings.
- Short-Term Assessment: Retention was measured immediately after learning. Future studies should include delayed tests to evaluate long-term effects.
- Real-World Application: Focused on controlled settings, it's unclear if retention improvements enhance real-world language use. Future research should address this gap.

4.5 Future Research Directions

To advance current findings, future research could focus on:

- AI-Driven Adaptive Learning: Leveraging AI to tailor difficulty levels and animations based on individual progress, using machine learning to create targeted content.
- Longitudinal Retention Studies: Assessing long-term impacts of animation-based etymology through extended tracking beyond immediate recall tests.
- Cross-Language Comparisons: Evaluating the effectiveness of this approach across languages like English, Chinese, and other morphologically rich systems to determine its universality.
- Integration with Other Modalities: Examining how animations pair with strategies like gesture-based learning, VR, or AR for enhanced multimodal education.

5. Conclusion

This study introduced a novel method for teaching English vocabulary to elementary students, combining etymological analysis with animations. The findings show this approach significantly improves word retention, comprehension, and engagement compared to text-based methods, supporting its effectiveness as a language learning tool. This method, using visual and linguistic cues to deconstruct and reconstruct words, enhances cognitive processing and long-term memory.Grounded in theories like dual coding, experiential learning, and the Zeigarnik effect, its dynamic animations foster conceptual understanding and curiosity-driven learning.

Beyond enhancing vocabulary acquisition, this study impacts second language acquisition, educational technology, and cognitive development. AI-driven platforms could tailor animations to learner profiles, cross-linguistic studies might confirm its universality, and interdisciplinary efforts could expand multimodal instruction's effectiveness. The study's limitations include its specific demographic and controlled setting, with unassessed long-term retention. Future research should explore longitudinal studies, cross-cultural analyses, and real-world language applications to expand on these findings.

In conclusion, this research paves the way for a transformative approach to vocabulary instruction. Combining etymology's analytical depth with animation's engaging visuals creates effective, enjoyable language learning methods. As digital tools grow in education, such strategies offer inclusive and enriching learning opportunities.

Further Reading

For an in-depth analysis, refer to the original study: [DOI=10.1142/9789814612883_0013].

Column 1: Why Etymology Matters in Language Learning

Subtitle: Building Connections Between Words and Meaning

Understanding the origins of words can serve as a powerful cognitive tool for language learners. Etymology, the study of word origins and histories, is not merely an academic endeavor, but a practical strategy for deepening vocabulary comprehension. For instance, recognizing that centipede derives from "centi" (hundred) and "pede" (foot) enables learners to form logical connections between word structure and meaning. This approach aligns with cognitive theories suggesting that meaningful, context-rich learning enhances long-term retention. Additionally, etymology sparks curiosity. For young learners in particular, this sense of discovery can transform vocabulary acquisition from a rote task into an engaging and explorative experience.

Column 2: The Role of Animation in Cognitive Engagement

Subtitle: Visualizing Concepts to Enhance Retention

This column highlights the cognitive benefits of using animation in language learning environments. Animations are not solely for entertainment, they function as pedagogical tools that can significantly boost understanding and recall. Research in multimedia learning shows that well-crafted animations facilitate learning by visualizing abstract or complex concepts. For example, animations in the system demonstrate "hundred feet" for centipede, or illustrate the motion of a windmill, making word meanings more concrete and memorable. However, overcomplicated or fast-paced animations may hinder comprehension, especially for younger learners. Simplicity, pacing, and clarity are therefore essential design principles in educational animation.

Column 3: Active Learning Through Sentence Construction

Subtitle: Moving Beyond Memorization

Effective language learning goes beyond memorizing individual words. One module within the vocabulary system encourages learners to construct sentences using newly learned vocabulary, reinforcing understanding through application. This active learning strategy engages multiple cognitive processes, recall, contextualization, and creativity. For instance, composing a sentence like "The windmill turns in the wind" not only reinforces the meaning of windmill but also fosters confidence in syntactic construction and communication skills.

Column 4: Adapting to Cognitive Styles in Learning

Subtitle: Field-Dependent vs. Field-Independent Learners

Different learners process information in different ways. Field-independent learners tend to excel with abstract tasks and benefit from visual stimuli like animations. In contrast, field-dependent learners may need more structured guidance and contextual cues. The vocabulary learning system accommodates these differences by offering multiple learning modalities, including animations, static images, and sentence construction, allowing learners to engage with content in ways that best suit their cognitive preferences. This flexibility supports personalized and effective language instruction.

Column 5: The Global Challenge of English Education in Non-Native Contexts

Subtitle: Lessons from Japan's Approach

This column considers how local educational challenges reflect broader global trends in English education.

In countries like Japan, transitioning from a native language environment to English instruction poses persistent difficulties for learners. These include lack of exposure, limited confidence, and vocabulary retention issues. Recent initiatives in Japan have begun to address these barriers by introducing English education earlier in the curriculum and integrating technology into instruction.

The etymology-based animation system discussed in this study represents one such innovation. By combining visual learning with linguistic analysis, it offers a culturally sensitive and cognitively effective tool that could be adapted for similar contexts worldwide.

Column 6: Gamifying Language Learning

Subtitle: Turning Vocabulary Practice into Play

This column explores how game-based elements can increase learner motivation. Gamification, the integration of game-like features into educational activities, has shown promise in sustaining student engagement. In the vocabulary learning system, a Word Meaning Deduction Quiz challenges students to break down compound words using etymological clues. For example, deducing that iceberg consists of “ice” and “berg” (mountain) engages learners in both linguistic analysis and critical thinking. This playful interaction encourages repeated exposure and practice, transforming vocabulary acquisition into a more enjoyable and motivating experience.

Column 7: Designing for Accessibility in Educational Technology

Subtitle: Making Learning Tools Universal

Educational tools must be inclusive and accessible to all learners. The vocabulary learning system incorporates colorful animations and intuitive touch interactions to support young users. However, accessibility extends beyond interface design. Features such as auditory support for visually impaired learners, simplified language for beginners, and customizable instructions can further ensure that the system meets a wide range of needs. Looking ahead, adaptive technologies, such as difficulty-level adjustments based on student performance, could enhance accessibility and personalization, making the system even more inclusive.

10 Experiencing the Role of a Bully: A Serious Game for Anti-Bullying Education

1. Introduction

Bullying is a global issue impacting emotional health, academics, and well-being. This study introduces a serious game where students assume a bully's perspective, navigating moral dilemmas to reflect on the emotional, social, and legal effects of harmful actions.

This approach redefines moral education by focusing on the perpetrator's perspective, evoking guilt, fear, and moral reflection instead of solely fostering empathy for victims. It aligns with recent research in persuasive technology and immersive learning.

Bullying varies by cultural context. PISA data shows Japanese students report verbal ridicule and physical aggression, while relational bullying, like exclusion and rumors, is more common in the U.S. and U.K. These differences highlight the need for tailored educational interventions.

In Japan, bullying is linked to group dynamics influenced by cultural norms of conformity. MEXT highlights exclusion of "the different" as a key factor and stresses empathy and inclusion. Few tools tackle the moral challenges of being a perpetrator or encourage reflection on complicity in group-based aggression.

To address this gap, we created a serious game where students, as transfer students, face subtle pressure to join bullying. Through branching narratives, mini-games, and first-person choices, the game simulates social pressure and internal conflict. Choices result in either symbolic praise for resisting or simulated legal consequences for bullying, fostering moral dissonance and ethical reasoning.

In a field experiment with 21 fifth-grade students, the game evoked strong emotional responses. Quantitative data showed increased awareness and engagement, while observations revealed gender differences, female students often skipped intense mini-games, highlighting greater emotional sensitivity compared to male participants.

These reactions highlight ethical concerns. While the system aims to foster moral development through emotional activation, ensuring psychological safety remains a key challenge in designing serious games on sensitive topics. Unlike our earlier conference paper focused on experimental results, this chapter offers a broader, reflective view. It examines theoretical foundations, cultural context, emotional dynamics, and the educational ethics of using immersive technology to promote empathy and social responsibility.

DOI: 10.1201/9781003782735-13

This work contributes to discussions on serious games in moral education, providing a framework for designing emotionally intelligent environments that focus on both what students learn and their emotional connection to the learning process.

2. Theoretical Framework

Integrating serious games into moral education requires a solid theoretical basis to explain how immersive experiences drive behavioral change. Our approach draws on research in persuasive technology, experiential learning, virtual embodiment, and cognitive-emotional theories, which inform the anti-bullying system's design and implementation.

2.1 Persuasive Technology and Behavioral Change

This study centers on persuasive technology, which explores how digital tools influence behavior without coercion. B.J. Fogg (2003) described "computers as persuasive agents," emphasizing principles like credibility, social influence, reinforcement, and personalization to shape behavior.

Our game applies Fogg's strategies as follows:

- Praise: Players receive affirmation for resisting bullying, reinforcing prosocial behavior.
- Similarity and Liking: Characters are matched in gender and demeanor to the player, enhancing relatability and trust.
- Social Roles and Authority: Police officers appear at the narrative's conclusion, emphasizing the legal consequences of bullying.
- Tunneling: Players navigate moral dilemmas, with each choice reinforcing the ethical implications of bullying.

These strategies align with the Persuasive Systems Design (PSD) model (Oinas-Kukkonen & Harjumaa, 2009), which emphasizes supporting tasks, dialogue, credibility, and social influence. By integrating these elements, the game seeks to not only educate, but also to reshape attitudes toward bullying.

2.2 Experiential Learning and Moral Reflection

Allowing students to play as perpetrators draws on Kolb's experiential learning theory, emphasizing understanding through concrete experience, reflection, conceptualization, and active experimentation.

Playing as a bully creates a controlled space for students to:

- Experience the emotional and social consequences of harmful behavior
- Observe moral dilemmas from an internal vantage point
- Reflect on feelings of guilt, discomfort, or dissonance

- Conceptualize ethical norms through personal narratives
- Rehearse better decision-making in future scenarios

This reflective cycle is crucial in promoting deep learning, especially in emotionally complex domains like bullying. While many anti-bullying programs encourage empathy toward victims, our system complements this by fostering self-reflection and personal accountability.

Moreover, the choice to place students within the social context of peer influence is informed by research on bullying as a networked phenomenon. Veenstra and Huitsing (2021) emphasize that bullying is not simply an individual moral failure but rather a social dynamic shaped by roles, status hierarchies, and group norms. Through branching narratives and character dialogue, our system simulates social pressure and peer complicity, helping learners see how individual actions are intertwined with broader relational dynamics. This combination of personal moral reflection and networked social awareness represents a key innovation in how experiential learning can be applied to moral education through interactive media.

2.3 Virtual Embodiment and Emotional Engagement

A key theoretical basis is embodiment in VR, defined by Kilteni, Groten, and Slater (2012) as the integration of body ownership, agency, and self-location. This sense of "being in" the virtual body enables users to process experiences as if they were occurring in real life, enhancing emotional engagement and behavioral relevance. In moral contexts, this realism can amplify the emotional impact of decisions, fostering deeper reflection. Assuming a bully's role through a first-person interface fosters a stronger emotional connection to in-game events.

Empirical studies, like Slater et al. (2010), show that first-person embodiment in moral scenarios enhances empathy and self-regulation. Participants in their study were more likely to internalize consequences of morally charged actions when experienced in immersive virtual environments, suggesting that embodiment can transform abstract ethical lessons into emotionally salient experiences. Immersive experiences engage users emotionally, fostering deeper moral reflection and behavioral change beyond passive learning.

Bertrand et al. (2018) found that virtual embodiment, such as viewing oneself from another's perspective enhances empathy through immersive experiences. Their study showed that when participants observed their own actions from the viewpoint of a virtual victim, they exhibited stronger empathic responses and moral sensitivity. This finding supports the idea that shifting perspective in immersive settings can disrupt habitual thinking patterns and promote ethical insight. This supports our use of avatar embodiment and emotional scenarios to promote moral reflection. Our system leverages embodiment by using:

- First-person perspectives
- Avatar personalization
- Realistic social interactions
- Emotional feedback through narrative consequences

These design choices ensure that the learning is not abstract or detached, but personal and emotionally resonant, critical components in moral education.

2.4 *Emotion, Guilt, and Moral Cognition*

Emotions are vital in moral reasoning but often overlooked in traditional pedagogy (Haidt, 2001). Guilt, as an internal regulator, drives reparative actions when individuals recognize violations of their moral standards. In our system, guilt is induced through:

- Depictions of the victim's emotional distress
- Social disapproval from in-game peers
- Legal consequences (e.g., arrest by a police officer)
- Reflective moments at narrative turning points

This design supports guilt induction as effective in promoting ethical behavior (Baumeister et al., 1994), while emphasizing caution to prevent emotional overload. Gender differences, noted in female students skipping intense scenes, will be explored further in later chapters.

2.5 *Game-Based Learning and Moral Development*

Our approach aligns with game-based learning, which uses interactive media to achieve educational goals. Gee (2003) highlights that games enable situated learning allowing players to learn by doing, exploring, and safely failing. In moral education, games help students explore ethics, assess consequences, and internalize values meaningfully. Serious games like SPARX, PeaceMaker, and GATE-BULL show the power of gamified interventions to influence attitudes and behavior. Our system extends this approach by highlighting the often-overlooked perspective of the perpetrator.

This chapter outlines the theoretical foundations of our system, integrating persuasive technology, experiential learning, emotional engagement, and virtual embodiment. These frameworks guide design decisions and evaluate educational impact. Subsequent chapters will detail their implementation and influence on design and outcomes.

3. System Design, A Serious Game for Anti-Bullying

Designing a serious game that lets children experience a bully's perspective demands balancing emotional impact and ethical responsibility. This chapter details the system's design, including structure, mechanics, personalization, persuasive elements, and the reasoning behind key choices.

3.1 *Game Concept and Educational Objectives*

This game shifts focus to the perpetrator, aiming to foster moral reflection by confronting the impact of harmful actions through a first-person view. Through immersive storytelling and mini-games, it evokes emotions like guilt and fear, encouraging empathy and behavioral change.

The educational objectives are threefold:

1. To raise awareness of the moral and legal consequences of bullying.
2. To simulate real-life social pressure and explore how it influences behavior.
3. To enable self-reflection by allowing players to observe the impact of their choices.

3.2 Narrative Structure and Game Flow

The narrative unfolds in a 3D virtual environment where the player interacts with 3D characters through first-person dialogue. Throughout the story, the player is prompted to engage in multiple bullying-related mini-games that simulate real-life peer pressure scenarios. The game starts with the player, a transfer student, being introduced to the classroom by a same-gender peer. This familiar and trusting interaction fosters emotional engagement and prepares players for future dilemmas.

The core gameplay uses a branching narrative where players face peer pressure through bullying mini-games, choosing to join or resist. At the final outcome screen, choices lead to two outcomes: praise from peers and teachers for abstaining, or a police officer highlighting the gravity of bullying for participating.

3.3 Mini-Games and Bullying Simulations

The mini-games replicate various forms of bullying observed in Japanese and international contexts:

- **Exclusion:** Players repeatedly press a key to push another student out of the classroom.
- **Verbal Attack:** Players choose phrases like "You're so annoying" or "Die already" to insult a classmate.
- **Ignoring:** Players avoid text bubbles such as "Hey!" and "What's your name?" symbolizing social neglect.
- **Backbiting:** Players click through gossip dialogues, representing relational bullying often seen among girls.

Visual and audio cues enhance realism, while the mechanics remain intentionally simple to ensure accessibility for elementary students and foster emotional engagement.

3.4 Personalization and Gender-Specific Scenarios

- To boost immersion and relatability, the system includes avatar customization, allowing players to select their gender. This choice affects character design and the mini-games encountered, reflecting research on gender-based bullying behaviors: boys often engage in physical or overt verbal aggression.

- While girls lean toward relational aggression like exclusion or gossip.

By tailoring experiences, the game mirrors students' realities, creating meaningful scenarios and supporting the Similarity principle in persuasive design, which enhances emotional resonance.

3.5 Persuasive Design Elements

The game design incorporates persuasive strategies from Fogg's persuasive technology framework:

- **Praise:** Positive feedback from in-game characters and authority figures rewards players who resist bullying.
- **Social Influence:** Characters provide encouragement or pressure, mirroring real-life peer dynamics.
- **Authority:** A police officer appears at the end to underscore the gravity of bullying through legal framing.
- **Emotional Framing:** Visual cues, character expressions, and voice acting convey emotions like sadness or fear, highlighting the consequences of the player's choices.

These elements work together to promote prosocial decision-making through experiential learning, rather than direct instruction.

3.6 Ethical Safeguards

Given the sensitive nature of the subject, the system incorporates ethical design features to prioritize student well-being:

- **Skip Function:** Players can skip mini-games if they feel uncomfortable, a feature often used by female participants in intense scenarios.
- **Neutral Feedback:** Choices to engage in bullying prompt reflective rather than shaming feedback.
- **Pre-game and post-game instructions:** Teachers introduce the game with context and facilitate discussions afterward to process emotions and reinforce learning.

These measures account for learners' emotional diversity and aim to ensure a safe, supportive environment while addressing morally complex content.

This thoughtfully designed serious game turns a challenging topic into an emotionally impactful learning experience. By integrating narrative branching, personalization, moral consequences, and persuasive technology, it fosters deeper reflection on bullying, values, and decision-making. The next chapter will outline the methodology and classroom implementation used to evaluate its effectiveness.

4. Research Methodology

The anti-bullying game was assessed through a mixed-methods study in a Japanese elementary school. This chapter outlines the research design, participants, data collection, and ethical safeguards. Combining quantitative, qualitative, and physiological data, the study aimed to understand how children cognitively and emotionally responded to embodying a bully in a simulated environment.

4.1 Research Context and Objectives

This study was designed to answer the following central questions:

1. Can a perpetrator-based first-person game enhance children's understanding of bullying's moral and legal consequences? Does the system elicit emotions like guilt, fear, or sadness, that contribute to moral reflection and learning?
2. Are there behavioral patterns, including gender-based differences, in students' responses to bullying scenarios?

The study took place in a fifth-grade classroom at a public elementary school in Japan. This age group, emotionally impressionable and capable of grasping moral dilemmas, was ideal for empathy-focused learning.

4.2 Participants

Twenty-one fifth graders (11 boys and 10 girls) participated in the study with full support from the school and parental consent. Participation was voluntary, and students could skip activities if needed. The class had no known bullying incidents, reducing the risk of triggering distress, while emotional reactions were closely monitored.

4.3 Procedure

The study was conducted during a regular class period and involved the following phases:

- **Introduction:** The teacher presented the project as an educational activity on bullying, explaining that the game would simulate school life and encourage reflection on decision-making.
- **Gameplay:** Students played the game on computers connected to external displays for 15–20 minutes, making decisions in bullying mini-games that resulted in either a "praise" or "arrest" ending based on their choices.
- **Physiological Monitoring:** Students used a "NAOS QG" mouse to track heart rate during gameplay, revealing emotional arousal during pivotal moments like bullying prompts or witnessing consequences.
- **Post-Game Questionnaire:** After gameplay, students filled out a structured questionnaire using a five-point Likert scale to evaluate:
    - Understanding of bullying issues

- Emotional reactions (e.g., fear, sadness)
- Reflections on their decisions
- Usability and clarity of the game

1. Video Recording and Observation

With consent, sessions were recorded for analysis, tracking players' hesitation, expressions, and in-game actions, alongside real-time responses and spontaneous student comments.

2. Debriefing and Discussion

At the session's end students shared their thoughts, verbally or in writing while the teacher led a brief discussion to provide emotional closure and reinforce key lessons.

4.4 Instruments and Measures

- Questionnaire: The items were crafted to evaluate both affective and cognitive aspects of the experience. Examples include:
  - "I understood the seriousness of bullying."
  - "I felt guilty or sad during the game."
  - "I would try to stop bullying if I saw it in real life."
- Heart Rate Data: Peaks and fluctuations indicated emotional arousal, time-synced with in-game events to pinpoint scenes that triggered strong reactions.
- Behavioral Indicators: Hesitation, skipping mini-games, and visible reactions (e.g., frowning, pausing) were noted as indicators of emotional engagement.

4.5 Observations from the Field

While quantitative data provided structured insight, some of the most illuminating findings emerged through direct observation:

- **Gender-Based Reactions:** A notable number of female students chose to skip certain mini-games, particularly those involving verbal aggression or exclusion. This tendency was not mirrored by male students, who more often proceeded through the scenarios with minimal hesitation.
- **Emotional Sensitivity:** Some students appeared visibly disturbed by specific scenes. In one case, a girl hesitated for nearly 30 seconds before skipping a scene involving backbiting. While no direct verbal reactions were observed, several students' facial expressions and hesitant gestures suggested internal discomfort or uncertainty about continuing with certain scenes.
- **Moral Ambiguity:** Several students expressed confusion or discomfort when their actions were rewarded with points, even though understanding that those actions were morally wrong. This highlighted the importance of clear in-game framing, which was improved in subsequent versions of the system.

- **Immersive Engagement:** Despite its simple interface, the game elicited high levels of emotional immersion. Students leaned forward, occasionally sighed, and showed expressions or body language indicating emotional reactions, such as frowning or pausing—particularly during intense scenes. These behaviors suggest that the system succeeded in creating a meaningful and emotionally engaging learning context.

4.6 Ethical Considerations

Given the emotionally charged nature of the content, ethical safeguards were prioritized:

- A skip function was embedded into the system, allowing students to bypass uncomfortable scenarios without penalty.
- Participants were briefed before the game about its themes and were told they could stop at any time.
- Teachers monitored gameplay and were prepared to intervene if a student became upset.
- A post-game discussion provided emotional closure and ensured that students could express any lingering concerns.

This study was conducted with school administration oversight. Although university-level ethics review wasn't required, all standard practices for research involving minors were rigorously followed.

This chapter detailed the methodology used to evaluate the serious game in a classroom setting, combining physiological, behavioral, and self-reported data with qualitative observations to understand both what students learned and how they emotionally responded. The next chapter analyzes the study's results, examining the game's impact on emotional engagement, behavioral intentions, and moral awareness.

5. Findings and Analysis

This chapter outlines the field study's results on how the serious game influenced students' emotions, behavior, and moral reasoning. Key patterns emerged from questionnaires, physiological data, and observations, including gender-based differences, hesitation, and signs of moral awareness. Student feedback was drawn from written and observed responses.

5.1 Emotional Responses: Engagement, Discomfort, and Guilt

A key objective was to evoke emotions like discomfort, guilt, or empathy to inspire moral reflection. Heart rate analysis showed spikes during high-stakes moments, especially in relational bullying mini-games, indicating heightened emotional arousal.

Data from the post-game questionnaire further supported this:

- 17 of 21 students reported feeling "uncomfortable" or "guilty" when choosing to engage in bullying actions.
- 15 students noted their surprise at how realistic the simulated bullying felt. Female students were more likely than male students to select "strongly agree" for items such as "I felt sad during the game" and "I didn't want to hurt others."

These findings indicate that the game was effective in evoking emotional responses, particularly around scenarios involving verbal or social exclusion, and they served as a cognitive entry point for reflection.

5.2 Gender Differences in Game Behavior

Behavioral data revealed that female students more frequently hesitated or skipped scenes, especially those involving direct aggression or social exclusion compared to male students.

- Observation records noted: 6 of 10 female students skipped at least one mini-game, compared to only 1 of 11 male students.
- Girls often paused before deciding, showing visible discomfort such as looking away, whispering to themselves, or quietly asking, "Do I have to do this?"
- Boys navigated gameplay more fluidly, with fewer signs of hesitation, often approaching tasks as straightforward objectives.

These findings align with prior studies showing that girls are more sensitive to interpersonal harm and prone to empathic distress in moral decision-making. Both genders reported emotional reactions, but discomfort was more evident in the behavior of female students.

5.3 Reflections and Learning Outcomes

The free-response section of the post-game questionnaire provided valuable insights, with several students expressing emotional responses and personal realizations in writing. Selected examples include:

- "I didn't know being mean could feel so bad, even in a game."
- "I think if someone tells me to do bad things, I can say no now."
- "It was scary when the police officer came. I didn't want that to happen."

These comments highlight how the game conveyed the harms of bullying while fostering self-reflection and moral insight. Many students noted peer influence in their decision-making, expressing that they felt conflicted when "everyone else was doing it." This suggests the game helped them explore the social dynamics and pressures shaping ethical choices.

5.4 Behavioral Shifts and Post-Game Intentions

Though formal follow-up interviews or tracking were not conducted, several students shared extended reflections in the questionnaire's open-ended section. For example:

- "I want to be able to say no if I'm asked to join in bullying."
- "I'll try to stop myself from saying things that hurt people."

These comments, though limited in number, point to a level of moral engagement that goes beyond the moment of gameplay. They reflect a desire to act differently in real-life scenarios, indicating that the game may have contributed to shifts in moral perspective and behavioral intention, even if only indirectly.

5.5 Observations on Game Design and Emotional Load

Alongside its strengths, the study revealed several areas in which the game's design could be improved to ensure clarity and psychological comfort:

- Reward Confusion: Some students expressed discomfort or confusion at receiving points for completing bullying mini-games, even when they recognized the actions as morally wrong. One student wrote: "It felt strange to get a reward after doing something bad."
- Emotional Impact of Arrest Scene: While no students required intervention, observation records note that some showed signs of emotional tension or surprise during the police scene at the end.
- Emotional Load Management: In several cases, students hesitated significantly or chose to skip scenes involving emotional distress, indicating the need for flexible pacing and emotional safety measures.

These issues underscore the importance of ethical calibration, designing emotionally engaging content that challenges students without overwhelming them. Future iterations of the system could include optional emotional warnings, varied endings, or teacher-adjustable pacing.

In summary, the findings of this study suggest that a first-person, perpetrator-perspective serious game can successfully promote emotional engagement, reflection, and early forms of moral reasoning among elementary students. Gender-based differences indicate that emotional sensitivity and threshold vary across learners, reinforcing the need for adaptive or flexible design.

By combining emotional immersion with structured moral consequences, the system provided students with an experiential learning environment that encouraged them to think deeply about the social and emotional dimensions of bullying. In the next chapter, we will contextualize these findings within existing scholarship and discuss their broader educational and ethical implications.

6. Discussion

The findings of this study underscore the complex interplay between emotional engagement, moral reasoning, and educational design in technology-assisted anti-bullying education. This chapter interprets those findings through the lenses of persuasive technology, experiential learning, and moral psychology, while also reflecting on the broader pedagogical and ethical implications. The discussion highlights both the strengths and the limitations of using a perpetrator-perspective serious game in the context of elementary education.

6.1 Emotional Engagement as a Catalyst for Moral Reflection

The system aimed to evoke emotions like discomfort, guilt, and anxiety to encourage self-reflection on moral issues. High heart rates and verbal reluctance among participants confirmed its effectiveness in delivering emotionally impactful experiences.

These findings support Haidt's (2001) theory of moral intuition, which argues that emotion often precedes rational judgment in moral decisions. His social intuitionist model further suggests moral judgments stem from emotional instincts followed by rationalization. Instead of teaching abstract rules, the game fostered embodied engagement, letting students emotionally and physically experience the impact of harmful actions.

Emotional engagement must be balanced, as overly intense experiences can distress sensitive students. Observed hesitation and scene-skipping among female students highlight how emotional overload may affect psychological safety and learning effectiveness. Future designs should focus on both emotional impact and regulation to support learner agency and control.

6.2 The Educational Value of the Perpetrator Perspective

A unique aspect of this system is its decision to let students play as the bully, a bold and sensitive choice designed to help them confront the moral conflict of harmful behavior firsthand. This design follows Kolb's (1984) experiential learning theory, where students learn through action and reflection. By simulating complicity, the game helped them explore why people bully, the effects of peer pressure, and the impact of harming others, questions beyond the scope of lectures. However, placing students in a bully's role carries ethical risks, such as normalization or desensitization. Strong emotional framing, like victim expressions and legal consequences, mitigated these risks but further refinement is needed to emphasize moral lessons over potential thrills.

6.3 Gender and Emotional Thresholds in Moral Gameplay

The study revealed gender-based differences in responses to emotional scenarios. Female students showed more hesitation, scene-skipping, and verbal signs of discomfort, while male students engaged more directly. These patterns align with cognitive and emotional development differences noted in prior research. Eisenberg et al. (2006) found that girls tend to exhibit greater empathic concern and emotional sensitivity in social situations, particularly those involving interpersonal harm. Similarly, Chaplin and Aldao (2013) noted that girls are more likely than boys to express internalizing emotions such as sadness and guilt, especially in contexts of moral decision-making.

These differences suggest the need for adaptive learning paths. Strong emotional immersion may benefit some but cause others to disengage. Features like skip options, adjustable pacing, or alternate versions can help tailor the experience to individual needs.

These findings raise questions about differing expressions of empathy. Girls may show discomfort through avoidance, while boys might internalize it. Both patterns are crucial for designing emotionally sensitive learning environments.

6.4 Practical Implications for Anti-Bullying Education

This study highlights the potential of serious games in moral education, especially when traditional methods fail to emotionally engage students. Effective implementation requires a teacher or facilitator to frame the activity, guide reflection, and manage emotional responses.

The game should be part of a broader instructional framework, with structured post-game discussions to help students process their experiences and link lessons to real-life situations. Parental involvement, through consent and discussion guides, is also crucial for reinforcing support at home.

Though designed for Japanese students, the game's principles may require modification for other cultural contexts, where norms around bullying, authority, and emotions vary. Future possibilities include integrating adaptive modeling techniques, as seen in Pérez et al. (2023), who used simulations and computational modeling to assess cyberbullying dynamics and personalize feedback based on user input.

By incorporating such methods, it becomes possible to tailor ethical learning experiences to individual students' decision-making patterns, enabling more personalized and effective moral education.

6.5 Design Considerations and Ethical Safeguards

Future system iterations should offer multiple narrative paths with adjustable emotional intensity, clearer moral framing, optional in-game reflection prompts, emotional checkpoints for self-assessment, and teacher customization for scenes, pacing, and feedback.

In summary, ethically managed emotional engagement can enhance young learners' moral reasoning and empathy. While placing students in a perpetrator's role poses risks, thoughtful design provides a unique way to address bullying's social dynamics. Future iterations could integrate adaptive technologies and social modeling to better support diverse learners.

This study explored how a serious game, allowing students to embody a bully, could deepen awareness of bullying and moral responsibility. By integrating persuasive technology, experiential learning, and affective computing, it created impactful experiences that encouraged reflection on decisions, roles, and the consequences of harmful actions. The findings highlight four contributions:

- Shifting focus from victim to perpetrator enables students to confront ethical dilemmas firsthand.
- Emotionally calibrated design emphasizes the role of emotion as a key driver of learning.
- Gender-based differences in gameplay call for adaptive systems sensitive to varied emotional needs.
- Practical guidance underscores the importance of structured facilitation and emotional support in classrooms.

These findings suggest integrating emotion-centered learning into moral education, with serious games emphasizing ethical complexity over simple content delivery. Designers should balance player agency with ethical clarity and ensure adaptability across cultures and emotional contexts.

The study had limitations, including a small, context-specific sample and a lack of long-term behavioral data. Emotional responses were assessed indirectly and could benefit from detailed affective analysis. Future research could examine longitudinal effects, emotion-adaptive design, and cross-cultural differences in moral gameplay reactions.

7. Conclusion

This study examined a serious game enabling elementary students to embody a bully's perspective within an ethically guided and emotionally calibrated setting. Rooted in persuasive technology, experiential learning, and moral psychology, the system promoted emotional engagement and ethical reflection through immersive gameplay.

The game evoked discomfort and guilt, especially in scenarios of social exclusion or verbal aggression. Observed gender differences in emotional thresholds emphasized the need for adaptive design.

Students showed greater awareness of bullying's impact and expressed intentions to change their real-life behavior. This research introduced a new approach to moral education by blending emotional experience, learner agency, and structured reflection.

The game's design effectively fostered introspection and critical thinking on social behavior. Future work could focus on scaling, localizing, and adapting these experiences for diverse learners, as well as examining their long-term impact on moral development and behavior.

Further Reading

For a detailed analysis, refer to the original study: [DOI=10.1007/978-3-031-97177-8_4].

Column 1: The Psychology of Guilt in Learning

Subtitle: How Emotional Responses Shape Behavioral Change

Guilt, a driver of moral growth, can enhance anti-bullying education by prompting reflection and internalizing ethical values within a safe and simulated setting. Research shows guilt activates empathy-related brain regions (Baumeister et al., 1994; Haidt, 2001).

In our system, guilt is elicited through consequences such as a victim's emotional expressions or the arrival of a police officer, carefully balanced to ensure emotional impact while avoiding distress. This is key for sensitive students, some of whom chose to skip intense mini-games.

Column 2: Peer Pressure in the Digital Classroom

Subtitle: Simulating Social Dynamics Through Gameplay

Peer pressure strongly influences children's behavior, often driving bullying to gain approval or avoid exclusion. Our game simulates this dynamic with characters nudging players through praise, similarity, and casual invitations to join bullying actions.

These mechanics let students experience peer pressure in a safe setting, encouraging them to explore resistance. The branching narrative shows contrasting outcomes: legal and moral consequences for conformity, and social rewards for resistance, fostering moral agency for real-life decisions.

Column 3: Gender Differences in Bullying Behavior

Subtitle: What Gameplay Reveals About Emotional Thresholds

Bullying behaviors often differ by gender. Boys tend toward physical or verbal aggression, while girls lean toward relational tactics like exclusion or gossip. In gameplay, boys embraced action-based tasks, whereas girls hesitated or skipped scenarios involving social manipulation. These patterns reflect varying emotional thresholds and empathy expressions, with girls more sensitive to social consequences.

Adaptive designs, offering flexible pacing, skip options, and reflection prompts, are vital for accommodating diverse emotional needs in learning environments.

Column 4: The Role of Gamification in Emotionally Charged Education

Subtitle: Motivating Reflection Without Trivialization

Gamification, using elements like points and rewards, is common in education but requires caution for sensitive topics like bullying. Poor implementation might reward harmful behavior, causing moral confusion.

In our system, points act as narrative markers, not moral judgments, though some students felt uneasy receiving points after bullying scenes. Clear framing of rewards is essential to align gamification with ethical learning, ensuring it transforms abstract dilemmas into impactful, emotionally resonant experiences.

11 Motivating Athletic Performance: A Throwing Training System with Immersive Feedback

1. Introduction

Modern children spend more time indoors, which has led to reduced physical activity and declining motor skills like throwing. In Japan, fitness assessments show boys' softball throw distances dropped by 6.4 meters and girls' by 3.8 meters from 1985 to 2013, with declines continuing into 2023. Sixth-grade averages are now 25.8 meters for boys and 13.8 meters for girls, far below past records. According to the World Health Organization (2019), approximately 81% of adolescents aged 11–17 worldwide do not meet the recommended guideline of at least 60 minutes of moderate-to-vigorous physical activity per day. This widespread inactivity is attributed to factors such as urbanization, reduced outdoor play opportunities, increased screen time, and changing lifestyle patterns.

Throwing, unlike walking or running, is a complex skill requiring coordination across joints and body segments (Fleisig et al., 1995). Developmental motor learning highlights the need to practice such skills during sensitive childhood periods (Haywood & Getchell, 2019). Without proper guidance and positive experiences, children risk motor deficits and negative attitudes toward physical activity (Weiss, 2000). This study introduces a feedback-enhanced throwing training system to tackle technical and motivational challenges in skill acquisition. Unlike traditional methods, it uses real-time visual and auditory effects, such as animated "speed lines" and celebratory sounds, to provide immediate and engaging feedback, encouraging improved performance. This approach aims to enhance skill development and intrinsic motivation. Children who feel inadequate in sports often disengage, leading to a cycle of failure (Ntoumanis, 2010). Game-like feedback simulates success and affirms effort, fostering competence and confidence.

The system evolved in two phases: an initial version emphasizing basic feedback like throw distance visualization and speed-line animations, and an enhanced version adding multimodal features such as form visualization, dynamic sounds, and layered visuals. Both versions were tested with elementary students using quantitative and qualitative measures. The study integrates motor learning, interaction design, and educational psychology. It applies Self-Determination Theory (Deci & Ryan, 2000), focusing on autonomy, competence, and relatedness to boost intrinsic motivation. Design principles from serious games and gamification, including immediate feedback, progressive challenges, and reward systems, are used to enhance user engagement. In this study, these elements are applied to

DOI: 10.1201/9781003782735-14

provide emotionally meaningful feedback that reinforces motivation and sustained participation (Michael & Chen, 2005; Hamari et al., 2014; Deterding et al., 2011).

This study makes four contributions: showcasing real-time, emotionally resonant feedback's role in boosting performance and motivation, applying serious game principles to motor skill development, emphasizing the need for personalized feedback systems, and illustrating scalable technologies for real-world educational challenges. By merging feedback with emotional experience, it shifts focus from correction to empowerment, enhancing both movement and confidence.

2. Related Work

This research builds on prior work in motor skill acquisition, motion capture in sports training, serious games, gamification, and sensory feedback. Key findings from these fields are reviewed to highlight the gaps addressed by this study.

2.1 Motor Skill Development Challenges in Children

Throwing is a complex motor skill requiring coordination, timing, and balance, unlike walking or running. Haywood and Getchell (2019) note that motor skills develop best during "sensitive periods," and a lack of instruction can lead to lasting proficiency deficits.

Teaching throwing is challenging in physical education, as many children, particularly those with low motor competence, struggle with technique, leading to frustration and disengagement (Robinson et al., 2015; Stodden et al., 2008).

Robinson et al. (2015) emphasized that motor competence is crucial for children's health development, while Stodden et al. (2008) proposed a developmental model linking motor skills to physical activity engagement, suggesting that low competence may trigger a negative cycle of inactivity and health risks.

Declining throwing ability in Japanese children, especially girls, underscores the need for better teaching methods (MEXT, 2013). Post-pandemic studies reveal worsened motor skill performance due to reduced activity levels (Veldman et al., 2023) and increased sedentary behavior during lockdowns (López-Bueno et al., 2020), highlighting the importance of scalable interventions in schools and homes.

2.2 Motion Capture and Feedback Systems in Educational Settings

Advances in motion capture, like Microsoft Kinect, enable real-time tracking of joint movements without markers, offering non-invasive, cost-effective options for analyzing human movement in schools (Lange et al., 2009). Studies show immediate, personalized feedback enhances motor learning (Sigrist et al., 2013).

Mousavi et al. (2024) revealed how dart-throwing kinematics differ between virtual and real environments, offering insights for designing effective motion-based training systems. Their findings highlight the need to account for contextual and perceptual constraints in digital motor learning environments.

However, many existing systems are still overly technical and rigid, making them unsuitable for young learners or those with low sports confidence. Feedback systems in education should balance clarity and emotional engagement to support both understanding and motivation.

Recent developments in AI-integrated motion capture systems have enabled adaptive, real-time performance analysis. Wang & Qiu (2019) demonstrated an AI-based pose estimation system for personalized coaching, and Zhang et al. (2024) reviewed applications in physical education, emphasizing the importance of individualized feedback to support diverse learners in both rehabilitation and school contexts.

2.3 Gamified Approaches and Motivational Theories in Physical Education

Serious games, designed for purposes beyond entertainment like education and behavior change, have gained prominence in physical education. Michael & Chen (2005) categorized serious games into types based on goals and context, providing frameworks for integrating them into structured learning. Research shows they boost motivation, procedural learning, and cognitive engagement when thoughtfully integrated into programs (Gee, 2003; Susi et al., 2007).

Gamification applies game design elements like points, leaderboards, and rewards to boost engagement and behavior in non-game contexts (Deterding et al., 2011). In physical education, it encourages participation, tracks progress, and reduces exercise avoidance (Domínguez et al., 2013). Grounded in Self-Determination Theory (Deci & Ryan, 2000), it enhances intrinsic motivation by fulfilling autonomy, competence, and relatedness needs, with game-like feedback supporting sustained engagement.

Skill-based scoring and progress indicators can boost competence, while celebratory feedback like visuals and sounds affirm effort and enhance success perception. Though user customization and peer interaction were absent in this system, studies show such features enhance motivation by supporting autonomy and relatedness.

Effective gamification depends on aligning game elements with meaningful learning tasks. Platforms like Exergame+ and PE-Gamify have implemented point systems, badges, and dynamic visuals to sustain physical activity engagement among elementary students.

These findings highlight the long-term potential of game elements when aligned with curriculum goals. Studies such as those on platforms like Exergame+ and PE-Gamify have demonstrated increased physical activity among elementary students through visual and reward-based feedback.

2.4 Multisensory Feedback for Engagement in Motor Learning

Strategic visual and auditory feedback enhances learning by improving memory, motivation, and reducing cognitive load in motor tasks (Shams & Seitz, 2008).

In game-based learning environments, visual effects such as speed trails and celebratory animations not only increase engagement but also encourage repeated effort by reinforcing emotional responses (Mekler et al., 2017; Hamari et al., 2014).

This is particularly valuable for children, who often require affective reinforcement to persist in challenging physical tasks.

Poorly designed sensory feedback can overwhelm users with low skills or cognitive overload. Effective implementation requires balancing cognitive demand and motivation through collaboration in educational psychology and user-centered design.

Plass et al. (2015) emphasized the importance of aligning feedback with learner goals to reduce cognitive overload while enhancing engagement. Feedback resonates more when aligned with learners' emotional states and performance context (Janelle et al., 2018) and when structured to enhance learning outcomes (Hattie & Timperley, 2007).

3. Development and Pilot Testing of a Basic Feedback-Based Throwing System

To explore motion capture's potential in youth athletic training, a simple prototype was developed, focusing on basic throwing mechanics. It assessed whether real-time feedback could enhance children's performance in a short session, detailing its design, implementation, and outcomes.

3.1 Overview of the Initial System Design

The initial throwing training system, designed for elementary students, served as a proof-of-concept to enhance throwing distance and form while addressing their cognitive, physical, and motivational needs.

The system used Microsoft Kinect to track throwing motions in real time, comparing them to an ideal model.

Feedback, focused on throw distance, included displayed lengths and simple sound cues to reinforce performance.

3.2 Technical Implementation

The system used the Kinect SDK to capture 3D skeletal data, comparing users' joint angles frame-by-frame with those of experienced throwers. A threshold-based evaluation assessed the form as acceptable, partially correct, or incorrect, triggering feedback accordingly.

Key joints analyzed included the shoulder, elbow, hip, and knee, as these are critical for throwing mechanics (Fleisig et al., 1995).

3.3 User Interface and Feedback Design

The interface was designed to be simple, colorful, and engaging, displaying throw distance, offering audio prompts like "Nice throw!" or "Try again!", and using a visual meter to show motion accuracy. Character avatars celebrated successful throws, fostering motivation.

While immersive effects like "speed lines" were absent in this version, clear and positive feedback supported basic engagement.

3.4 Experimental Setup and Participants

A pilot study was conducted at a public elementary school in Japan with 28 participants (14 boys and 14 girls) from the 4th and 5th grades.

The evaluation included three stages:

1. A baseline throwing trial without feedback.
2. A 15–20 minute training session with the system.
3. A post-training throw to measure improvement.

Afterward, a brief questionnaire gathered participants' opinions on enjoyment, ease of use, and perceived progress.

3.5 Results and Observations

Throwing distances improved after training, with boys gaining 0.8 meters and girls 0.6 meters on average. Over 85% of participants found the system "fun" or "very fun," and 71% felt their throwing had improved, enjoying the distance display and verbal encouragement.

Teachers observed greater engagement, laughter, social interaction, and spontaneous competition, creating a lively learning environment. Such qualitative observations suggest that the system's simplicity and visual rewards effectively fostered a playful and collaborative learning atmosphere.

Some confusion about the form comparison meter led to its redesign in the next system iteration.

3.6 Discussion and Identified Limitations

The early system showcased the use of markerless motion tracking and real-time feedback to improve children's throwing practice, combining distance visualization, basic form evaluation, and emotional reinforcement for engagement and short-term progress.

However, limitations included:

- A lack of nuanced form analysis
- Absence of visual animations for self-correction
- Static feedback without adaptation
- Indoor space constraints affecting natural throwing

These insights guided the next development phase, adding motivational effects and refining the interface for clearer feedback (see Chapter 4).

4. Enhanced System with Immersive Visual and Auditory Feedback

After testing the initial system, it became evident that while basic feedback improved performance, it lacked the emotional engagement needed to sustain motivation.

This led to the enhanced system, featuring immersive visual, auditory, and linguistic feedback for a more engaging training experience.

This chapter details its design, implementation, and evaluation.

4.1 Overview of the Enhanced System

The second system addressed prior limitations, adding emotionally resonant feedback to boost engagement and self-efficacy.

It introduced three modes:

- Form-based visual feedback showing movement accuracy via joint analysis
- Onomatopoeic auditory cues like "whizz" and "boom" for rhythmic reinforcement
- Special visual effects emphasizing effort and success (Sumi & Tsukamoto, 2016).

This approach draws on Bandura's (1997) concept of self-efficacy, where belief in one's capabilities enhances motivation and task persistence.

4.2 Feedback Modes: Form, Onomatopoeia, and Special Effects

4.2.1 Multimodal Form Guidance: Movement Instruction through Animation and Onomatopoeia

This mode combines real-time joint movement assessment, animated demonstration of the ideal throwing form, and auditory guidance using onomatopoeia to support children's form learning through both visual and auditory channels.

First, using Microsoft Kinect, the system performs real-time skeletal analysis, evaluating the user's joint angles and movement patterns. The accuracy of motion is visualized using color gradients and clear icons, making it easy for young learners to understand their performance intuitively.

Furthermore, to enhance understanding of the movement, an animation displaying the ideal throwing form is shown. This allows users to visually learn the correct motion as a model and compare it with their own form.

In addition, the system incorporates onomatopoeic cues such as "whoosh," "snap," and "bang," commonly used in Japanese sports instruction, to convey the rhythm and power of movement. These mimetic sounds help children, especially those responsive to auditory stimuli, to grasp timing and movement quality in an intuitive, embodied way.

Grounded in Bandura's (1997) theory of self-efficacy, this mode not only aids in accurate motor execution but also promotes a sense of accomplishment and confidence, thereby fostering sustained motivation.

In summary, this mode supports motor skill acquisition through a multimodal approach integrating visual, auditory, and kinesthetic feedback.

4.2.2 Special Effects Feedback

Dynamic animations offered the most visually immersive feedback after each throw, embodying success, intensity, and progress in an emotionally engaging way. This version featured and tested three types of visual effects:

- Speed Lines, a streaking trail followed the hand's motion, dynamically illustrating real-time throw velocity. Its length and brightness adjusted to reflect throw quality, emphasizing speed and momentum.
- Phoenix Animation, a glowing phoenix appeared and soared across the screen after a successful throw, symbolizing power, transformation, and emotional impact.
- Crowd Cheers, animated characters cheered and celebrated the thrower's success, offering peer recognition and social encouragement.

These effects served as emotional rewards and explored how various aesthetic and symbolic representations impact children's engagement and motivation.

4.3 Visual Feedback Design and User Reactions

Speed Lines offered the clearest depiction of motion dynamics, directly linking throwing effort to visual output. The Phoenix effect provided a symbolic, fantastical reward, while Crowd Cheers highlighted social recognition.

Figure 1 shows the Speed Lines effect as an example of real-time motion feedback. The figure illustrates the hand's movement trail during throwing, helping to link physical effort with a dynamic visual response. Pilot tests found children responded well to all three effects, though preferences varied. Nearly half favored Speed Lines for its clear link to physical effort, while others appreciated the Phoenix's symbolism or the social reward of Crowd Cheers. This highlights the broad appeal of effects closely tied to effort, like Speed Lines. These preference variations underscore the value of flexible feedback systems that adapt to individual motivational styles and aesthetic preferences.

4.4 Experimental Design and Results

A controlled experiment involved 32 children (16 boys and 16 girls), aged 9 to 11, who were randomly assigned to one of three feedback conditions:

- Condition A: Form feedback only
- Condition B: Form + Onomatopoeia
- Condition C: Form + Onomatopoeia + Special Effects

In Condition C, participants experienced one of three special effects (Speed Lines, Phoenix, or Crowd Cheers), to compare their motivational impact. Each child completed three throwing rounds, with pre- and post-training data collected.

Fig. 1 Speed Lines Feedback: Real-Time Visualization of Throw Velocity
This figure illustrates the "Speed Lines" feedback mechanism, in which animated streaks radiate from the hand trajectory to represent throw velocity and motion. Designed to deliver immediate and emotionally engaging feedback, the effect reinforces the connection between physical effort and performance. As one of three immersive feedback styles tested in the system, it aims to motivate users by visualizing success in a dynamic and rewarding way.

Participants in Condition C showed the greatest improvement in throwing distance, with an average gain of 1.2 meters. The observed differences in performance and motivation indicate promising trends for future investigation. Moreover, 81% found the visual effects more enjoyable or motivating. Speed Lines were the favorite (47%), followed by Phoenix (31%) and Crowd Cheers (22%).

These findings indicate that immersive visual feedback, tailored to aesthetic preferences, can greatly boost children's engagement and persistence in physical training.

5. Discussion and Theoretical Implications

This chapter combines theoretical and empirical perspectives to analyze the study's findings. It examines how the throwing training system's design, spanning its basic and enhanced versions, aligns with motor learning, intrinsic motivation, and educational game design theories evaluating its effectiveness within child-centered physical education and motivational feedback frameworks.

5.1 Theoretical Foundations of Motivation and Feedback Design

The throwing training system combines motor learning theory and motivational psychology. Feedback plays a key role in enhancing physical performance, helping learners master skills like overhand throwing through practice and guidance that links movement patterns to outcomes. Clear, immediate feedback aids throwing form correction and reinforces motor schemas, especially for young learners (Schmidt & Wrisberg, 2008). Feedback effectiveness relies not only on content but also on motivation. Self-Determination Theory (Deci & Ryan, 2000) highlights that intrinsic motivation flourishes when autonomy, competence, and relatedness are supported. In physical education, these needs often go unmet for children who feel "unathletic" or struggle with traditional methods. Engaging, playful feedback, like cheering sounds or visual rewards, can address these gaps and maintain long-term engagement.

Research on serious games and gamification highlights their ability to enhance motivation and engagement. Serious games, created for purposes beyond entertainment, and gamification, using game-like elements in non-game contexts, have proven effective. Celebratory visuals tied to achievements boost enjoyment and motivation, particularly among younger learners (Michael & Chen, 2006; Deterding et al., 2011; Hamari et al., 2014; Mekler et al., 2017). This system emphasizes effort and improvement through multimodal reinforcement reflecting progress to build competence. For children with coordination challenges, even small gains are celebrated with immediate, emotionally impactful feedback, breaking cycles of discouragement common in traditional physical education (Ntoumanis, 2001).

The training system goes beyond correction, fostering encouragement by aligning feedback's timing, relevance, and emotional impact. It supports motor learning and psychological motivation—key elements for sustained skill development. This approach also draws on the concept of self-efficacy—emphasizing that when learners believe their efforts lead to success, they are more likely to persist.

5.2 *Psychological Effects of Visual Feedback: The Case of Speed Lines*

The "Speed Lines" animation, designed to visualize throwing velocity, effectively boosted children's motivation. Animated streaks followed the hand's trajectory, growing longer and more vivid with increased speed, offering instant, intuitive feedback that linked actions to outcomes. The Speed Lines' motivational impact stems from reinforcing a sense of agency. By directly responding to the child's motion, they strengthened the feeling of "my action caused this." Research shows that such connections between actions and outcomes boost motivation and persistence, especially in sports where control and ownership are vital (Bandura, 1997; Haggard & Tsakiris, 2009).

The Speed Lines extended the throwing motion, closely mirroring hand and arm trajectories to form a sensorimotor link. This heightened children's movement awareness and embodiment, supporting improvements in motor coordination and self-perception, particularly during developmental stages (Gallagher, 2005).

The Speed Lines acted as an emotional reward, with children enjoying the visual effect itself. Many eagerly repeated throws to "see the streaks again," highlighting its intrinsic appeal. This aligns with research showing emotionally engaging visuals boost motivation and participation (Hamari et al., 2014; Mekler et al., 2017).

The Speed Lines promoted a flow-like state during practice by combining a clear goal, immediate feedback, and an appropriate challenge level, fostering focused and enjoyable immersion.

Psychological factors like agency, embodiment, emotional resonance, and flow made the Speed Lines engaging and effective, motivating children to practice while building emotional connection, self-expression, and a sense of achievement, even for those with low athletic confidence.

5.3 *From Basic to Enhanced: A Developmental Perspective on System Evolution*

The throwing training system evolved in two phases, exploring feedback's role in motor learning and motivation. The basic version, featuring only "Speed Lines" and distance feedback, improved children's throwing distance significantly, highlighting how simple, synchronized, and emotionally resonant cues can enhance performance. The enhanced version introduced onomatopoeic sounds, celebratory animations, and a redesigned form evaluation interface to sustain motivation and create a game-like experience. Children using the multimodal system showed improved performance, enjoyment, and motivation, especially when visual, auditory, and linguistic cues were combined.

Among the feedback elements, Speed Lines remained the most motivating, preferred by 47% of children. Additional effects, like the Phoenix (31%) and Crowd Cheers (22%), boosted engagement further, highlighting the broad appeal of simple visuals and the targeted impact of layered animations.

Multimodal feedback can boost both attention and emotional investment, but effective design requires aligning feedback with user needs, skill level, and context (Hamari et al., 2014; Mekler et al., 2017). The two system phases show a progression from basic functionality to emotional enrichment. The basic version proved minimal feedback could drive skill improvement, while the enhanced version demonstrated the value of sensory and motivational layering, serving distinct purposes: technical reinforcement and emotional engagement.

This progression highlights key lessons for educational tech design: start with simple, meaningful feedback and expand iteratively based on learner response. Feedback should not just inform but create an experience, helping learners see, feel, and believe in their improvement.

5.4 *Individual Differences and Personalization*

While the system proved broadly effective, user studies revealed individual differences in responses to feedback. Preferences varied across visual, auditory, and linguistic modes, influenced by personality, social behavior, and gender. For instance, while some children enjoyed intense effects like speed lines, others, especially introverted or sensitive individuals, found them overwhelming. Gender differences also emerged, as some girls hesitated to throw publicly, with playful and affirming feedback helping reduce discomfort and boost participation.

These findings emphasize the importance of personalization in educational feedback systems. Aligned with Universal Design for Learning (UDL), effective systems should offer flexible engagement options tailored to learners' strengths, needs, and comfort. For instance, allowing users to choose feedback modes, visual, auditory, or both, can reduce anxiety and boost motivation. Self-Determination Theory (Deci & Ryan, 2000) also highlights autonomy as vital for intrinsic motivation.

Small customizations, like selecting avatars or adjusting feedback intensity, enhance ownership and control, fostering engagement and persistence. These options support autonomy, a core element of Self-Determination Theory, by allowing learners to feel in control of their learning environment. Future adaptive systems could tailor experiences by recognizing disengagement or anxiety and adjusting feedback style in real time through learner modeling or emotion-sensing technologies. Additionally, inclusivity should address factors like cultural background, gender norms, and past experiences, acknowledging how social expectations shape confidence and motivation. Personalization, as a core design principle, can help educational technologies support the diverse emotional, cognitive, and social needs of all learners.

5.5 *Implications for Educational Technology Design*

The study highlights key implications for designing educational technologies in physical education. Feedback serves two main roles: offering task-specific information to improve performance and acting as a motivational stimulus to enhance engagement, enjoyment, and persistence. Effective feedback supports skill development with timely, specific, and clear performance cues. In line with motor learning principles, even simple visual effects like speed lines helped children improve throwing distance, showing that straightforward, action-based feedback can be highly effective.

Feedback's second function is to foster emotional engagement.Visually rewarding and affirming feedback creates meaningful learning experiences, as seen in the enhanced system, where combined visual, auditory, and verbal cues boosted enjoyment, effort, and participation. This aligns with theories like Self-Determination and Flow, emphasizing emotionally resonant environments. Additionally, effective design can begin with simple, scalable elements. The basic system's success shows lightweight, theory-driven tools can significantly impact learning. Systems can then expand iteratively with multimodal feedback and adaptive personalization. This system is practical for real-world educational settings, requiring no specialized equipment. It can be used in schools, homes, or programs and suits diverse learners, including those in special education, thanks to its intuitive design. The study highlights how feedback bridges cognitive goals with emotional experiences. Future systems should enhance emotionally intelligent feedback—using visuals, sound, and user control—to boost engagement, mastery, and long-term learning.

5.6 Limitations and Future Refinements

Despite promising results, the study's limited scope—short-term interventions with few school-aged participants—raises questions about its generalizability across ages, cultures, and settings. Longitudinal research is needed to assess if improvements in motivation and motor performance persist over time.

Although tested in a school setting, the system's limited interaction duration leaves its impact during extended use unclear, including effects on engagement, fatigue, or novelty. Future studies should assess responses across multiple sessions and longer timelines.

Additionally, feedback in the enhanced system was static and not tailored to individual preferences or emotional states. Adaptive features that adjust feedback intensity, content, or modality based on real-time data, such as movement accuracy or disengagement, could enhance personalization and effectiveness.

The system focused on short-term motivational and performance outcomes, overlooking factors like social dynamics, peer interaction, and long-term self-efficacy. These are crucial in group settings, where peer visibility and performance anxiety can affect participation, as seen in children hesitant to perform publicly.

The study did not assess accessibility for learners with disabilities or sensory processing differences. Though designed to be inclusive, further work is needed to ensure the system is effective and customizable for all learners, including those with special needs.

In summary, the study offers valuable insights into emotionally resonant feedback but highlights the need for longitudinal research, adaptive personalization, inclusive design, and cross-cultural validation to maximize its educational potential.

6. Conclusion and Future Work

This study examined how emotionally resonant feedback in a gamified throwing training system supports motor skill development and motivation. Two system versions, basic and enhanced, were tested to assess the impact of simple visual cues versus rich multimodal responses on children's performance and engagement. Results showed lightweight feedback improved throwing distance, while layered feedback increased emotional involvement and enjoyment, highlighting the potential of accessible educational technologies rooted in clear feedback principles and learner-centered design. The study highlighted individual differences in feedback response, influenced by personality, sensitivity, and social dynamics, emphasizing the need for personalization and inclusivity. Future systems should allow customization of feedback styles and intensity, considering diverse needs like gender-based differences.

The system's simple, intuitive design shows promise for real-world use in schools, programs, or homes, providing an engaging tool for physical skill development with minimal setup. Future research could explore skill retention and transfer over time, while adaptive systems may enable greater personalization. Cultural variation and accessibility should also be examined to ensure equity and effectiveness. In conclusion, this study shows feedback in physical education can inform actions, boost confidence, and foster enjoyment, empowering learners through cognitive and emotional design.

Further Reading

For a detailed analysis of this research, refer to the original study: [DOI= 10.1007/978-3-319-49616-0_13].

Column 1: The Evolution of Gamified Sports Training

The merging of sports training and gamification is a growing field. Early programs used basic rewards like points and badges to motivate, but digital advances now allow for immersive tools like augmented reality (AR), virtual reality (VR), and motion capture systems. AR overlays help athletes refine movements, while VR safely replicates real-world environments for skill learning. For youth training, gamification turns drills into engaging activities. For example, the throwing system in this study uses motion tracking and interactive feedback to develop skills while making exercise enjoyable for children.

Column 2: The Motivational Power of Visual and Auditory Effects

Visual and auditory elements in gamified learning systems act as both teaching tools and motivators. Visual stimuli, like color changes or animations, enhance engagement and memory by creating immersive experiences. Similarly, auditory effects, such as cheers or sound effects, trigger the brain's reward system, reinforcing behaviors. In the throwing system, features like "Speed Lines" provide instant feedback, while celebratory animations link physical effort to success. Future updates could customize these effects to optimize motivation and balance.

Column 3: Striking a Balance – When Do Animations Become Overstimulating?

Flashy animations in the system boosted motivation but also caused overstimulation for some users, leading to distraction. Bright visuals captured attention but raised the issue of balancing excitement with clarity. Excessive sensory input, particularly for younger learners, may lead to cognitive overload. Future updates could include adjustable animation intensity, enabling customization for individual needs to ensure effective and sustainable motivational feedback.

12 | Enhancing Spatial Cognition in Sports Through Virtual Reality Training

1. Introduction

In competitive sports, athletes must demonstrate not only physical prowess but also advanced cognitive abilities, especially spatial cognition, which plays a vital role in team-based performance. Spatial cognition allows players to interpret their surroundings, anticipate others' actions, and make informed decisions under pressure.

1.1 The Centrality of Spatial Cognition in Team Sports

Spatial cognition helps athletes identify positions, anticipate movements, and make strategic decisions. Soccer midfielders utilize bird's-eye view cognition to process both immediate surroundings and broader configurations (Shepard & Metzler, 1971). Elite athletes excel at switching from a first-person perspective to an allocentric view, enabling quicker decisions, efficient movements, and improved tactical awareness (Mann et al., 2007; Vickers, 2007).

1.2 Limitations of Traditional Training Approaches

Spatial cognition in sports is often developed indirectly through gameplay and experience-based coaching, but this approach has limitations. Team drills require large spaces and many participants, making frequent sessions challenging. Additionally, conventional training lacks individualization, as cognitive skills like spatial reasoning are acquired incidentally rather than through focused exercises, leading to uneven and unstructured development among athletes.

Developing perspective-switching skills, like shifting from an egocentric to a bird's-eye view, is often slow and informal, taking years of experience without standardized methods for feedback or improvement. Real-world training limitations make rapid perspective shifts impractical, leaving few opportunities for structured reflection or correction. This lack of tools highlights a gap in training spatial cognition effectively.

1.3 The Emergence of Virtual Reality in Sports Training

Recent advances in immersive technologies have established Virtual Reality (VR) as a transformative tool in sports science. VR enables athletes to train in realistic 3D environments, isolating and enhancing cognitive skills. Systems like STRIVR help quarterbacks practice reading defensive formations (STRIVR Labs, Inc.), and

DOI: 10.1201/9781003782735-15

NeuroTracker improves situational awareness using 3D dynamic object tracking (Faubert, 2013; Romeas et al., 2016). Research in Japan and Europe developed VR systems to train spatial perspective transformation in soccer and basketball by reconstructing layouts from a first-person to bird's-eye view (Shimizu & Sumi, 2019).

1.4 Why VR Matters Now: Technological and Cognitive Convergence

The adoption of VR-based cognitive training in sports is driven by advances in technology, validation through research, and improved feedback capabilities. High-resolution head-mounted displays (HMDs), motion tracking, and platforms like Unity and Unreal Engine have made immersive simulations more accessible.

Recent studies, including Kittel et al. (2024) and Richlan et al. (2023), have shown that VR-based tactical training improves decision-making accuracy and situational awareness in soccer and basketball scenarios. These studies used immersive simulations to present dynamic, game-like contexts that require real-time choices, revealing cognitive performance benefits over traditional video methods. Additionally, VR delivers precise, real-time feedback, enabling data-driven skill development and individualized improvement beyond traditional methods.

1.5 Towards a New Paradigm in Perceptual-Cognitive Training

Perceptual-cognitive skills are now central to optimizing athletic performance, with virtual reality (VR) driving this shift. Unlike video-based systems, VR enables embodied simulation, where athletes use natural movements to train perspective-switching abilities. This approach helps bridge the gap between first-person perception and higher-order spatial reasoning. The next chapter examines this approach in greater depth, drawing on insights from spatial cognition, neuropsychology, and sports science to establish its theoretical and empirical foundations.

2. Theoretical Foundations and Related Research

Examining VR training's impact on spatial cognition in sports involves insights from cognitive psychology, neuroscience, sports science, and human-computer interaction. This chapter outlines the concept of spatial perspective transformation and highlights relevant research shaping VR-based training systems.

2.1 Spatial Cognition and Perspective Transformation

Spatial cognition involves mental processes like rotation, memory, navigation, and perspective-taking (Shepard & Metzler, 1971; Shelton & Gabrieli, 2002). In team sports, perspective transformation, shifting from a first-person to bird's-eye view, is key for situational awareness and decision-making (Vickers, 2007).

Under pressure, this ability defines expert performance and is supported by neural activity in the parietal and prefrontal cortices. Shelton and Gabrieli (2002) demonstrated this through fMRI tasks involving imagined perspective shifts and spatial memory, showing activation patterns linked to spatial transformation.

2.2 Shared Mental Models and Situation Awareness in Sports

Situation awareness, as defined by Endsley (1995), involves three hierarchical stages: the perception of environmental elements, comprehension of their meaning, and projection of their future status.

Shared mental models (Eccles & Tenenbaum, 2004) refer to the common understanding among team members about roles, goals, and spatial configurations. These models enable faster coordination and reduced communication needs during play.

Theories of situation awareness and shared mental models highlight how elite teams synchronize spatial and dynamic representations.

Perspective transformation, especially to a bird's-eye view, bridges perception and shared strategy, enabling coordinated team performance.

2.3 Prior Approaches to Cognitive Training in Sports

Athletes' perceptual-cognitive skills are enhanced through methods like video occlusion training, anticipatory cue recognition, and pattern recognition (Farrow et al., 1998; Williams et al., 2002). The 3D-Multiple Object Tracking (3D-MOT) system improves attention control and decision accuracy but doesn't address spatial perspective shifting, vital for tactical team sports (Legault & Faubert, 2012; Romeas et al., 2016).

Eye-tracking studies reveal skilled athletes focus more efficiently on key zones, informing better training designs (Bard & Fleury, 1976; Kredel et al., 2023).

2.4 Virtual Reality as a New Platform for Cognitive Training

Virtual Reality (VR) is revolutionizing sports training by enhancing perceptual and cognitive skills. Unlike traditional methods limited by logistics and injury risks, VR offers immersive, repeatable environments simulating gameplay. Recent VR systems focus on processes like perspective transformation and attention allocation. Notably, Shimizu and Sumi's (2019) system trains users to switch from a first-person to bird's-eye view, improving spatial reasoning and relational positioning crucial for team sports.

The interactive nature of VR enables real-time feedback and performance tracking, helping athletes refine cognitive strategies. Customizable difficulty and environments cater to all skill levels, from novices to elites. While long-term effects require further study, early findings show VR's potential as a complementary tool to physical training, targeting cognitive mechanisms often hard to train in traditional settings.

2.5 Advancing VR Training: Bridging Egocentric and Allocentric Spatial Skills

While prior research established VR's role in enhancing perceptual-cognitive skills, few systems focus on transforming perspectives from egocentric to allocentric views or provide real-time interaction, feedback, and performance tracking. The VR system discussed here addresses these gaps with an iterative protocol, observing spatial layouts, reconstructing them from memory in a bird's-eye view, and using visual feedback for reflection. It offers scalable difficulty, objective scoring, and immediate error feedback to foster skill development and progress tracking.

The training environment prioritizes individual practice, removing the need for complex team drills or physical setups. This improves accessibility and widens its application to fields like emergency response, military operations, and surgical navigation, where precise spatial understanding is critical.

This chapter reviewed the theoretical and research basis for VR systems in spatial cognition training, integrating insights from cognitive psychology, sports science, and HCI. The next chapter delves into the VR training system's design, components, and workflow.

3. System Design and Implementation of the VR Training Program

The VR training system enhances athletes' ability to convert egocentric visuals into an allocentric bird's-eye view, essential for spatial cognition in fast-paced sports. It focuses on intuitive interaction, cognitive challenges, and real-time feedback within a structured virtual environment.

3.1 System Overview

The training system, developed with Oculus Rift and Oculus Touch, and Unity 3D follows three phases: Tracking, Reproduction, and Review.

In Tracking, users observe moving player objects from a first-person view, engaging with head movements.

In the Reproduction phase, users rebuild the layout by placing colored spheres on a virtual grid using hand controllers, based on their memorized positions from the previous view.

Finally, the Review phase provides feedback by comparing the original and reconstructed layouts, fostering error recognition and learning.

3.2 Tracking Phase: Perceiving the Environment from First-Person View

In the Tracking Phase, users observe dynamic movements of players in a virtual sports court from a first-person perspective. They actively track 4–6 objects moving in all directions, requiring spatial awareness and concentration. Physical head movements replicate real-world engagement, reinforcing spatial encoding. After 5–10 seconds, objects stop, and users memorize their positions and distances, training quick and accurate spatial assessment.

3.3 Reproduction Phase: Constructing a Bird's-Eye View from Memory

After the Tracking Phase, users transition to Court B, viewed from a bird's-eye perspective, starting the Reproduction Phase. Using Oculus Touch controllers, participants place spherical objects based on their memorized positions from Court A.

The top-down view reduces spatial ambiguity, such as occlusion (e.g., hidden objects) and depth distortion (e.g., misjudged distances), encouraging analytical spatial reasoning. A time limit simulates real-world decision-making pressure, enhancing spatial recall under stress.

Accuracy is scored by comparing placements to a reference layout, awarding points based on proximity, with a maximum score of 100 across all trials.

3.4 Review Phase: Visual Feedback and Error Reflection

In the Review Phase, users scoring below 100 view side-by-side visuals comparing Court A's actual positions with their reconstructed placements in Court B. This comparative display visually highlights spatial discrepancies, such as misaligned distances or swapped object locations, enabling users to identify and reflect on specific errors. The phase fosters cognitive reflection and encourages performance review, with options to retry and improve through targeted feedback.

3.5 Interaction Design and User Experience Considerations

The VR training system prioritizes usability and accessibility, enabling users of all experience levels to train comfortably. Setup includes HMD calibration and a simple two-object tutorial to reduce VR discomfort. Task complexity scales from two to six objects for gradual learning. Immediate score-based feedback fosters motivation, while optional gamified features such as progress tracking and high scores enhance engagement and retention by triggering users' sense of achievement and competition.

3.6 Technical Implementation Summary

The VR training system uses the Oculus Rift headset for natural 6DOF head tracking and Oculus Touch controllers for precise 3D interaction. Developed with Unity 3D, it integrates head orientation, hand gestures, and trigger buttons for input, with visual and haptic feedback enhancing immersion. A scoring mechanism compares reconstructed layouts with a reference model, awarding points for accuracy. The system also logs session data, such as object placement accuracy, time taken, and user movements, for behavior analysis and effectiveness evaluation.

4. Experimental Design and Evaluation

A controlled experiment with university students evaluated the VR training system's effectiveness in improving spatial perspective transformation. This chapter outlines the design, participants, tasks, and evaluation metrics, focusing on whether the system enhanced the ability to convert first-person visuals into a bird's-eye view.

4.1 Participants and Procedure

Twenty-two male university students with varying ball sports experience participated. They were divided into two groups: experimental (trained with the VR system) and control (no training). Pre- and post-tests were conducted for both. A questionnaire on team sports background ensured balanced group composition, improving the study's internal validity.

The experiment spanned four days. On day one, participants completed a pre-test to measure baseline spatial cognition, and the experimental group began VR training. Training continued on days two and three, while the control group had no activities. Both groups completed a post-test on day four.

Experimental group sessions began with a simple two-object tutorial, progressing to tasks with 4–6 objects to increase cognitive load. Each session included Tracking, Reproduction, and Review phases for iterative practice and feedback. Breaks were allowed to minimize fatigue and VR-induced discomfort.

4.2 Pre- and Post-Test Tasks

Evaluation tasks adapted from Shelton and Gabrieli (2002) assessed participants' ability to convert spatial layouts from an egocentric to an allocentric view.

Their original study used fMRI to show that such perspective transformation engages the parietal and prefrontal cortices, highlighting the neural basis of spatial cognition.

Each trial featured two stimuli: a first-person image briefly shown for spatial encoding, followed by a bird's-eye image that was either accurate or modified. Participants judged the second image as "correct" or "incorrect," with randomized trials ensuring active engagement. Performance was measured by response accuracy, reflecting spatial transformation ability. A practice trial preceded the test for procedural clarity.

4.3 Evaluation Metrics

The study's primary performance metric was accuracy in identifying whether the bird's-eye view matched the spatial layout observed from the first-person perspective, reflecting participants' ability to switch between egocentric and allocentric spatial frames. Secondary metrics included total correct responses, improvement from pre-test to post-test, and qualitative feedback on cognitive changes and user experience. For the experimental group, VR training sessions provided additional data scored on a 100-point scale based on object placement accuracy during the Reproduction Phase, offering deeper insights into spatial memory and reconstruction skills.

4.4 Data Analysis

To evaluate the VR training's impact on spatial cognition, a two-factor mixed-design ANOVA examined group (experimental vs. control) and time (pre-test vs. post-test) variables. Bonferroni correction controlled for Type I error, and main effects analyses explored significant interactions. Results showed a meaningful interaction, $F(1, 20) = 5.11, p < .05, \eta^2 = 0.21$, with experimental group participants improving significantly, $F(1, 20) = 8.56, p < .01, \eta^2 = 0.30$. The observed effect sizes ($\eta^2 = 0.21$ and 0.30) suggest moderate impacts, indicating that even short-term VR interventions can yield meaningful cognitive improvements in spatial perspective-taking.

4.5 Summary of Results

The experimental group showed significant post-test improvement, with mean scores rising from 5.55 to 7.09, while the control group's scores increased minimally from 5.45 to 5.64. This confirms the VR training's effectiveness beyond test-retest effects. Participants reported improved spatial awareness and strategic thinking, supporting the system's role in enhancing spatial cognition and perspective transformation.

This chapter outlined the evaluation framework and results. The next chapter will discuss the findings, implications, limitations, and real-world applications.

5. Discussion

This discussion builds on the findings of Sumi and Okuyama (2024) research in Frontiers in Psychology, which introduced a VR system for enhancing spatial cognition through egocentric-to-allocentric perspective transformation. It revisits the findings, situates them within the broader literature, and examines their implications, limitations, and future potential.

The study explored a VR training program aimed at improving the ability to transform egocentric visual input (first-person perspective) into an allocentric representation (global, bird's-eye view). This skill is essential in many contexts, such as sports, where players must make strategic decisions by integrating direct perception with inferred environmental understanding.

The study showed that short-term VR training significantly improved spatial perspective transformation, with participants in the experimental group achieving higher post-test scores than the control group. Engaging repeatedly in egocentric-to-allocentric transformation tasks enhanced spatial encoding and reconstruction. The structured training phases, Tracking, Reproduction, and Review, facilitated these improvements through iterative, feedback-rich learning. Participants also reported heightened spatial awareness and strategic reasoning.

These findings align with prior research, such as Shelton and Gabrieli's (2002) work on neural adaptability in spatial perspective transformation.

Their fMRI research showed that tasks involving perspective transformation activate the parietal and prefrontal cortices, supporting the neural basis of spatial cognition. They also align with VR studies like Shimizu and Sumi's (2019), which demonstrated improvements in spatial reasoning through immersive training. Unlike 3D-MOT research, which focuses on attention and tracking, this study uniquely targets spatial reference transformation, highlighting VR's potential for honing this distinct cognitive skill. 3D-MOT systems primarily train dynamic attention allocation and visual tracking across multiple moving objects, rather than spatial perspective shifts.

This study stands out for training users to reconstruct spatial layouts from memory while switching between distinct spatial frames, unlike earlier methods focused on visual recognition or tracking. Its interactive design, scoring, and feedback combine perceptual stimulation with reflective cognitive engagement, resulting in improved test outcomes and strategic thinking.

Beyond academics, the study has practical implications, especially in team sports where players monitor movement and field dynamics. It shows that VR can effectively train bird's-eye spatial understanding, offering scalable, individualized programs free from physical and logistical constraints. Applications extend to areas like piloting, surgery, and emergency response, where precise spatial decisions under pressure are crucial.

The study's findings face limitations due to a small, homogenous participant sample of male university students, brief training duration, and the absence of full-body movement, team dynamics, or live decision-making in the experimental environment. These factors restrict generalizability and real-world applicability, especially in complex, embodied scenarios.

Future research should consider longer training programs, diverse participants, and real-world gameplay data. Incorporating motion tracking, physiological sensors, and neuroimaging could deepen understanding of cognitive adaptation and skill internalization.

In conclusion, Sumi and Okuyama's (2024) study confirms that immersive VR environments can effectively train spatial reference frame transformation, enhancing egocentric-to-allocentric shifts. This chapter situates the findings within academic and practical contexts, highlighting VR's potential in advancing spatial reasoning for sports and beyond. While further validation is needed, the work marks a key step in developing structured cognitive training tools for complex spatial tasks.

6. Conclusion

This chapter outlined the rationale, design, and evaluation of a VR training system aimed at improving spatial cognition by transforming egocentric visuals into allocentric representations.

Built on observation, memory-based reconstruction, and feedback loops, the system demonstrated significant gains in perspective transformation tasks through immersive, short-term training. Participants showed improved test results, heightened spatial awareness, and strategic thinking, advancing research in cognitive psychology and VR-based learning. By addressing a gap in sports cognition training, the system leveraged immersive VR to target spatial frame transformation—a skill crucial not only in team sports but also in fields such as aviation, surgery, and emergency response.

Despite promising results, limitations include short training duration, a homogeneous sample, and the lack of full-body interaction and social context. Future studies should extend training periods, diversify participant demographics, and integrate real-world data and multimodal input (e.g., motion tracking, physiological sensors, neuroimaging).

This work positions immersive VR technology as a scalable and adaptive platform for structured cognitive training, linking perceptual experience with abstract spatial reasoning in measurable and transferable ways. It highlights the growing potential of VR to cultivate high-level cognitive abilities in sports and beyond.

Further Reading

For a detailed analysis of this research, refer to the original study: [DOI=10.3389/fpsyg.2024.1504838].

Column: Exploring the Potential of VR in Sports Training

Virtual Reality (VR) is transforming sports training by refining cognitive and perceptual skills in controlled, repeatable environments. Unlike traditional methods, VR simulates high-fidelity game scenarios, enabling targeted training of processes like object tracking, pattern recognition, and egocentric-to-allocentric spatial transformations.

The VR system in this chapter demonstrates this by engaging users in perspective-switching tasks, enhancing their ability to internalize spatial layouts for strategic decision-making. Its adaptability allows for sport-specific contexts, adjustable difficulty, and real-time feedback, catering to athletes of all levels, from beginners to experts.

VR offers a safe space for athletes to explore high-pressure scenarios and complex plays, reducing risks and logistical challenges. This deliberate practice builds confidence and situational awareness.

However, VR's training effectiveness in sports remains under study. While early results show improvements in spatial awareness and decision-making, physical realism limitations like tactile feedback and unpredictability may hinder transfer to on-field performance.

Rather than replacing physical training, VR serves as a valuable complement, enhancing skills through perceptual-cognitive rehearsal alongside traditional drills. Future platforms with haptic interfaces, team simulations, and adaptive feedback promise even greater utility.

In summary, VR is an evolving and promising tool for sports training, enabling athletes to engage with complex, cognitive scenarios and improve gameplay dynamics. Ongoing research and collaboration will be essential to unlocking its full potential for enhancing athletic performance.

13 Game with a Purpose: Building a Visual Effect Dictionary Through Engaging Gameplay

1. Introduction

Visual effects like steam, glow, or shimmer enhance digital content by providing intuitive cues about an object's mood or status, such as warmth from ramen steam or mystery from a glowing treasure chest. Their meanings vary with context. Steam may suggest heat for soup but cold for dry ice, showing the importance of cultural and situational factors. This variability challenges systems to consistently map language to visuals, highlighting the need for a structured framework to connect adjectives, nouns, and effects. This chapter builds on Hirai and Sumi's (2019) original prototype, which demonstrated the feasibility of collecting (adjective, noun, effect) triplets using a narrative-based GWAP. While that early study introduced the core concept, the present work reexamines and systematizes it as a robust framework for constructing culturally and contextually grounded visual effect mappings.

This research introduces the Visual Effect Dictionary, a structured knowledge base linking language to visual forms in context. Using a Game with a Purpose (GWAP) framework, participants provide semantic judgments through engaging gameplay, enabling large-scale, nuanced associations difficult to achieve with surveys or manual annotation.

Building on Hirai and Sumi's (2019) prototype, this study emphasizes context-sensitive representation, semantic structure, and cultural variability. It explores visual semantics, multimodal meaning, and interactive knowledge acquisition, capturing intuitive and culturally grounded interpretations often inaccessible to traditional methods. Upcoming chapters detail prior work, system design, data collection, and broader implications for understanding and designing expressive, context-aware media systems.

2. Related Work

Connecting language to visual effects, especially with affective and cultural nuances, requires insights from structured knowledge acquisition, game-based data collection, text-to-visual generation, and responsive design. This chapter reviews commonsense knowledge collection, the evolution of text-to-visual systems, and research on affect and cultural semantics, forming the basis for expressive, context-aware mappings.

DOI: 10.1201/9781003782735-16

2.1 Structured Knowledge Acquisition and GWAP Approaches

The structured acquisition of commonsense knowledge has been pivotal in AI research. WordNet (Miller, 1995) organized the lexicon into synsets for semantic tasks, while Cyc (Lenat, 1995) encoded everyday knowledge via logical predicates. Despite their impact, both systems relied on manual methods that struggled with scalability and cultural diversity.

Crowdsourced initiatives like Open Mind Common Sense (Singh et al., 2002) and ConceptNet (Liu & Singh, 2004) expanded participation, gathering large-scale knowledge bases with simple assertions. However, these approaches faced limitations in consistency and context-sensitive depth.

The introduction of Games with a Purpose (GWAP) by von Ahn & Dabbish (2008) revolutionized knowledge acquisition by making it engaging and fun. For example, the ESP Game validated image labels through player agreement, while Verbosity gamified commonsense fact generation. These approaches boosted data volume, reliability, and user participation. GWAPs are particularly well-suited for collecting visual effect data because they leverage intuitive, affect-laden judgments that users can make quickly and without formal instruction. Unlike surveys, which require reflective explanation, or annotation tasks that demand consistency, GWAPs tap into spontaneous, culturally grounded impressions, ideal for capturing subjective visual semantics.

Building on GWAP, our research explores affective and visual semantics by capturing how users link adjectives, nouns, and visual effects in context-sensitive, culturally grounded ways. For instance, "delicious" might evoke a glossy apple or steaming ramen, revealing subjective interpretations beyond traditional taxonomies.

Anime de Blog (Sumi, 2007) highlights participatory knowledge collection by turning user text into animated visuals, enriching a database of visual effect mappings with each use. Similar to GWAPs, it shows how lightweight, user-facing tools can sustainably gather semantic insights in affective and visual domains.

Expanding on this, Effect Game uses a narrative-based GWAP to collect nuanced semantic data as (adjective, noun, visual effect) triplets. By embedding this in gameplay, users provide intuitive, scalable judgments seamlessly. The result is a dynamic, culturally adaptable knowledge base that captures subtle, affect-rich associations often beyond formal systems.

2.2 Text-to-Visual Systems and Multimodal Representation

Translating linguistic expressions into visuals has been a complex challenge across fields like NLP, computer graphics, and multimodal interaction. Early systems, like WordsEye (Coyne & Sproat, 2001), mapped nouns to 3D models and adjectives to properties like color but struggled with metaphorical and affective interpretation due to rigid ontologies.

Interactive e-Hon (Sumi, 2005; 2009) offered modular tools for creating visual narratives, reusing story components like characters and props. Though primarily storytelling-focused, it paved the way for more dynamic text-to-visual mappings in multimodal communication.

Anime de Blog (Sumi, 2007) allowed users to generate animated blog entries by analyzing text inputs and associating nouns and verbs with corresponding characters and actions, gradually building a visual vocabulary through user interaction. It combined symbolic modeling with participatory learning, serving as a precursor to later approaches.

Recent advancements in generative models like DALL·E 2 (Ramesh et al., 2022), Stable Diffusion (Rombach et al., 2022), and Imagen (Saharia et al., 2022) have revolutionized text-to-visual systems by generating realistic images using diffusion-based architectures. Video synthesis has further evolved with tools like Make-A-Video (Singer et al., 2022), Phenaki (Villegas et al., 2022), and Sora (OpenAI, 2024), enabling dynamic visual storytelling from textual input.

Generative systems excel at creating visuals but operate as opaque black boxes, making semantic mappings unclear and difficult to modify. They also reflect training biases, often favoring Western perspectives and missing cultural nuances. Furthermore, their distributed representations lack structured or editable semantic knowledge, limiting interpretability and cultural adaptation in areas like education and accessibility.

To address this, our research offers a structured alternative that complements generative models. By using precise triplets (adjective, noun, visual effect), it enables transparent, adaptable meaning representation with affective and cultural depth, combining symbolic modeling and data-driven generation.

2.3 Affective Computing, Kansei Engineering, and Cultural Semantics

Early text-to-visual systems focused on literal semantics, but research now explores affective, subjective, and culturally influenced meanings. Visual elements like color, motion, and texture carry emotional connotations crucial for expressive design and cross-cultural understanding.

Affective computing (Picard, 1997) examines how machines recognize and elicit emotions using cues like warm colors or gentle motion, influencing systems like animated avatars. Kansei Engineering (Nagamachi, 1995) designs products to evoke emotional responses, linking impressions like "elegant" or "clean" to features such as texture or shape. It emphasizes that emotional interpretation varies across cultures and demographics.

Psychological studies show that brightness and saturation influence emotional perception, correlating with pleasure, arousal, and dominance (Valdez & Mehrabian, 1994). These findings emphasize the cultural and perceptual nuances of visual design, as color or texture evoke varied associations depending on the viewer's background.

Our research incorporates these perspectives through the Effect Game, focusing on whether visual effects "feel right" in context. For example, does a glowing apple suggest "deliciousness," or would steam better suit ramen? The system collects and compares cultural interpretations via structured triplets tied to user inputs, enabling cross-cultural semantic insights, such as comparing the adjective "fresh" across regions or demographics.

By combining affective computing and Kansei Engineering with a GWAP framework, our system gathers intuitive, emotionally rich, and culturally sensitive knowledge at scale. This approach surpasses conventional text-to-image models by enabling a more human-centered and expressive take on multimodal semantics.

2.4 The Continued Relevance of GWAP-Based Structured Knowledge

While various methods, from rule-based ontologies to generative AI—have linked language to visuals, challenges remain in achieving interpretable, context-sensitive, and culturally grounded knowledge. Generative models like DALL·E 2 and Stable Diffusion create realistic outputs but lack transparency and adaptability.

GWAP-based systems, like ours, address these gaps by combining transparency, structure, and user participation. Semantic data is tied to explicit gameplay judgments, creating a scalable, traceable, and explainable knowledge base enriched by narrative-driven interaction.

Our system reveals affective and culturally specific interpretations often missed by black-box models, capturing how cultures visualize concepts like "cleanliness" or "deliciousness" and making these associations explicit, editable, and analyzable. This is vital for education, design, media, and intercultural communication.

It also offers pedagogical value, using structured mappings of adjectives, nouns, and effects as teaching tools for language, visual literacy, and metaphor comprehension. Unlike generative models, the triplet format allows learners to explore why certain effects suit specific expressions.

Finally, our system emphasizes ethical data participation through opt-in contributions, supporting transparent, culturally inclusive, and human-centered AI development.

GWAP-based structured knowledge systems provide unique strengths that generative models cannot replicate, including semantic clarity, cultural inclusivity, affective depth, and ethical participation. These qualities are vital for advancing intelligent and socially responsible AI. The next chapter explores how Effect Game embodies these principles through a dynamic, game-based semantic data collection platform.

3. System Design and Methodology

This chapter presents the design, structure, and implementation of Effect Game, a GWAP developed to gather affective and contextual knowledge for creating a Visual Effect Dictionary. Through gameplay, users contribute structured data by linking adjectives and nouns to visual effects, capturing intuitive, culturally sensitive semantics that are challenging to obtain via manual annotation or automated methods.

3.1 Concept and Goals of the System

The system aims to build a knowledge base linking adjectives to visual effects based on noun context. For example, "delicious ramen" might be represented by steam, while "delicious apple" suggests gloss. To capture these nuanced, context-dependent associations, a game-based platform allows users to provide judgments interactively and intuitively. The system is designed as a Game with a Purpose (GWAP), enabling users to contribute affective, semantic knowledge in an enjoyable and scalable way. The interactive format encourages voluntary participation and supports the collection of intuitive and culturally grounded associations that are difficult to obtain through surveys or static annotations.

By combining structured data collection with narrative-driven gameplay, the system fosters natural judgments while minimizing cognitive load, making it accessible to a wide range of users.

This design supports the dual goals of entertainment and knowledge acquisition, building a foundation for a context-aware Visual Effect Dictionary.

3.2 Game Scenario and Interaction Design

The gameplay combines narrative and data collection. Users assist a weakened protagonist by selecting food items to restore their strength. When prompted to "enter a delicious food," players choose a noun, represented by an emoji, from a list of 78 options.

The system then asks simple binary questions, such as "Is it a fruit?", to confirm or expand commonsense knowledge related to the selected noun. These questions serve both to verify existing assumptions and to gather new associations. Answers are scored based on consistency with other users' responses, encouraging shared knowledge formation.

Next, users evaluate visual effects applied to the selected food. For instance, a glowing apple might be presented with the question, "Does this look delicious?" Agreements strengthen associations, while disagreements prompt the system to offer alternative effects or record divergent interpretations, enriching the database of visual pairings.

3.3 Visual Effect Mapping and Data Representation

The system uses a limited set of semantically rich visual effects, such as steam, sparkle, glow, and mist, chosen for their intuitive emotional and cultural associations with food. Users interpret these effects based on context, allowing the system to build a structured knowledge base of (adjective, noun, visual effect) triplets through gameplay.

These triplets are stored for future applications such as context-aware quizzes, adaptive effect generation, and visual communication research. A key feature of the system is its ability to capture diverse interpretations. By aggregating user judgments and using a scoring mechanism, the system prioritizes widely agreed-upon associations.

At the same time, it preserves minority responses, which may reflect culturally unique or personally nuanced meanings. These are retained as alternative interpretations, potentially informing comparative studies or adaptive design systems that require semantic flexibility.

3.4 Gameplay Dynamics and Knowledge Incentivization

The system uses a lightweight combat-style game mechanic to motivate user participation. After completing quizzes, user answers determine the strength of an energy beam used to attack an enemy. This mechanic is metaphorical: the beam represents the power of collective semantic agreement. Beam power is based on alignment with majority responses; stronger alignment leads to more powerful attacks. If the beam surpasses the enemy's health, which is randomly set between 60 and 100, the enemy is defeated.

This gamified feedback loop reinforces the value of semantic consensus and encourages users to think carefully about how visual effects relate to meaning. It also sustains engagement by turning abstract annotation into an emotionally satisfying experience.

In addition, the system dynamically updates questions and introduces new visual effects or concepts based on response patterns in the database. This ensures that each session remains fresh, personalized, and contributes to ongoing knowledge expansion.

3.5 Implementation and Deployment

Effect Game, a web-based application built on Unity, integrates real-time data storage, NMeCab for text analysis, and IBM Watson for optional speech interaction. Unity provides cross-platform rendering and animation capabilities, while NMeCab handles Japanese morphological parsing, supporting free-text inputs if enabled. Emoji inputs are normalized and aligned with WordNet concepts.

User contributions, stored with timestamps and scores, undergo validation through repeated play. This data structure supports tracking semantic reliability over time and enables refinement of the Visual Effect Dictionary through iterative input.

The system supports cross-cultural adaptation by using language-independent input modalities such as emojis and binary-choice questions. This allows users from different linguistic backgrounds to interact naturally without requiring translation or language-specific annotation schemes.

The design emphasizes intuitive participation by minimizing the need for typing and abstract categorization. Instead, it relies on familiar metaphors like food, emojis, and simple yes/no decisions to encourage broad engagement.

It seamlessly combines gameplay with knowledge collection, fostering intuitive participation.

The next chapter evaluates its effectiveness and usability through user experiments.

4. Evaluation and Results

To evaluate the Effect Game's effectiveness in acquiring context-sensitive semantic knowledge, we conducted a controlled experiment. This chapter details the experimental design, gameplay data collected, the evolution of semantic structures over repeated sessions, and insights from a post-game user questionnaire.

4.1 Experimental Setup

The experiment had eight participants, each playing three sessions over three days. They selected inputs from eight food-related emojis (e.g., apple, pizza, ice cream), representing a variety of food types.

Each session presented adjective-noun combinations like "delicious + apple" or "spicy + curry and rice." During gameplay, users were asked to complete two types of tasks: answering binary questions to verify commonsense knowledge (e.g., "Is it a fruit?") and judging whether a visual effect matched the selected adjective-noun pair. These tasks allowed the system to evaluate both factual and intuitive semantic alignment.

The game presented effects visually over emoji-based representations of food, and responses were recorded in real time. Data were analyzed after the first and third sessions to observe how semantic associations evolved. Figures illustrating gameplay (Fig. 1) and feedback (Fig. 2) provide visual reference for these mechanics.

4.2 Initial Data Analysis (After First Gameplay)

After the first session, user judgments showed consistent patterns. In commonsense knowledge (○/× format), combinations receiving strong agreement included: dish with dumplings, pizza, and curry; spicy with curry; dessert with ice cream; and fruits with apple and orange, aligning with WordNet hierarchies. These results confirm that the system can elicit widely accepted categorical knowledge through simple, intuitive interaction.

New insights also emerged, such as associating sweet with cake and apple. In visual judgments (Yes/No format), "shiny" was frequently selected as a plausible effect for items labeled sweet, cold, or round, suggesting a default association with freshness or quality. In contrast, combinations such as powder with fruits or shiny with spicy were often rejected, indicating mismatched or culturally implausible associations.

These findings indicate the system's dual capacity: to reinforce established knowledge and to surface novel, culturally influenced interpretations. The visual

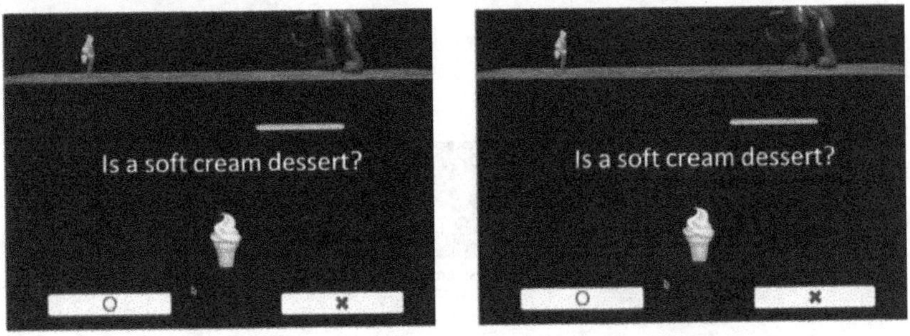

Fig. 1 Gameplay interfaces for knowledge elicitation.
The left panel shows a commonsense knowledge quiz (○/× format), prompting users to verify categorical relationships (e.g., "Is this a fruit?"). The right panel displays the visual effect quiz (Yes/No format), asking whether a presented effect appropriately matches the adjective-noun pair.

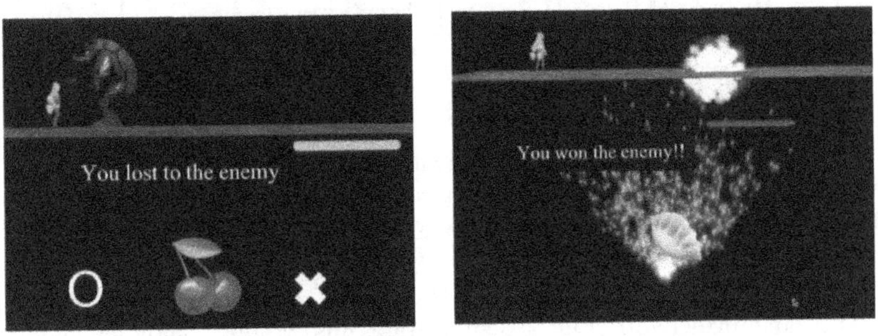

Fig. 2 Visual feedback indicating battle outcome in the game.
The left image shows the player successfully defeating the enemy using a high-scoring energy beam, while the right image depicts a failed attack due to weak semantic alignment. These feedback screens incentivize user engagement through gamified reinforcement.

effect evaluation, in particular, provided insight into participants' intuitive semantics that might not align with taxonomic structures like WordNet.

4.3 Evolution of Data Structures (After Three Play Sessions)

By the third gameplay session, structured data showed strong participant consensus, with many combinations exceeding 15 points. Key pairings included dish with curry, spicy with curry, dessert with soft cream, sweet with cake and apple, and round with orange, reflecting WordNet-like semantic clusters. The consistency across users indicates the system's capacity to consolidate emerging interpretations into stable semantic structures.

Visual effect judgments also became more nuanced. For instance, spicy was more often linked to dish, powder to dessert, and shiny to fruits and round. These combinations reflect a refinement of aesthetic-semantic alignment, as participants increasingly agreed on contextually appropriate visual metaphors.

Negative associations, like steam with fruits and shiny with spicy, were consistently noted and avoided.

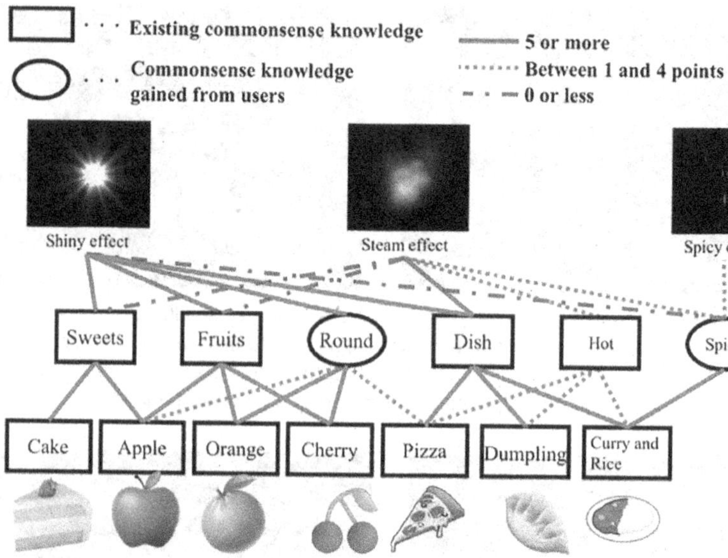

Fig. 3 Refined semantic network after three gameplay sessions per participant. Compared to Figure 6, this network exhibits greater density and consistency in associations, reflecting evolving user consensus and the discovery of new visual effect–word pairings over time.

The semantic network (Fig. 3) demonstrates this evolution, showing increased density and coherence compared to the first session. These trends highlight how repeated gameplay not only diversifies the visual vocabulary but also strengthens culturally informed, context-specific interpretations.

4.4 User Feedback and Questionnaire Analysis

After the third gameplay session, participants responded to a questionnaire about usability and system impressions. Regarding visual effects for "delicious," 87.5% found multiple appropriate options, while 12.5% were unsure, confirming the system's alignment with subjective expectations.

When asked about the diversity and contextuality of visual effects, several participants commented that effects like "shiny," "steam," and "sparkle" each evoked different emotional tones depending on the food item—indicating that users were actively interpreting affective meaning, not just matching appearances.

For replay interest, 62.5% expressed willingness to play again, and 37.5% were uncertain. On entertainment value, 62.5% rated the game as interesting or very interesting, supporting its effectiveness as a GWAP.

However, usability feedback revealed areas for improvement. Only 12.5% rated it "easy to use," while 62.5% found it "somewhat difficult to use." Participants suggested expanding noun options, enhancing attack animations, and allowing multiple visual effects per trial. These suggestions highlight the importance of intuitive interface design in maintaining engagement and ensuring that semantic judgments remain fluid and expressive.

Additionally, comments emphasized a desire for richer narrative integration and more fluid transitions between game phases, pointing to the need for a smoother, more immersive user experience.

4.5 Key Findings and Reflections

The experimental results show that Effect Game effectively captures nuanced, context-sensitive semantic relationships through engaging gameplay. In three sessions, participants constructed a meaningful visual-semantic network, validating existing linguistic structures and contributing culturally relevant insights.

The gradual shift from general associations (e.g., shiny = delicious) to more specific mappings (e.g., steam for curry, powder for desserts) illustrates the system's capacity for semantic refinement through interaction.

This refinement mirrors natural language use, where meaning adapts to context and shared cultural assumptions.

These findings affirm the potential of GWAP-based methods for affective and perceptual knowledge collection. While user participation was positive, the study also revealed limitations related to system usability and content depth.

Importantly, the results suggest that playful interaction supports the emergence of tacit cultural knowledge, insights that are often difficult to elicit through traditional surveys or static annotation.

By grounding these insights in user-generated (adjective, noun, visual effect) triplets, the system enables structured yet flexible meaning representation.

Future enhancements should focus on interface refinement, gameplay variation, and expanded content to maintain engagement and scalability.

Figures included in this chapter, Fig. 1 (gameplay interface), Fig. 2 (feedback effect), and Fig. 3 (semantic network), visually reinforce these findings.

5. Discussion

The previous chapter showed that even with few participants, the system effectively captured context-sensitive visual interpretations. This study was motivated by the idea that even when using the same adjective, such as "delicious", the mental image evoked can vary greatly depending on the noun it modifies. For instance, "delicious apple" may suggest a glossy sheen, while "delicious ramen" evokes steaming warmth. Our system was designed to explore and collect such variations interactively.

Initially, users favored generic effects like "shiny" for "delicious," but over three sessions, more specific pairings emerged, such as steam for hot dishes, powder for desserts, and sparkle for cold sweets like soft cream. This progression highlights the system's ability to refine affective meaning through interaction.

These results position the system as more than a data collection tool, as it serves as a participatory platform for building a semantic knowledge base rooted in emotion, culture, and context. The following sections connect these findings to theoretical insights, assess methodological contributions, and outline future directions.

5.1 Evolving Semantic Judgments Through Gameplay

In the initial gameplay session, participants commonly chose the visual effect shiny to represent delicious, particularly for apple, cake, and soft cream, reflecting cultural associations of glossiness with freshness or quality. This aligns with Norman (2002), who emphasizes how surface attributes such as gloss can elicit positive emotional responses in product design. Over time, preferences grew more context-specific: steam for hot dishes like curry, powder for cake suggesting powdered sugar, and sparkle for cold sweets like soft cream.

This semantic refinement happened naturally, allowing tacit cultural intuitions to emerge. The resulting network of (adjective, noun, visual effect) triplets captures both consensus and minority perspectives. These triplet-based associations also resemble the structured approach of Lieberman et al. (2007), who proposed semantic visual dictionaries to map user-understandable concepts to interface elements, supporting interpretability and user-driven refinement.

Unlike static ontologies such as WordNet (Miller, 1995), this system reflects the flexible and affective nature of contextual meaning, and demonstrates how participatory gameplay can facilitate semantic evolution through culturally grounded interaction.

5.2 Cultural Semantics and Cross-Cultural Interpretability

Visual interpretations of adjectives are shaped by cultural and contextual factors. For instance, red symbolizes love in Western cultures but signifies celebration in China. Similarly, gold may evoke luxury in one culture but appear excessive in another, and white signifies purity in the West but mourning in East Asia (Madden, Hewett, & Roth, 2000). Floral imagery also varies: lilies symbolize purity in the West but are associated with funerals in parts of East Asia.

To address this variability, our system uses culturally neutral emoji and visual effects as interaction tools, enabling diverse, localized interpretations. While the current study focused on Japanese users, the system's multilingual design allows cross-cultural applications.

Aligned with Kansei Engineering's focus on emotional response in product design (Nagamachi, 1995), our approach extends this concept. It incorporates cultural interpretation, enabling the design of emotionally and culturally resonant content. This helps uncover how emotion and meaning are co-constructed within specific cultural contexts.

This framework supports creating a semantic atlas of visual metaphors, comparing how adjectives like delicious are tied to steam, shiny, or sparkle across cultures. By visualizing these associations, the system can highlight both commonalities and divergences in metaphorical thinking and emotional resonance.

Region-specific visual dictionaries could be developed over time and integrated into design workflows for adaptive media, user interfaces, marketing, and education, enabling culturally tailored applications.

5.3 A Human-Centered Semantic Framework in the Age of Generative AI

Recent generative AI advancements, including text-to-image models like DALL·E 2 (Ramesh et al., 2022), Stable Diffusion (Rombach et al., 2022), and video-focused systems such as Sora (OpenAI, 2024), have achieved high visual fidelity and strong alignment with linguistic prompts. Surveys such as Zhang et al. (2023) demonstrate that these systems perform well in many image generation tasks but often operate as opaque black boxes, limiting transparency, cultural adaptability, and user-guided control, factors that are especially critical in domains like education and cross-cultural communication.

In contrast, our Visual Effect Dictionary uses explicit (adjective, noun, effect) triplets derived from human gameplay input, enabling semantically interpretable, emotionally grounded, and culturally adaptable mappings. This structured approach complements generative models by addressing their limitations.

This framework provides several key benefits:

- **Semantic traceability:** Each triplet is backed by identifiable user input and can be audited or edited manually, in contrast to latent representations in neural models.
- **Cultural adaptability:** Region-specific differences, such as glossiness for "delicious" in Japanese culture vs. warmth or richness in others, can be preserved and compared.
- **Control and integration:** The Dictionary can function as a semantic filter or grounding layer for generative models, guiding them toward more context-sensitive and emotionally resonant outputs.

Our approach complements generative AI by adding structure, transparency, and user interpretability. The Visual Effect Dictionary can enhance image or video generation pipelines by providing cultural nuance and human intention, which are difficult to capture in purely data-driven models.

By embedding participatory human processes, this system reimagines AI as a co-constructed, interpretable, and socially grounded tool for meaning-making.

5.4 Theoretical and Methodological Contributions

This research demonstrates how gameplay enables semantic co-construction in emotion-rich and culturally embedded domains, extending the concept of Games with a Purpose (von Ahn & Dabbish, 2008) into areas involving subjective, affective meaning-making. Rather than focusing on binary correctness, the system facilitates interpretive engagement, allowing users to collectively shape a knowledge base through playful, narrative-driven interaction.

User input is structured into explicit (adjective, noun, visual effect) triplets, making tacit judgments accessible and analyzable. These triplets reflect both majority consensus and minority variations, enabling the system to capture nuanced, culturally grounded associations that escape traditional ontologies such as WordNet (Miller, 1995).

The resulting knowledge base contributes to several interdisciplinary fields:

- In product design and interface aesthetics, it offers insights into how adjectives like "elegant" or "fresh" are visually interpreted across cultures.
- In affective computing, it supplies a rich set of emotionally tagged visual associations.
- In cross-cultural psychology, it reveals how visual metaphors differ based on sociocultural background.

This aligns with principles of human-centered AI, emphasizing interpretability, inclusivity, and co-creation. The Visual Effect Dictionary is not just a dataset, but a methodology, a structured, participatory process for collecting culturally and emotionally resonant semantic knowledge.

5.5 Future Directions and Application Scenarios

The system and dataset developed in this research open up multiple paths for future exploration and application.

Semantic Domain Expansion

While the prototype centered on delicious and food-related nouns, its framework extends to broader affective domains. Adjectives like anxious, elegant, or friendly could pair with nouns from fields like spaces, emotions, or behaviors, supporting a richer, more comprehensive affective-semantic resource.

Cross-Cultural Semantic Mapping

Expanding the system across languages and cultures would allow for systematic comparisons of affective visual meanings, providing valuable insights for international design, cultural psychology, and education.

To support such analysis, future versions of the system could implement metadata tagging for each semantic triplet, such as region, language background, and age group. This metadata would allow researchers to identify demographic patterns (e.g., whether "fresh" evokes glossiness in one culture and brightness in another), enabling comparative visualization and cross-linguistic insight.

Integration with Generative AI

The Dictionary can integrate with generative pipelines as a semantic control layer, ensuring outputs are context-sensitive, culturally grounded, and less prone to bias.

This approach empowers users by guiding generation with affective and cultural nuance, especially in co-creative systems and human-in-the-loop workflows.

Educational and Creative Applications

The system holds promise for language learning (e.g., teaching how visual metaphors are used in different cultures), visual literacy training, metaphor instruction, and design education. It can also inspire artists, writers, and UX designers to explore expressive affective metaphors and support more emotionally grounded user engagement.

System Enhancements

Future iterations could include multiplayer modes for collaborative meaning-making, dynamic difficulty adjustment for personalized engagement, and an expanded library of visual effects for finer semantic distinctions.

Support for voice or gesture input could enhance accessibility and usability, ultimately transforming the Visual Effect Dictionary into a dynamic, participatory tool for a multicultural, media-rich world.

6. Conclusion

This research presents a novel method for gathering affective, culturally nuanced visual semantics through interactive gameplay. Using a narrative-driven Game with a Purpose, it enables users to intuitively link adjectives, nouns, and visual effects to convey nuanced meanings. The resulting Visual Effect Dictionary captures both shared associations and contextual variations shaped by emotion and culture.

Unlike static ontologies or opaque AI models, the system emphasizes human judgment, transparency, and collaboration. Experiments revealed that even limited participation, just three sessions per user, led to meaningful refinements in the semantic network, capturing nuanced affective interpretations that static ontologies or survey methods might overlook.

As multimodal expression becomes key in education, communication, and media, systems like Effect Game empower users to actively shape meaning. It exemplifies GWAPs as participatory tools for encoding diverse, contextual knowledge, evolving into a dynamic, human-centered semantic resource.

Column 1: Why Does "Shiny" Mean "Delicious"?

Food advertisements often showcase glossy finishes to emphasize freshness and quality. Participants in our study similarly linked the effect "shiny" with the adjective "delicious," particularly for items like apples and cakes, reflecting intuitive perceptions of freshness and appeal. This association reflects intuitive cues of edibility but varies by culture, where glossiness might connote greasiness or artificiality.

Our research reveals that such visual metaphors are context-dependent, shaped by food type and cultural background. By gathering diverse inputs through gameplay, we can build a more adaptable and nuanced model of affective semantics.

Column 2: Contributing by Playing — The Future of Meaning-Making Through Games

Serious tasks often feel dull, but what if playing a game could help create knowledge or analyze culture? Games with a Purpose (GWAP) transform gameplay into meaningful data collection, as seen in tools like ESP Game for image labeling.

Effect Game takes this further, gathering rich semantic knowledge through story-driven gameplay, where players unknowingly shape word meanings and metaphors. This innovative approach could impact education, media design, AI, and cultural preservation, turning play into purposeful meaning-making.

Column 3: What Generative AI Lacks, A Dialogue About Meaning

Generative AI like ChatGPT and DALL·E excels at creating text and visuals but often lacks transparency in semantic reasoning. The Visual Effect Dictionary addresses this by making mappings visible and editable through user consensus. Judgments like "shiny" for "sweet + apple" are recorded and shared, fostering a dialogue about meaning. This system complements generative AI by offering explainable, culturally sensitive, and human-centered guidance.

Column 4: Visualizing "Delicious" in Japanese

The concept of "delicious" varies by food and cultural context—steaming ramen, shiny glazed fruit, or warm desserts. In Japanese, "oishii" (おいしい) conveys diverse meanings like sweetness, freshness, or nostalgia. Our study found "apple + delicious" linked to "shiny" for gloss, while "curry rice + delicious" paired with "spicy" or "steam" for heat and richness.

This dynamic metaphor highlights cross-linguistic differences, where "delicious" evokes unique sensory cues across cultures. The Visual Effect Dictionary captures these subtleties, enabling deeper cross-cultural semantic understanding.

Part 4
XR and Beyond: The Future of Learning

As emerging technologies reshape our world, they also open new frontiers in education. Virtual reality (VR), mixed reality (MR), and digital twins are creating immersive, interactive spaces where learners can engage with content in previously unimaginable ways. These environments enable students to visualize abstract concepts, explore real-world phenomena, and develop critical thinking and creative skills through embodied experience.

This part highlights pioneering research on the use of XR and related technologies in educational contexts. Chapters explore how MR can support STEM learning by extending spatial reasoning, how generative art can enrich programming education through visual creativity, and how digital twins combined with VR can bring geographic concepts to life in virtual environments.

Through these innovations, the chapters demonstrate how next-generation technologies are redefining what learning looks like, offering new possibilities for education that is immersive, adaptive, and deeply engaging.

14 Beyond Flatland: Mixed Reality Geometry for Immersive STEM Learning

1. Introduction

Traditional math education often relies on 2D depictions of 3D shapes, requiring students to mentally visualize cubes or spheres. This approach imposes a cognitive strain, as geometry, being spatial and visual, is taught abstractly. Many learners, especially younger ones, struggle with this disconnect, which diminishes engagement and understanding. Although Sweller (1988) does not specifically address 2D-to-3D transformations, his cognitive load theory implies that requiring learners to mentally convert 2D representations into 3D forms can impose unnecessary demands on working memory—particularly for novices.

This research proposes teaching 3D geometry in 3D. By introducing tools for directly manipulating virtual shapes, such as grabbing, rotating, and unfolding them, students could engage more intuitively, eliminating the burden of mental translation and fostering curiosity and exploration.

Advances in immersive technology, particularly Mixed Reality (MR), enable the integration of virtual objects into physical spaces. Unlike fully immersive Virtual Reality (VR), which blocks out the physical world, MR allows learners to see and interact with both virtual objects and their physical environment, for example, by manipulating a virtual cube on a real desk. This approach is ideal for education, allowing interaction with both real and digital elements.

This chapter introduces a novel MR-based system using the HoloLens 2 headset, designed for studying 3D geometric figures. HoloLens 2 was chosen for its advanced spatial mapping and hand-tracking capabilities, which make it especially suitable for interactive educational settings. It provides hands-on interaction with models, enhancing spatial reasoning and conceptual understanding for a more engaging learning experience. The upcoming chapters explore immersive learning principles, the design of the MR system, and experiment results with students. They also examine cognitive differences and broader impacts on STEM education. By transitioning from abstract methods to interactive experiences, this work aims to transform geometry teaching into a spatial and engaging approach.

2. Theoretical Background

Before delving into specific cognitive skills and instructional approaches, it is essential to establish the theoretical foundation that supports the integration of

DOI: 10.1201/9781003782735-18

Mixed Reality in geometry education. This section outlines the key concepts in spatial reasoning, cognitive development, and educational technology that inform the design and application of immersive learning tools.

2.1 Spatial Reasoning and Cognitive Development

Spatial reasoning, the ability to mentally visualize and manipulate shapes and spatial relations, is key in mathematics and STEM fields, strongly linked to problem-solving and achievement (Clements & Battista, 1992; Mix & Cheng, 2012). According to Piaget's theory of cognitive development, concrete spatial understanding emerges during the concrete operational stage (ages 7–11), while abstract reasoning develops in the formal operational stage (12 and above) (Piaget, 1964).

Research shows spatial reasoning can be cultivated through dynamic, interactive environments (Uttal et al., 2013). These environments include hands-on activities like block play, puzzle solving, and digital manipulation tools. Early interventions targeting these skills have lasting benefits for cognitive development and math proficiency (Clements & Sarama, 2011), highlighting the potential of Mixed Reality in education. This developmental window, spanning late concrete operational to early formal operational stages, makes upper elementary and early secondary students ideal candidates for spatial learning through Mixed Reality. MR supports concrete interaction while scaffolding abstract reasoning, bridging the gap between developmental stages.

2.2 Geometry Education and the Limitations of 2D Representation

Traditional geometry teaching often relies on static 2D diagrams, requiring students to mentally translate flat images into 3D forms, a challenge for those with weaker spatial skills (Battista, 2007). This translation process imposes a cognitive burden, particularly for novice learners who have not yet developed strong mental rotation or visualization abilities.

Despite its importance, geometry is often introduced too late in early education, missing key developmental opportunities (Jones, 2012). Introducing geometry concepts during the late concrete operational stage (ages 10–12), when students can handle concrete representations but are just beginning to engage with abstraction, may offer optimal learning benefits.

Early engagement boosts mathematical and spatial reasoning (Clements & Sarama, 2011). Mixed Reality offers a developmentally appropriate solution by providing embodied, manipulable 3D experiences that support both concrete and emerging abstract reasoning. It reduces the need for mental dimensional translation by allowing learners to directly interact with virtual solids, grasping, rotating, and unfolding them in physical space. This interactive experience fosters spatial intuition and aligns with the developmental needs of learners transitioning from concrete to formal thinking.

2.3 Mixed Reality in Educational Contexts

Mixed Reality (MR), blending elements of Virtual Reality (VR) and Augmented Reality (AR), enables interaction with 3D digital content in physical spaces. Unlike fully immersive VR, MR allows users to remain aware of and interact with their physical surroundings while engaging with virtual objects, making it particularly suitable for classroom learning.

Research highlights MR's ability to enhance engagement and learning by leveraging multimodal environments that activate visual, auditory, and tactile senses, promoting deeper cognitive processing (Annetta et al., 2024). These multimodal inputs align with dual coding theory (Paivio, 1986), which suggests that learning improves when verbal and nonverbal information are processed together.

Rohendi et al. (2025) found that middle school students using MR tools for geometry showed improved motivation, interactivity, and comprehension of abstract concepts. In these studies, students used mobile AR apps to manipulate cubes, prisms, and pyramids, thereby transforming static lessons into tangible, hands-on experiences.

The benefits of MR extend beyond K–12 education. Adams et al. (2022) reported increased motivation and understanding in medical training using the Microsoft HoloLens for anatomical studies. Fonkalsrud et al. (2025) showed that midwifery students appreciated MR's support for mastering complex topics like fetal positioning, highlighting its value as a supplementary tool to traditional instruction.

In all these contexts, MR serves not only as a visualization tool but also as a scaffold for active, embodied learning. Its immersive affordances help bridge the gap between abstract and concrete understanding, particularly critical during transitional developmental stages.

Further studies have explored specific affordances of MR in higher education. Banjar et al. (2023) reviewed its use in 3D visualization for tasks such as molecular modeling and spatial design, where traditional 2D methods often fall short. Ogunseiju et al. (2024) warned of potential cognitive overload from poorly designed MR systems, underscoring the importance of simplicity and instructional guidance based on Cognitive Load Theory. Goagoses et al. (2024) demonstrated how MR fosters emotional and social engagement, enhancing presence, collaboration, and motivation—especially in STEM subjects.

2.4 MR for Geometry and Spatial Reasoning

Geometry, with its inherently spatial and visual nature, is particularly well-suited for Mixed Reality applications. Tarng et al. (2023) demonstrated that AR-based geometry systems significantly improved both performance and reduced cognitive load among 5th-grade students. Similarly, Rohendi et al. (2025) reported that real-time manipulation of 3D shapes enhanced spatial understanding and student engagement.

Azzam et al. (2024) found that MR modules led to significant improvements in spatial reasoning skills. Their findings highlight the importance of direct interaction with geometric solids, which allows learners to rotate, dissect, and reconfigure shapes, reinforcing spatial intuition and addressing common misconceptions.

Such embodied interactions are especially beneficial during the late concrete operational and early formal operational stages, when learners are transitioning from tangible, perception-based reasoning to more abstract, logical thinking. MR provides a developmentally aligned environment that supports this shift through hands-on, immersive experiences.

Additionally, MR offers immediate visual feedback and encourages exploratory learning, two elements that foster learner agency and intrinsic motivation. These qualities are essential not only for understanding geometric concepts but also for building long-term competence in STEM disciplines.

Backed by developmental psychology and empirical research, MR emerges as a promising tool for making 3D geometry intuitive, engaging, and accessible across age groups and educational levels.

3. System Design

Building on the theoretical foundations of spatial reasoning and immersive learning, this section describes the design of an MR-based geometry system. The system is tailored to support students' conceptual understanding through direct interaction with 3D figures.

3.1 Design Principles and Pedagogical Goals

The system aims to close the cognitive gap between 2D representations and students' spatial understanding of 3D figures. Traditional methods often demand the mental conversion of flat diagrams into three-dimensional forms, placing strain on working memory and leading to misconceptions (Battista, 2007). By using Mixed Reality (MR), the system presents geometric shapes as interactive holograms, allowing embodied interaction that aligns with how humans naturally learn through perception and action (Wilson, 2002; Barsalou, 2008). Students manipulate virtual shapes in physical space, reducing the need for mentally converting 2D representations into 3D forms and fostering engagement.

Our design is guided by three pedagogical principles:

1. **Embodied interaction:** Learning through hands-on engagement with virtual objects, such as grasping, rotating, and cutting. This approach draws on embodied cognition theory, which emphasizes that cognitive processes are deeply rooted in physical experience.
2. **Progressive scaffolding:** Supporting learners' cognitive development by gradually introducing more complex spatial tasks. This principle is inspired

by Vygotsky's zone of proximal development and the concept of scaffolding (Wood, Bruner, & Ross, 1976).

3. **Situated Learning:** Engaging with geometric concepts in realistic contexts to enhance understanding and transferability, in line with situated learning theory (Lave & Wenger, 1991).

The system, optimized for Microsoft HoloLens 2, uses advanced spatial mapping, hand tracking, and eye tracking to facilitate smooth 3D interaction. Its intuitive and safe design makes it ideal for elementary and junior high school classrooms.

3.2 Core Features and User Interface

The MR system uses an interactive holographic interface layered onto real-world surroundings. Key features include:

- Hand Tracking: Enables manipulation of virtual objects, reinforcing spatial understanding through tactile interaction.
- Eye Tracking: Aligns object placement with the student's gaze, reducing cognitive load and aiding navigation. This feature is grounded in dual coding theory (Sweller, 1988), which posits that reducing extraneous processing, such as manual object alignment, frees cognitive resources for meaningful learning.
- Spatial Anchoring: Secures holograms to surfaces for realistic and stable interaction.
- Palm-Activated Menu: Provides easy access to tools like "Cut," "Unfold," and "Paint" by looking at the palm. This design aligns with user-centered design principles, minimizing cognitive effort and streamlining tool access (Norman, 1988).
- Tutorial Mode: Offers guided instruction with visual and auditory feedback, easing students into MR interactions. The use of multiple sensory channels supports Dual Coding Theory (Paivio, 1986), which suggests that combining visual and verbal information enhances comprehension and recall.

These features collectively support young learners by minimizing interface complexity while enabling rich, intuitive interaction. The integration of gesture, gaze, and voice creates a multimodal experience that not only improves usability but also strengthens learning by reducing cognitive barriers.

3.3 Learning Content Modules

The system addresses three fundamental categories of geometric problems commonly found in curriculum-based assessments and classroom teaching. These modules are grounded in research on spatial reasoning, which has shown that interactive, visual tasks enhance learners' mental transformation and geometry comprehension (Uttal et al., 2013).

3.3.1 Building Block Problems

These tasks involve analyzing multi-cube structures, challenging students to count painted cubes or uncover hidden faces that are not visible in 2D diagrams, like the Building Block 2 Problem (Figure 1). Such activities enhance skills in spatial decomposition, surface area estimation, and navigation of occluded geometry, strengthening mental rotation and visual-spatial fluency. Research has shown that block-based spatial reasoning tasks improve spatial visualization and decomposition skills, both of which are critical for success in STEM fields (Newcombe, 2010; Uttal et al., 2013). MR enables learners to view structures from multiple angles and interactively explore hidden areas, reducing ambiguity and cognitive overload.

3.3.2 Cutting Problems

In cutting tasks, students work with 3D solids like cubes or pyramids to perform planar slices and identify the resulting cross-sections. These tasks are traditionally challenging due to the need to visualize intersecting planes, but they become

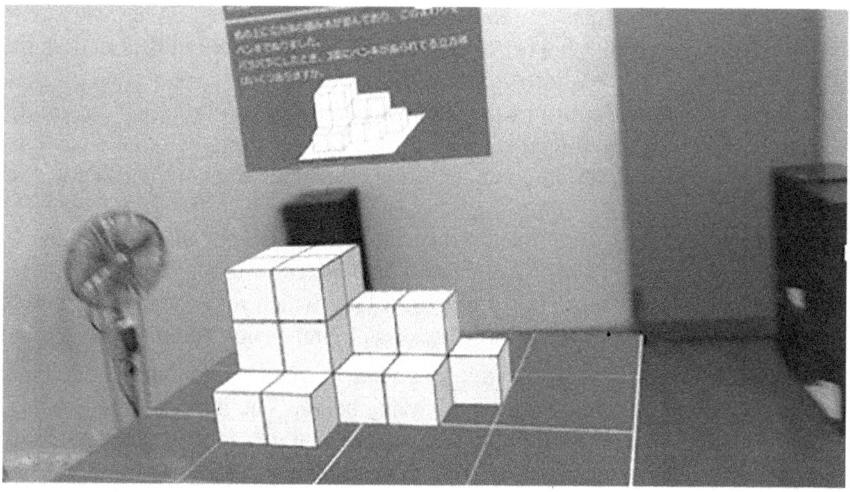

Fig. 1 Building Block 2 Problem, an Interactive Mixed Reality Visualization
This figure showcases a 3D representation of a cubic block structure arranged on a table, illustrating the system's ability to visualize geometric problems in an immersive environment. The task challenges learners to calculate the number of cubes painted on three sides, a concept often difficult to grasp in traditional 2D diagrams. Through the MR interface, learners can rotate, zoom, and disassemble the virtual structure to explore hidden faces and develop a comprehensive understanding of the spatial relationships. This interactivity fosters hands-on engagement and enhances spatial reasoning, making abstract mathematical concepts more accessible and intuitive. By allowing students to manipulate and analyze the structure dynamically, the system bridges the gap between theoretical instruction and practical comprehension, a key feature of the Mixed Reality learning approach.

intuitive with MR. Students can interactively slice objects, view cross-sections in real time, and adjust orientations.

Studies by Cohen and Hegarty (2007) highlight that learners often struggle to mentally simulate cross-sectional views, making direct visual support highly beneficial. MR provides this support by rendering immediate and accurate visual feedback, helping learners overcome limitations in mental imagery and spatial inference.

3.3.3 Unfolding Problems

In this module, students unfold 3D shapes like cubes or prisms into their 2D nets. These are commonly referred to as "net problems" in mathematics education. Traditional methods often rely on paper cutouts, limiting interactivity and clarity. With MR, students drag faces outward to create nets, explore how faces connect, and verify unfolding sequences with visual feedback in real time.

Net problems have been shown to be particularly difficult for learners due to the need for dynamic spatial transformations (Boakes, 2009). MR enables students to experiment with multiple unfolding paths, view nets from different angles, and refold shapes, fostering hypothesis testing and flexible spatial thinking.

This shift from static to interactive representations encourages deeper conceptual understanding and reduces reliance on rote memorization.

3.4 Interaction Design Considerations

While developing the MR system, we prioritized user experience and age-appropriate design to ensure effective learning and accessibility for elementary and junior high school students. The following considerations informed our interaction design:

- **Age-Adapted Interaction:** Simplified gestures like pinching and dragging were chosen to suit younger learners. This aligns with Shneiderman's (1998) user interface design principles, which emphasize simplicity and direct manipulation, especially for novice users.
- **Minimized Cognitive Load:** Tasks were broken into manageable steps with gradual scaffolding to prevent cognitive overload. This reflects cognitive load theory (Sweller, 1988), which suggests that instructional design should reduce extraneous processing and adapt complexity to the learner's cognitive stage.
- **Feedback and Error Recovery:** Visual highlights, haptic responses, and undo options were incorporated to create a frustration-free learning experience. These features are consistent with Norman's (1988) principles of error-tolerant and discoverable interfaces, critical for maintaining learner confidence.
- **Multi-Modal Feedback:** The combination of visual cues, spatial audio, and interactive holograms supports learners with diverse needs and preferences. This approach is supported by dual coding theory (Paivio, 1986), which shows that presenting information via multiple sensory channels can improve comprehension and recall.

These interaction design elements aim to lower barriers to engagement while encouraging active exploration and learner autonomy. They also promote emotional and social engagement, which Goagoses et al. (2024) identified as essential components of meaningful MR-based learning experiences.

4. Experiments

The MR-based geometry system addresses challenges in spatial reasoning and 3D comprehension, leveraging cognitive theories and immersive learning advances. This chapter details experiments evaluating its impact on learning, engagement, and interaction among elementary and high school students in real classroom settings.

4.1 Research Objectives and Questions

This study evaluated the impact of Mixed Reality (MR) on enhancing students' 3D geometry understanding, focusing on spatial reasoning, task performance, and engagement compared to paper-based methods. It also explored how age, gender, and cognitive style influenced learning outcomes and interactions. Four key questions guided the investigation:

1. Does MR-based learning improve students' performance on spatial reasoning tasks involving three-dimensional shapes?
2. Are there discernible differences in learning outcomes between elementary and junior high school students?
3. In what ways do students interact with the MR system—particularly in terms of exploration, persistence, and strategy?
4. Do cognitive style or gender influence the way students use and benefit from the system?

These questions were designed to evaluate not only academic gains but also behavioral and cognitive dynamics in MR-based learning environments.

4.2 Participants

Participants were recruited from Japanese public schools, including 28 junior high school students (13–14 years old) and 13 fifth grade students (10–11 years old). All had basic geometry knowledge but no prior MR experience. Informed consent was obtained from parents and schools, adhering to ethical standards for research with minors.

This age range allowed for comparison between late concrete operational and early formal operational stages of cognitive development, offering insight into developmental readiness for MR-based spatial learning.

4.3 Experimental Procedure

Students participated in two MR learning sessions using the HoloLens 2, following a pre-test/post-test design with cognitive assessments and feedback. A pre-test evaluated skills in building block visualization, cutting, and unfolding tasks. The first session included a tutorial and guided practice, while the second featured more complex problems and self-directed exploration. A post-test assessed progress, and participants completed the Group Embedded Figures Test (GEFT) to classify cognitive styles. Selected students provided feedback through surveys or interviews.

This structured design enabled both quantitative and qualitative data collection, providing a well-rounded understanding of the system's effectiveness.

4.4 Interaction and Behavioral Observations

Researchers gathered detailed observational data, tracking task duration, feature usage (e.g., slicing, rotating), and interaction patterns. Younger students displayed curiosity, exploring object manipulation, while older students worked systematically with fewer interactions. Field-independent learners engaged with multiple system functions freely, whereas field-dependent ones relied on tutorials and visual cues. Gender differences showed boys exploring more extensively and girls completing tasks more linearly, but both groups maintained task focus and demonstrated comparable engagement.

These observations suggest that the MR environment supports diverse learning preferences, enabling both exploratory and structured learners to succeed.

4.5 Learning Outcomes

Analysis of pre- and post-test data showed key trends:

- **Building Block Tasks:** Both age groups improved, with enhanced visualization of hidden surfaces through MR manipulation.
- **Cutting Tasks:** Modest gains were observed, as predicting cross-sectional shapes remained challenging, especially for younger students.
- **Unfolding Tasks:** Elementary school students showed slight improvement, while junior high school students exhibited minimal change, possibly due to reduced novelty.

Field-independent learners excelled in exploratory tasks, while field-dependent ones benefited from structured guidance. Gender differences in interaction styles did not impact performance, indicating the system's adaptability to diverse learning approaches.

Overall, MR-based learning promoted spatial thinking across diverse profiles, with notable gains in visual inference and manipulation. The system's flexibility allowed learners with varying cognitive and behavioral styles to engage meaningfully with geometric concepts.

5. Discussion

This study highlights the benefits of Mixed Reality (MR) in teaching 3D geometry, with students showing significant improvement in spatial figure interpretation, especially in building block tasks. The MR interface enabled dynamic exploration of 3D models, enhancing comprehension of hidden surfaces and volumetric relationships—particularly for students struggling with spatial tasks.

These findings align with Clements and Sarama (2011), who advocate for early spatial learning interventions to boost mathematical thinking. Their developmental framework emphasizes the importance of introducing spatial reasoning activities during the transition from the concrete to the formal operational stage, when students are particularly receptive to hands-on, visual learning.

The system also heightened learner engagement, as elementary school students showed curiosity and persistence in tasks like slicing and unfolding. This supports Annetta et al. (2024), who demonstrated that MR fosters both cognitive and motivational gains, emphasizing its cross-disciplinary educational value. In our study, this was evident not only in geometry comprehension but also in increased attention and willingness to explore.

Despite promising results, limitations were evident. Students struggled to predict cross-sections in dynamic slicing tasks, highlighting the high cognitive demands despite MR visualization. Unfolding tasks benefited elementary school students with low pre-test scores but showed limited impact for junior high school students, likely due to prior familiarity. The intervention's short duration restricted assessments of long-term retention and transfer, while usability issues occasionally challenged field-dependent learners.

These findings refine our understanding of MR's educational role, supporting prior studies like Banjar et al. (2023) and Maas & Hughes (2020), which highlight MR's benefits for spatial visualization and motivation, even extending to elementary school students when developmentally appropriate. Strong improvements in building block tasks align with Tarng et al. (2023) and Rohendi et al. (2025), who found AR and MR environments enhance geometric understanding.

However, modest results in cutting and unfolding tasks emphasize that novelty alone doesn't ensure comprehension in abstraction-heavy tasks, such as cross-sectional reasoning. Ogunseiju et al. (2024) similarly cautioned that insufficient scaffolding in MR systems could lead to cognitive overload, underscoring the importance of adaptive, step-by-step guidance for complex operations.

Age group differences revealed key insights. Elementary school students interacted more broadly and engaged with MR's novelty, while junior high school students were more focused and efficient but less exploratory. This pattern aligns with developmental psychology: younger learners in the concrete operational stage benefit more from perceptual and physical manipulation, while older learners in the formal operational stage require higher cognitive challenge to sustain engagement.

Cognitive styles also influenced outcomes. Field-independent learners thrived with MR's exploratory features, while field-dependent learners benefited more from structured prompts, consistent with Clements and Battista's (1992) findings on spatial reasoning. Field-independent learners, those who process information with minimal reliance on external cues, navigated the interface with greater autonomy, whereas field-dependent learners relied more on visual guidance and tutorials.

Gender-related interaction patterns, as noted in prior studies like Fonkalsrud et al. (2025) and Goagoses et al. (2024), showed boys engaging in trial-and-error exploration while girls approached tasks systematically, completing them efficiently. While these general trends were observed, individual differences within each gender group were also notable, underscoring the system's flexibility. These behaviors did not affect learning outcomes, indicating MR's adaptability to diverse approaches.

Our findings reinforce MR's role in bridging the gap between 2D representations and 3D geometry understanding. By enabling interaction with spatial models, grasping, cutting, and unfolding shapes—MR reduces the cognitive burden of inferring 3D properties, as supported by Battista (2007) and Jones (2012). However, its effectiveness varies by learner characteristics, such as cognitive style, gender, and developmental stage. Future MR systems should incorporate age-sensitive and adaptive designs, offering responsive scaffolding that personalizes learning and supports cognitive diversity.

6. Conclusion

This chapter examined the design, implementation, and evaluation of a Mixed Reality (MR)-based learning system to enhance understanding of 3D geometry. Addressing the disconnect between 2D representations and 3D spatial concepts, the system provided learners with an intuitive, immersive environment to manipulate geometric figures in real time, grasping, rotating, slicing, and unfolding shapes for direct interaction.

Classroom experiments showed significant improvements, particularly among elementary school students, in visualizing and reasoning about 3D forms like building blocks. The immersive environment fostered engagement and supported diverse learning behaviors. However, challenges in tasks requiring abstract spatial reasoning, such as slicing or interpreting nets, highlighted the need for conceptual guidance. Learner differences in age, gender, and cognitive style further underscored the importance of adaptive MR systems tailored to individual needs.

This work highlights the importance of spatial reasoning in STEM education, with MR as a powerful tool to support it. Geometry, a foundational link to science, engineering, and technology, thrives in environments emphasizing visualization, manipulation, and embodied understanding. MR transforms spatial concept learning by making it immersive and intuitive.

Future developments should include adaptive feedback, scaffolding, and long-term studies to assess retention and transfer. Collaborative features, teacher dashboards, and curriculum alignment could enhance its impact. Expanding MR's use across subjects requiring spatial reasoning and visualization would further its educational relevance. By moving beyond static representations, MR can make geometry more engaging and foster essential 21st-century spatial and technological literacies.

Column 1: Beyond the Classroom – Real-World Applications of Mixed Reality and Spatial Learning

Teaching 3D figures with Mixed Reality (MR) connects classroom learning to real-world applications across various professions. Exploring how these technologies are used in fields like architecture, medicine, and gaming highlights their broader value and offers students a deeper appreciation for immersive spatial learning.

Architecture and Engineering

Architects and engineers use 3D modeling tools to simulate and refine structures, developing spatial reasoning essential for design and planning. Similarly, MR and VR are revolutionizing medical training, allowing surgeons to interact with holographic anatomical models. These technologies enhance skills like rotating, dissecting, and reconstructing 3D forms, directly benefiting areas like medical imaging and surgical preparation.

Gaming and Entertainment

In game design, MR and VR create immersive 3D environments that require spatial skills like assembly, scene visualization, and object interaction. These abilities, similar to those practiced in MR-based geometry lessons, are essential for game development, animation, and user experience design.

STEM Education

Understanding 3D relationships is vital across STEM disciplines. Chemistry involves visualizing molecules, physics models forces in 3D space, and biology examines anatomical and ecological systems. MR integration bridges abstract concepts with hands-on learning, helping students engage with and understand spatial structures.

Everyday Problem-Solving

Spatial thinking extends beyond academics, aiding everyday tasks like packing, organizing spaces, or navigating unfamiliar areas. Consistent practice with MR systems enhances school learning while fostering lifelong cognitive skills transferable to various real-world challenges.

15 Mixed Reality and Generative Art in Mathematics and Programming Education

1. Introduction

Immersive technologies are revolutionizing education by making abstract concepts like mathematics and programming more tangible. Traditional methods, which often depend on internal visualization, can overwhelm those with limited spatial skills, especially when studying 3D geometry. To address this, we propose an interactive system using Mixed Reality (MR) and generative art. This system transforms static representations into dynamic experiences, enabling learners to explore, adjust, and interact with mathematical objects in real time. By grounding abstract ideas in direct perception and physical action, this approach reduces cognitive load and enhances conceptual grasp. It fosters accessibility, creativity, and deeper understanding by leveraging visual intuition.

1.1 Background and Motivation

Mathematics and programming often struggle to make abstract concepts, like 3D geometry, comprehensible. Flat 2D images fail to fully capture the spatial complexity of these objects, requiring learners to construct internal mental models—an unevenly effective process influenced by individual spatial reasoning abilities (Battista, 2007; van Hiele, 1959). Tools like the Mental Cutting Test (MCT) are used to assess such differences by measuring learners' ability to visualize 3D cross-sections, a key STEM skill (Sorby, 2009).

To address these challenges, we developed a Mixed Reality (MR) system that immerses users in a 3D environment. Learners can interact with geometric shapes, manipulate their parameters, and view them from multiple perspectives. This supports embodied cognition, where thinking is rooted in perception and action (Wilson, 2002), and makes abstract content directly experienceable.

Mixed Reality (MR) merges digital and real-world elements, enhancing spatial learning by enabling the manipulation of complex structures. Generative art, grounded in algorithmic processes (Galanter, 2003), serves as a creative bridge between mathematics, programming, and visual design. By integrating these elements in a constructionist framework (Papert, 1980), our system supports learning-by-making, where conceptual understanding emerges through iterative interaction.

Using MR, learners can intuitively explore parametric shapes like the torus. Generative art enhances the aesthetic and creative appeal of the models, inviting

DOI: 10.1201/9781003782735-19

both analytical and imaginative engagement. This approach aligns with STEAM principles (Henriksen, 2014; Resnick et al., 2009), encouraging holistic, hands-on learning that connects logic, art, and personal expression.

1.2 Challenges in Traditional Education

Traditional teaching methods in geometry and programming often rely on rote learning and abstract symbols, leading to fragmented understanding (Presmeg, 1986). Geometry instruction typically presents 3D shapes as static 2D projections, offering limited spatial cues. Meanwhile, novice programmers must bridge the gap between abstract code and concrete outcomes, an often difficult leap (Grover & Pea, 2013).

These approaches contradict constructivist learning theory, which asserts that understanding arises from active manipulation and experience. Static diagrams and symbolic representations offer limited opportunities for exploratory learning.

By combining generative art with MR, our system offers an immersive, interactive environment where learners receive real-time feedback from algorithmic or mathematical changes. This iterative feedback loop supports deeper learning, allowing learners to develop intuitions through trial, error, and refinement, which is a core principle of experiential education.

1.3 Research Focus and Contributions

This study introduces an MR learning system combining generative art with mathematics and programming education, using Microsoft HoloLens 2. Learners interact with a 3D torus model that dynamically responds to parameter changes. The system features two modules: one covering the torus's volume and surface area calculations, and the other explaining the algorithms behind its creation.

A comparative experiment with 22 university students evaluated the system. Participants alternated between MR and paper-based learning, with pre- and post-tests and torus drawings assessing outcomes. While test scores showed no significant differences, students using MR created more detailed, spatially accurate drawings, highlighting improved 3D visualization skills (Furuichi & Sumi, 2024). Most participants expressed a preference for MR, citing its clarity and engagement. These findings suggest that MR systems may offer qualitative benefits, such as improved spatial fidelity and intuitive engagement, which are critical for domains requiring abstract reasoning and visual thinking.

2. Related Work and Theoretical Background

To situate our approach, we first review prior research on spatial reasoning in geometry education, followed by literature on programming pedagogy, generative art, and mixed reality. Each of these domains offers key insights into how learners engage with abstract concepts through visual, interactive, and constructive experiences.

2.1 Spatial Reasoning and Geometry Education

Grasping three-dimensional (3D) structures is a major challenge in math education, as learners must mentally manipulate spatial forms through two-dimensional (2D) media like diagrams or static images. This demands advanced spatial reasoning skills, which vary considerably among individuals and frequently remain underdeveloped without targeted instruction (Battista, 2007). The van Hiele model highlights the progression from visual recognition to descriptive, relational, formal deduction, and ultimately rigorous reasoning (van Hiele, 1959). This framework underscores the value of manipulable visually rich environments in helping learners advance through these levels.

Visualization plays a critical role in geometry learning. Students with strong visual imagery abilities tend to perform better on spatial tasks (Presmeg, 1986). Immersive environments featuring interactive 3D models have been shown to effectively foster spatial understanding. Tools like the Mental Cutting Test (MCT) assess spatial visualization ability by testing learners' mental interpretation of 3D cross-sections, aiding instructional design (Sorby, 2009).

Mixed Reality (MR) enhances spatial cognition by enabling learners to interact directly with 3D objects through gesture-based interaction, bridging the gap between internal mental imagery and external physical representation. Multiple studies have confirmed MR's effectiveness in improving both spatial learning outcomes and student engagement (Johnson-Glenberg, 2018; Faridan, Kumari, & Suzuki, 2023).

2.2 Programming Education and Constructivism

Programming education often begins with abstract syntax and logic, which makes it difficult for novices to connect these elements to meaningful outcomes and contributes to high dropout rates in computer science (Guzdial & Ericson, 2016). Constructionism, as introduced by Papert (1980), offers a solution by engaging learners in creating artifacts like patterns or simulations, grounding abstract logic in tangible outputs. This approach inspired visual environments like Scratch (Resnick et al., 2009), which simplify entry and foster experimentation (Grover & Pea, 2013).

Generative art bridges programming and creativity, showing how code produces visual effects. By offering immediate feedback (Schön, 1983), it supports exploration and computational thinking. In MR environments, generative art evolves into an interactive canvas, allowing learners to "sculpt" with code and merge logical skills with artistic expression.

2.3 Educational Use of Generative Art

Emerging in the 1960s, generative art has gained renewed educational focus with tools like Processing and p5.js enhancing creativity and computational thinking (Messer, 2024). Mathematical topics like parametric curves, fractals, and trigonometric functions lend themselves well to generative exploration. In this study, learners manipulate a torus, defined by circular rotations—to see how parameter changes affect its form.

Generative art's real-time feedback mirrors the iterative nature of scientific experimentation, aligning with STEAM's integration of analytical and creative thinking (Henriksen, 2014). Unlike traditional tasks focused on correct answers, generative art-based activities foster divergent thinking, experimentation, and iterative design, which are key 21st-century skills (Rauth et al., 2010).

2.4 Mixed Reality in Educational Settings

MR technologies, like Microsoft HoloLens, enable interactive learning by blending physical and digital objects (Milgram & Kishino, 1994). Unlike Virtual Reality (VR), which fully immerses the user in a simulated world, or Augmented Reality (AR), which overlays information onto the physical environment, Mixed Reality (MR) allows continuous, context-aware interaction between the two. This approach enhances spatial cognition, memory, and engagement, especially in geometry education, by reducing cognitive load through manipulable holographic models (Bacca et al., 2014; Johnson-Glenberg, 2018).

Despite its benefits, integrating MR into education presents challenges such as technical constraints, usability, and curricular alignment. Therefore, empirical evaluations must consider both cognitive and behavioral impacts to optimize instructional design.

2.5 Contribution of the Current Study

Despite extensive research on MR, generative art, and constructivist programming environments, few studies have combined them into a unified system. This study designs an MR-based platform integrating mathematical theory, programming logic, and artistic creativity. Through quantitative and qualitative analysis, it evaluates how MR enhances spatial understanding, reflected in test scores, diagrams, and learner feedback. The study also demonstrates generative art's potential as a core STEM educational strategy for engaging with complex concepts.

3. System Design

Building on the theoretical foundations and related work discussed above, this section details the design and implementation of our Mixed Reality (MR)-based learning system. We describe its components, interaction mechanisms, and pedagogical principles, illustrating how the system integrates mathematics, programming, and generative art into a unified, experiential learning environment.

3.1 Overview of the MR Learning Environment

To address challenges in spatial understanding and code-concept mapping, we developed an immersive MR system using Microsoft HoloLens 2, comprising two modules:

1. **Mathematics Module:** Focuses on exploring the torus's volume and surface area through interactive visualizations.
2. **Programming Module:** Demonstrates the code generating the torus as generative art.

Presented in an MR environment, these modules allow learners to interact with 3D mathematical objects using gestures, blending computation, visualization, and embodiment for experiential learning. Generative art serves as both an educational tool and a visual metaphor, bridging formulas and sensory experience (Galanter, 2003; Papert, 1980). This dual-module system integrates a Mathematics Learning Module for exploring torus geometry, and a Programming Learning Module for visualizing generative code in real time. Users interact with 3D models via hand gestures and receive immediate visual feedback.

The design supports conceptual understanding by linking mathematical parameters to dynamic 3D visualizations, grounded in constructivist learning principles.

Rather than using static diagrams, the system promotes learning through embodied interaction, allowing learners to switch between modules and spatially engage with abstract mathematical concepts.

3.2 Hardware and Software Configuration

The system, built on Microsoft HoloLens 2, utilizes eye tracking, spatial mapping, and gesture recognition for intuitive interaction. Developed with Unity and the Mixed Reality Toolkit (MRTK), it ensures precise spatial registration. Inspired by algorithmic methods in platforms like Processing, the torus's parametric model allows real-time adjustments based on user input through an interactive interface.

3.3 User Interface and Interaction Design

To support first-time users, the system includes a guided tutorial with three key tasks:

1. **Button Interaction:** Users practice tapping virtual buttons with hand gestures, receiving visual feedback through a number counter.
2. **Air Tap and Hand Ray Alignment:** Users point with a hand ray and perform air tap gestures, confirmed by a numerical display.
3. **Object Manipulation:** Users grab, rotate, move, and scale 3D objects using pinching gestures, with gestures interpreted based on the selected part of the object, such as a vertex, edge, or face.

These tasks ensure all learners, regardless of XR experience, can interact effectively with the system.

3.4 Mathematics Learning Module

The mathematics module introduces torus geometry, covering formulas for volume and surface area. The interface includes an instructional slide panel and an interactive 3D torus model. Learners can navigate slides using "Next" and "Back" buttons and explore the torus by zooming, rotating, or translating it. Adjustment buttons (+1, +10, –1, –10) allow changes to parameters like inner and outer radius, instantly updating the torus's shape. Based on standard parametric formulations (Vince, 2004), this system enhances understanding by linking formulas to dynamic, visual representations.

3.5 Programming Learning Module

The programming module reveals the code behind the torus generation and includes:

- **Slide Panel:** Detailed explanations of programming logic.
- **3D Torus:** Functionally identical to the math module, allowing interaction.
- **Live Code Display:** Dynamically updates in response to changes made to the torus model.

Using the same +/– buttons, learners can synchronize adjustments with the code panel by pressing "Check," which highlights updated variables in real time. This strengthens the link between code and output, fostering computational thinking and illustrating cause-effect relationships (Resnick et al., 2009).

3.6 Design Principles and Educational Goals

The system follows these educational principles:

- **Embodied Learning:** Promotes physical interaction to enhance cognitive processing (Johnson-Glenberg, 2018).
- **Immediate Feedback:** Links actions to outcomes through dynamic visual updates.
- **Constructivist Engagement:** Encourages active exploration and variable manipulation (Papert, 1980).
- **Dual Coding:** Combines textual, visual, and kinesthetic inputs to support deeper learning (Clark & Paivio, 1991).

These principles make abstract mathematical and computational concepts more interactive and memorable, benefiting students with limited spatial reasoning or code visualization experience.

3.7 System Features and Learning Design Recap

The described MR system introduces an innovative approach to learning mathematics and programming through generative art. It utilizes Mixed Reality to immerse learners in dynamic 3D environments, where mathematical and code-based changes are instantly visualized.

The next chapter outlines the experimental evaluation, covering participant selection, testing tools, and data collection. It examines test performance, spatial representations, and learners' feedback.

4. Experiment

To investigate the educational potential of the MR learning system introduced in the previous section, we conducted a controlled experiment that combined quantitative and qualitative methods. This chapter outlines the experimental setup, procedures, and analytical approach used to evaluate the system's impact on spatial reasoning, geometric understanding, and user experience.

4.1 Research Objectives and Design

The experiment aimed to evaluate the effectiveness of a Mixed Reality (MR) learning system that combines generative art with mathematics and programming education. It focused on learners' understanding of 3D geometric concepts, spatial visualization, and their interaction experiences with the MR interface.

A within-subjects crossover design compared MR-based instruction with paper-based materials. Participants, divided into MR-first and paper-first groups, alternated between modalities. The study examined whether the MR system enhanced learning outcomes, improved 3D visualization skills, and influenced user perceptions of usability and learning effectiveness.

4.2 Participants

The study included 22 undergraduate students (17 male, 5 female) from a university in Japan, all were majoring in information science and had foundational knowledge of mathematics and programming, but no prior MR experience. Participants were divided into two groups: the MR-first group started with MR learning, followed by paper-based materials, while the paper-first group reversed this order. This crossover design enabled balanced comparisons, minimizing biases from prior knowledge or learning styles.

4.3 Experimental Procedure

Each participant conducted the experiment individually in a controlled setting, starting with the Mental Cutting Test (MCT) to assess spatial ability (Sorby, 2009), completing 25 items in 20 minutes. A pre-test followed, with five questions on the torus's volume, surface area, and properties, completed in two minutes.

In the first learning phase, MR participants took a tutorial to master hand gestures and object manipulation before exploring interactive math and programming modules. The paper-based group studied equivalent content via printed slides and diagrams.

Post-Test 1 assessed learning gains using different values from the pre-test and included a torus drawing task. Participants then switched modalities; MR-first learners moved to paper-based materials, and vice versa. Post-Test 2, which included another torus drawing task, was administered after the second phase. Finally, participants completed a usability questionnaire on interaction, interface, and learning efficacy.

4.4 Measures of Learning and Experience

To evaluate the learning interventions, both quantitative and qualitative measures were used:

- **Test Scores:** Pre-test and post-test scores (out of 5 points) assessed understanding and application of geometric formulas, highlighting improvements and differences between learning modalities.
- **Hand-Drawn Torus:** Drawings were evaluated by raters for three criteria: dimensionality, structural detail, and geometric fidelity to analyze spatial understanding.
- **MCT Results:** Participants were grouped into high and low spatial ability categories based on a 40% accuracy threshold, to examine modality effects on learning.
- **Usability Ratings:** A Likert-scale questionnaire measured ease of interaction and manipulation within the MR environment, with open-ended responses capturing user feedback on usability and educational value.

These measures provided comprehensive insights into both learning outcomes and user experiences.

4.5 Data Analysis Approach

Data were anonymized and analyzed using standard statistical methods: paired t-tests compared pre- and post-test scores, independent t-tests examined differences between MR and paper groups, F-tests assessed variance, and Kolmogorov–Smirnov tests were used to examine score normality.

Drawing analysis was conducted through inter-rater consensus for reliability, while usability survey responses were categorized into themes like interface ease, engagement, and cognitive benefits, offering a comprehensive view of learning outcomes and experiences.

4.6 Experimental Setup Recap

This experiment evaluated the educational impact of a Mixed Reality-based generative art system in geometry and programming. Using a mixed-methods approach, it assessed cognitive gains, spatial drawing, and user experiences. The next chapter details learners' responses to instructional formats and the MR system's influence on understanding, expression, and engagement.

5. Result

This chapter outlines the experimental results, focusing on four areas: (1) test score performance, (2) spatial representation through drawing, (3) the relationship between spatial ability and learning outcomes, and (4) learner feedback on the usability and educational value of the MR system. Findings are based on quantitative data and qualitative observations, demonstrating cognitive and experiential impacts.

5.1 Test Score Performance

Learners from both the MR-first and paper-first groups showed significant score improvements from pre-test to post-tests. MR-first participants improved from a mean score of 2.23 to 3.41 and 3.64, while paper-first participants progressed from 2.05 to 3.32 and 3.50. Paired t-tests confirmed all improvements were significant ($p < .05$). No notable differences were found between MR and paper-based methods, nor were any order effects observed, indicating comparable effectiveness in short-term knowledge acquisition across modalities.

5.2 Spatial Representation Through Drawing

Spatial representation tasks revealed key differences in visualization and expression. After the MR phase, most learners created detailed 3D drawings, including inner and outer radii and spatial depth, features often absent after the paper-based session. MR improved participants' ability to internalize and accurately represent the torus's form. Drawings were evaluated based on three dimensions: (1) dimensionality (2D profile vs. 3D depth), (2) structural accuracy (e.g., toroidal curvature and radii), and (3) geometric detail (such as correct axis orientation). These criteria ensured that improvements in illustration reflected conceptual understanding rather than drawing skill alone.

Figure 1 highlights this contrast, with MR-based drawings showing greater structural detail and dimensionality compared to flatter paper-based illustrations. Subjective feedback further supported this, with 86.4% of participants noting their MR-inspired drawings were "more three-dimensional" and reporting improved spatial understanding. These findings demonstrate MR's substantial impact on conceptualizing and externalizing spatial information.

5.3 Spatial Ability and Learning Outcomes

Participants were grouped by their Mental Cutting Test (MCT) scores to assess spatial cognition's impact on learning. While those with higher spatial ability performed better, both high- and low-ability groups showed comparable improvements, indicating learning gains across cognitive profiles.

Notably, the MR system provided added support for lower-ability learners, enabling them to create detailed 3D drawings of the torus. This suggests MR can function as a form of spatial scaffolding, providing perceptual anchors that reduce reliance on internal mental imagery, thus helping to level the playing field for learners with weaker spatial skills.

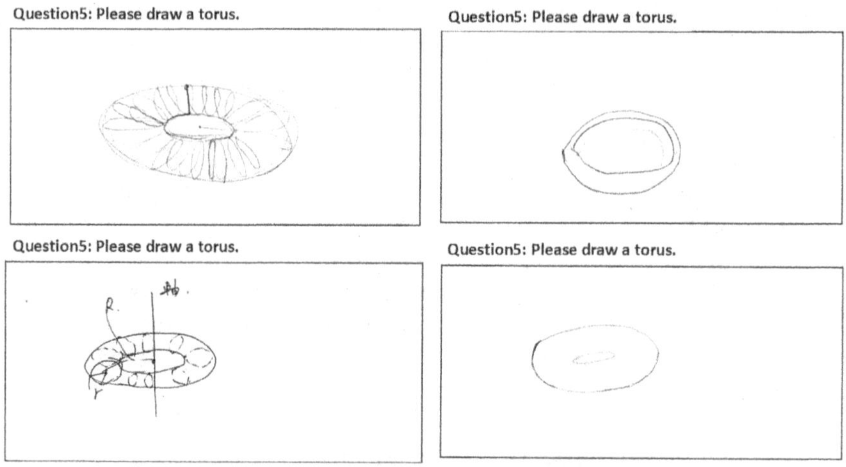

Fig. 1 Comparison of learner drawings after MR-based and paper-based instruction. The two drawings on the left were produced after the MR learning phase, while the two on the right followed the paper-based instruction. MR-based drawings exhibit clearer dimensionality, structural accuracy (e.g., toroidal curvature), and geometric detail, such as inner and outer radii. This contrast illustrates how Mixed Reality can enhance learners' ability to internalize and externalize complex 3D geometry, especially in terms of spatial understanding and representational fidelity.

5.4 Learner Experience and Usability Feedback

Participants generally praised the MR system, describing the interface as intuitive and enjoyable. Tasks like button pressing and rotating the 3D torus were highly rated, though object manipulation revealed minor issues with gesture recognition.

Learners strongly agreed that MR enhanced their understanding of the torus's structure and its connection to formulas, describing the experience as both immersive and novel. Many noted it clarified concepts they had struggled with. Although some cited technical issues like inconsistent hand tracking, these were minor inconveniences and did not diminish the system's value as a functional and engaging educational tool.

5.5 Main Findings and Insights

The study highlights the impact of MR on learning. While test scores showed similar improvements across methods, MR excelled in enhancing spatial visualization and representational accuracy. Learners demonstrated stronger 3D conceptualization, especially among those with lower spatial abilities, who benefited most from the immersive environment.

MR also fostered high engagement and satisfaction, emphasizing its role in sustaining interest and supporting STEM and STEAM education. Rather than replacing traditional methods, MR serves as a powerful supplementary tool, enriching accessibility and interactivity in the learning process.

These findings lay the foundation for designing adaptive MR learning tools tailored to learners' spatial profiles, as explored in the concluding chapter.

6. Discussion

This chapter interprets the study's findings, highlighting that while both MR and paper-based methods led to similar test score improvements, MR outperformed in spatial visualization, spatial expression, and learner engagement. These findings highlight the value of immersive technologies and generative art in modern mathematics and programming education.

6.1 Beyond Test Scores: The Value of Spatial Expression

Despite comparable test scores between MR and paper-based groups, MR showed clear advantages in representational skills, spatial reasoning, and creative engagement. Participants using MR produced more structurally detailed and spatially accurate 3D drawings, internalizing the torus's geometry deeply (Johnson-Glenberg, 2018; Clark & Paivio, 1991).

In response to Fowler's (2015) critique of pedagogical gaps in immersive technologies, the MR system integrates constructivist and experiential learning frameworks, serving as a cognitive scaffold for abstract concepts. It fosters understanding beyond standard tests, essential for mastering geometry and computational thinking.

The MR system also enhanced behavioral and emotional engagement, with students, particularly those with lower initial performance, showed increased persistence and curiosity. As Clements and Battista (1992) note, spatial learning varies by cognitive style, and MR environments offer adaptive pathways for diverse learner profiles, maximizing educational impact.

6.2 Mixed Reality as a Support for Low Spatial Ability Learners

Mixed Reality (MR) serves as a compensatory tool for learners with low spatial ability. Participants with lower scores on the Mental Cutting Test (MCT), who typically struggle to visualize 3D objects, were able to produce detailed and accurate drawings after using the MR system. By offloading cognitive demands onto manipulable 3D environments, MR helps bridge gaps in spatial skills and promotes equitable access to STEM education (Sorby, 2009).

This approach is particularly effective because learners no longer need to rely solely on internal mental imagery. Instead, they can externalize their thinking through guided interaction, making abstract geometry more accessible.

These results are consistent with findings by Uttal et al. (2013), who demonstrated that spatial reasoning can improve through targeted interventions. MR offers an immersive platform for such interventions by providing learners who struggle with traditional methods an alternative, experience-based pathway to geometric understanding.

6.3 Generative Art and Constructivist Learning

Generative art, a core feature of the MR system, visually demonstrates the impact of changes to mathematical and programming parameters. This directly aligns with constructionist learning theory, which emphasizes the creation of meaningful artifacts as a foundation for deep understanding (Papert, 1980). Through exploration, reflection, and iterative engagement, generative art fosters creative problem-solving and design thinking (Henriksen, 2014).

By integrating mathematics, programming, and artistic expression, generative art supports the aims of STEAM education. It brings together analytical and aesthetic thinking, allowing learners to combine logical reasoning with intuition and creativity (Yakman, 2008).

6.4 Engagement and Affective Outcomes

Positive feedback on the MR learning experience highlights its role in fostering affective engagement. Many participants enjoyed the 3D interactions, finding the process immersive and motivating, which are factors known to enhance cognitive effort and memory retention (Csikszentmihalyi, 1990). Several learners described the experience as "fun" or "memorable," indicating heightened emotional involvement and curiosity.

This aligns with Dede's (2009) argument that immersive interfaces boost engagement by enabling meaningful interactions. The MR system's intuitive design fosters flow-like learning states, making it a tool not only for understanding complex content but also for sustaining interest in mathematics and programming.

6.5 Limitations and Design Considerations

While promising, the study had limitations. The small sample size (n = 22) affects generalizability, requiring larger, diverse populations in future research. Some participants faced gesture recognition issues during object manipulation, underscoring the need for interface improvements like precise hand tracking and error tolerance. Advancements in MR hardware, such as AI-driven gesture recognition, are expected to enhance usability.

The study primarily focused on factual knowledge, which limited the assessment of deeper learning. Future research should include evaluations of higher-order cognitive skills, such as spatial reasoning, creative thinking, and long-term retention.

In line with findings by Ogunseiju et al. (2024), suboptimal interface design can increase cognitive load. To address this, improvements such as tiered interaction complexity, adaptive feedback mechanisms, and multimodal controls are recommended. These refinements can enhance user accessibility and reduce frustration during task performance.

6.6 *Implications for Educational Practice*

The study highlights MR combined with generative art and constructivist pedagogy as a powerful educational tool. Rather than replacing traditional methods, MR serves to enhance visualization, engagement, and creativity.

Its interdisciplinary nature, linking mathematics, programming, and design, makes it well-suited for STEAM curricula and project-based learning environments. As MR technology becomes more accessible, its integration can improve educational inclusivity and quality. Professional development and training programs will be crucial for effective classroom implementation, and teacher involvement in customizing content and facilitating learning could further amplify its impact in real-world settings.

7. Conclusion and Future Work

This study highlights the integration of Mixed Reality (MR) and generative art as a transformative model for interdisciplinary learning. While paper-based methods effectively teach factual content, MR enhances spatial understanding, engagement, and creativity, especially benefiting learners with lower spatial ability.

Empirical findings show MR improved spatial representation skills, with participants producing accurate 3D drawings and expressing greater motivation. Generative art further deepened conceptual connections through visual and interactive elements, supporting constructionist learning.

Despite its success, limitations include small sample size, short-term assessment, and interface challenges like gesture recognition. Future research should focus on longitudinal studies, scalability, and adaptive personalization. Expanding MR applications to subjects like physics, art, and architecture could uncover broader benefits.

Ultimately, MR and generative art are powerful educational tools, capable of reshaping how abstract and computational concepts are taught as the technology evolves.

Further Reading

For a detailed analysis of this research, refer to the original study: [DOI= 10.1109/COMPSAC61105.2024.00330].

Column 1: Drawing in 3D, Why Sketching Still Matters in the Digital Age

In an era of digital tools and immersive technologies, sketching remains essential in disciplines like mathematics, architecture, and engineering. Beyond mere illustration, it externalizes mental models and reinforces understanding, particularly after dynamic MR experiences. Drawing a torus challenges learners to translate immersive interactions into accurate 2D forms, highlighting internalized geometry.

This process supports "dual coding," which links verbal and visual information, and activates spatial reasoning, abstraction, and perspective skills vital for academic success and design thinking. Research shows that MR sessions enhance sketch accuracy, making drawing a reflective practice that complements immersive learning. While MR enables interaction with math, sketching captures its essence, bridging experience and conceptual clarity in contemporary education.

Column 2: Beyond Right Answers – Fostering Divergent Thinking through Code and Art

Traditional mathematics education prioritizes precision and correct answers, yet creativity is equally vital. Generative art transforms code into visual expressions, encouraging exploration and iteration rather than fixed solutions. This open-ended approach shifts focus from solving problems to creating meaning, empowering students as knowledge creators.

In a Mixed Reality setting, generative art allows real-time experimentation, where changes to code parameters dynamically alter 3D shapes. This fosters reflection and divergent thinking, which are essential for innovation, flexibility, and originality. Beyond technical skills, it cultivates human-centered design abilities that are relevant to diverse fields.

Generative art merges logic with imagination, turning classrooms into creative studios. By encouraging divergent thinking, it becomes an essential tool for integrating creativity into technical literacy and reshaping education.

16 Immersive Geography Education Through Digital Twins and Virtual Reality

1. Introduction

Geography education often relies on static tools like textbooks and maps, which struggle to represent the dynamic spatial, temporal, and environmental complexity. Traditional methods make it difficult to help learners intuitively and systematically understand complex geographic concepts such as river morphology over time, regional differences in climate, and spatial patterns of vegetation. For example, students may study landforms through words or photographs, yet find it hard to grasp how such features exist within real terrains, how they extend, slope, or connect within physical environments.

These instructional limitations can lead to fragmented understanding and difficulty in forming coherent mental models.

Virtual Reality (VR) and Digital Twins offer promising alternatives. VR creates interactive, sensory-rich environments for learners to explore, while Digital Twins replicate real-world conditions using live or historical data. Together, these technologies not only support comparative analysis and contextual learning but also allow learners to explore various regions, investigate terrain interactively, and observe seasonal or historical climate changes in virtual space. This approach enables dynamic engagement with geographical phenomena across both space and time.

Moreover, the integration of real-world geographic and climate datasets enhances the realism and educational validity of these experiences.

The study introduces the Digital Twin Learning System (DTLS), which integrates VR with data-driven models to teach geography. Focused on Japan's climate and topography, the system allows users to explore regions through detailed 3D simulations, fostering comparative analysis, reducing cognitive load, and increasing motivation. By combining immersive visualization with authentic geospatial data, DTLS aims to transform geography education—making abstract concepts tangible, explorable, and accessible to diverse learners.

2. Theoretical Background and Related Works

Geography education is shifting from fact-based instruction to inquiry-driven learning, moving beyond textbooks and static maps which often lead to fragmented understanding. Immersive technologies like Virtual Reality (VR) and Digital Twin systems provide tools to cultivate spatial thinking and curiosity.

DOI: 10.1201/9781003782735-20

Digital twins are dynamic virtual representations that are synchronized with real-world data. Initially developed for engineering, they now enhance education by enabling learners to explore realistic simulations grounded in authentic data (Negri, Fumagalli, & Macchi, 2017; Fuller et al., 2020). Sepasgozar (2020) found that digital twins improve understanding and engagement in construction education through interactive 3D city simulations.

In the context of geography, digital twins allow comparisons of features such as climate and vegetation across both space and time. The Digital Twin Learning System (DTLS) uses real data to simulate meteorological differences between locations like Hokkaido and Okinawa, offering immersive, first-person experiences that deepen spatial understanding and engagement.

This chapter discusses the pedagogical limitations of traditional geography instruction, reviews the capabilities of VR and digital twin systems, and outlines how experiential learning theory and spatial thinking principles inform the design of immersive learning environments like DTLS.

2.1 Limitations of Traditional Geography Education

Traditional geography education has typically focused on memorizing facts, such as "Hokkaido is cold" or "Shizuoka's river meanders," using simplified diagrams and maps that often result in shallow understanding (Lambert & Morgan, 2010). While field trips can offer richer insights, they are often constrained by cost and logistical challenges (Rickinson et al., 2004). This disconnect leaves students with abstract knowledge, failing to cultivate a meaningful "sense of place" or "geographical imagination" (Catling & Willy, 2018).

Static instruction lacks interactivity and does not effectively support learners in understanding how geographical phenomena manifest and interrelate in real-world contexts. For example, while students may learn about terrain types through text or photographs, they often struggle to visualize how these features exist and interact within a broader landscape.

Simulations can help address this gap by allowing learners to experience geographic phenomena directly. For instance, visualizing the climates of Hokkaido and Okinawa during winter using real weather data fosters vivid, sensory comparisons. These immersive experiences reduce cognitive load and enhance retention through spatial memory.

2.2 Virtual Reality in Geography Education

Virtual Reality (VR) immerses learners in virtual environments, enabling the exploration of otherwise inaccessible regions through interactive, first-person navigation. Instead of static visuals, students actively engage with geographic phenomena, which enhances understanding and spatial skills.

Maher and Buchanan (2021) found that 360° VR improved map skills and orientation, boosting engagement and conceptual clarity. Czimre, Mucsi, and Török (2024) conducted a systematic review that highlighted the role of VR in improving geographical thinking, motivation, and spatial awareness. They found that interactive VR environments are more effective than passive videos in promoting inquiry and retention (Czimre et al., 2024).

Supporting embodied learning (Johnson-Glenberg, 2018), VR activates sensory and motor pathways, which reinforces cognitive processing. This multimodal approach benefits younger learners by translating abstract concepts into tangible experiences.

2.3 *Digital Twins in Educational Contexts*

Digital twins amplify VR's immersive potential by introducing real-time, data-driven simulations, which reflect changes across timelines using sources like meteorological and geospatial data (Negri, Fumagalli, & Macchi, 2017). Initially developed for aerospace, this concept, formalized by Grieves and Vickers (2017), supports monitoring, analysis, and complex system similation, has now been extended into education.

In learning contexts, digital twins foster experiential and systems-based thinking. Sepasgozar (2020) demonstrated their effectiveness in construction education, showing improved engagement and mental modeling through interactive simulations. Applied to geography, digital twins enable learners to simulate and explore real-world conditions across different regions and time periods. The Digital Twin Learning System allows students to interact with climate and vegetation datasets from areas such as Hokkaido and Okinawa, rendering data through VR for immersive, comparative exploration.

These systems enable active inquiry. Learners manipulate variables like location or time, testing hypotheses and analyzing outcomes. This approach mirrors scientific investigation, bridging abstract geography concepts with lived, interactive experiences, fostering deeper understanding and higher-order thinking.

2.4 *Experiential Learning in Immersive Environments*

Immersive tools like VR and digital twins are grounded in experiential learning theory, in which Kolb (1984) outlines a cycle of experience, reflection, conceptualization, and experimentation. These technologies offer direct experiences followed by opportunities for analysis, enhancing learning.

Chin, Wang, and Chen (2019) found that augmented reality improved performance and motivation by enabling learners to visualize and solve abstract problems. Southgate (2020) demonstrated VR's ability to foster inquiry and engagement through immersive, learner-driven activities.

The Digital Twin Learning System supports this cycle by allowing students to explore geographic systems, simulate rainfall, and reflect on its impact, fostering deeper conceptual understanding through interactive and guided tasks.

2.5 *Spatial Thinking and the Role of Immersion*

Spatial thinking is a core component of geography education, involving visualization, geospatial data interpretation, and reasoning about scale and orientation (National

Research Council, 2006). Interactive simulations greatly enhance spatial reasoning. Ishikawa and Kastens (2005) showed significant improvements in children's spatial skills through navigable virtual environments, such as "flying" through landscapes or "walking" along rivers.

Building on Johnson-Glenberg's (2018) embodied learning principles, VR and digital twins link physical interaction with abstract content, enhancing memory and understanding. The Digital Twin Learning System immerses students in spatial tasks, like comparing regions or analyzing features, and creates rich cognitive scaffolds for transferable knowledge.

By immersing learners in tasks such as cross-regional comparisons, temporal analysis of weather data, and exploration of terrain, the Digital Twin Learning System builds rich cognitive scaffolds that support transfer of spatial knowledge to more advanced levels of geographic thinking.

3. System Design and Implementation

Immersive technologies like VR and Digital Twins offer significant advantages for geography education. Their integration requires sound design, technical robustness, and learner-friendly interfaces. This chapter details the Digital Twin Learning System's architecture and application, emphasizing regional analysis, experiential learning, and spatial reasoning grounded in real-world data.

Fig. 1 Interactive Climate and Topography Exploration

This figure illustrates the Digital Twin system's immersive representation of Hokkaido and Okinawa, enabling learners to compare regional differences in climate, vegetation, and landforms. The visualization integrates real weather data, such as temperature, wind, and precipitation, to dynamically simulate geographic phenomena. Users can switch between a bird's-eye view for wide-area comparisons and a first-person perspective for detailed terrain exploration, which is supported by PLATEAU 3D city models. This interactive interface allows learners to manipulate variables like time and environmental conditions, fostering a deeper understanding of spatial relationships and regional contrasts in Japan's diverse geography. By engaging learners with vivid simulations, the system bridges the gap between theoretical study and practical understanding of climate and topography. .

Specifically designed for Japanese elementary school students, the system combines 3D geospatial models with meteorological data to explore diverse climates and landscapes, particularly comparing Hokkaido's cold, snowy terrain with Okinawa's subtropical features. This enables learners to observe and compare geographic conditions in a realistic, interactive environment, fostering multisensory engagement with abstract concepts. Figure 1 illustrates this functionality.

3.1 Objectives and Design Principles

The Digital Twin Learning System was designed to foster spatial thinking through immersive visualization of geographies, promote experiential learning via dynamic data interaction, and support comparative regional analysis aligned with the Japanese curriculum, emphasizing reflection and inquiry. Specifically, the system allows learners to zoom, rotate, and navigate through geospatial terrains, observe seasonal variations in weather, and compare climatic conditions between regions.

These features are structured to encourage students to ask questions such as "Why is it snowing in one place but in another?" and "How might this affect people's lives?" Interfaces were simplified for elementary school students, prioritizing intuitive interaction. The system enables macro- and micro-level perspectives, grounded in real-world datasets for authenticity, and adaptable to diverse learning scenarios.

3.2 System Architecture Overview

The system architecture integrates components for data acquisition, simulation, rendering, and user interaction. Meteorological and topographic datasets from sources like the Japan Meteorological Agency are processed and fed into a simulation engine that dynamically adjusts visual parameters.

Rendered environments appear on a Unity3D-based platform, which manages spatial geometry, terrain textures, and weather effects. A user interface enables selection of regions, timeframes, and modes, with modular expansion allowing future additions of regions, data types, and features.

3.3 Digital Twin Development

The digital twins for Hokkaido and Okinawa integrate diverse data sources to support realistic simulations. Digital elevation models (DEMs) shape landforms, while satellite imagery and land classification data render vegetation and urban features. Meteorological data from the Japan Meteorological Agency (2018) provide real temperature, precipitation, and seasonal variations, ensuring that the simulations reflect authentic environmental conditions.

Each twin adapts to the selected time of year. For instance, January shows Hokkaido's snowy terrain and Okinawa's green subtropical landscape. Real-time data synchronization dynamically generates features, enhancing realism and encouraging evidence-based observations. This fidelity to real-world data helps learners develop scientific thinking skills, as they base interpretations and hypotheses on accurate, time-stamped environmental inputs.

3.4 Virtual Reality Integration

The system's VR functionality enhances engagement by enabling first-person exploration of regions like mountainous terrain or coastal plains. Head-tracking functionality ensures a natural viewing experience, while learners navigate using gaze-based interactions or controllers.

Interactive features include environmental pop-ups showing data like temperature and altitude. Users can seamlessly switch between VR and desktop modes, minimizing cognitive overload and motion sickness, especially for younger learners.

3.5 User Interface and Interaction Design

The interface design prioritized simplicity and clarity, based on user testing with students and teachers. A map-based selector lets users choose regions like Hokkaido or Okinawa, while a temporal slider adjusts conditions to reflect the selected date.

The comparison mode allows users to explore regions either side by side or through a toggle-based interface. Informational overlays and audio prompts offer contextual guidance, and reflective tasks prompt learners to analyze and synthesize their experience after exploration.

3.6 Application Scenario: Comparative Climate Exploration

One key use of the system is comparing regional climates, such as Hokkaido and Okinawa on a specific date, such as January 15th. The simulation generates realistic landscapes and conditions, such as snow-covered fields and clear skies in Hokkaido, and lush green terrain and light rainfall in Okinawa.

Through first-person exploration, students reflect on temperature contrasts and their impact on clothing, housing, and transportation, fostering analytical and empathetic engagement with geographic diversity, in alignment with curriculum standards. This comparative inquiry is not limited to environmental features but extends to understanding cultural adaptations and regional lifestyles, enriching learners' socio-geographic perspective.

4. Evaluation and Learning Outcomes

Immersive learning systems show promise in enhancing engagement and understanding, especially for abstract or spatial topics. This study evaluated the Digital Twin Learning System through experiments with elementary school and university students, analyzing methodology, outcomes, and differences in learning effects across age groups and modalities.

4.1 Elementary School Implementation

The classroom trial at a Japanese elementary school involved 27 students (10 fifth graders, 17 sixth graders) using monitors and a shared Meta Quest 2 VR headset to explore climate differences, river morphology, and vegetation zones.

Learning effectiveness, assessed via tests and questionnaires, showed significant improvement in vegetation knowledge (fifth grade: $t(9) = 3.074$, $p = 0.007$; sixth grade: $t(16) = 2.582$, $p = 0.01$), but no gains in climate or river morphology. These gains were particularly pronounced when students actively explored the 3D digital twin landscapes, such as forests and hills, during immersive sessions, in which they investigated and observed the distribution of plant life across different regions. Despite limited test score improvements, students rated the system highly for enjoyability (4.2/5), clarity (4.1), and ease of understanding across topics, highlighting its motivational and perceptual benefits.

4.2 University Student Experiment

An experiment with 20 university students (ages 19–24) compared VR-based learning to paper-based materials. Both groups showed significant improvements in river morphology (VR: $t(10) = -7.475$, $p < 0.001$; paper: $t(8) = -6.107$, $p < 0.001$), with no statistical difference in post-test scores ($t(18) = 1.906$, $p = 0.073$). However, VR-based learners, who explored terrain features by virtually walking through river valleys or over plateaus, produced more vivid, sensory-rich descriptions of river forms and landscape interactions. In contrast, paper-based responses tended to be shorter and more abstract.

Questionnaire findings favored VR, with 55% preferring it for enjoyment, visualization, and memorability, despite reported challenges such as motion sickness and control difficulties. The ability to investigate specific regions dynamically within a VR map allowed learners to internalize spatial relationships more intuitively than with static illustrations. These results highlight VR's potential for enhancing expressive learning through immersive experiences.

4.3 Comparative Summary and Reflections

The experiments showed varied outcomes for immersive learning. Elementary school students gained the most in motivation and perceived clarity, with measurable content mastery limited to vegetation. University students, while showing similar test score improvements as traditional methods, provided richer, self-generated explanations in river morphology, reflecting deeper engagement.

Consistent with research by Johnson-Glenberg (2018) and Southgate (2020), immersive environments foster learner agency and expressive exploration. VR participants often described their learning as a process of "discovering" patterns or features by moving through the landscape, akin to real-world fieldwork, such as when noticing changes in vegetation while virtually traveling from mountainous to coastal areas. This highlights how immersive learning aids inquiry-based exploration and internalizes spatial concepts in ways that static tools cannot replicate.

4.4 Summary of Findings

The evaluation of the Digital Twin Learning System showcased distinct strengths. Elementary school students reported high levels of enjoyment and clarity, favoring the immersive format over textbooks. While notable knowledge gains were seen mainly in vegetation topics, many students noted that "seeing and investigating places" helped them better understand why vegetation or climate varied across regions. The system boosted perceived comprehension and interest in climate, rivers, and vegetation.

University experiments revealed immersive learning's qualitative benefits. Though VR and paper-based methods yielded similar test score improvements, VR users provided richer, personalized explanations, demonstrating deeper engagement. Immersive, exploratory interaction with the digital twin environment made abstract geography content feel more real and meaningful, enhancing both motivation and expressive ability. The system enhanced motivation for younger learners and expressive skills for advanced students, highlighting the need for thoughtful integration, tailored scaffolding, and ongoing refinement to maximize its educational potential.

5. Discussion and Future Directions

The evaluation of the Digital Twin Learning System across both elementary school and university settings highlights its ability to enhance geographical understanding through immersive environments. The system supports both foundational and advanced levels of learning, with outcomes shaped by learner characteristics and instructional design.

This chapter examines these findings from both theoretical and practical perspectives, exploring how digital twin and VR technologies can help transform geography education. It also addresses implementation challenges and suggests future improvements for broader adoption.

5.1 Summary of Learning Outcomes and Reflections

Elementary school students found the immersive system more enjoyable and understandable than textbooks, with notable learning gains in vegetation topics. While climate and river improvements were less clear, observations showed increased engagement, curiosity, and discussion.

University students displayed marginal test score differences between VR and paper groups, but VR learners provided more vivid, context-specific explanations, particularly of the area of river morphology, which reflected deeper spatial understanding.

The system's immersive VR allowed learners to virtually stand in regions, explore landscapes, and experience seasonal dynamics. Combined with real data, this realistic interaction fostered personalized and meaningful geographic understanding. These first-person experiences, grounded in real-world maps, enabled learners to "investigate" and observe environments directly, rather than merely memorizing facts, leading to deeper, embodied comprehension.

5.2 Theoretical Interpretation: Experiential and Spatial Learning

These findings align with Kolb's (1984) experiential learning cycle, where concrete experience, reflection, and experimentation drive understanding. Johnson-Glenberg (2018) emphasizes that immersive environments activate multimodal cognitive pathways, enhancing memory and conceptual depth. In her framework, higher levels of bodily engagement, such as when learners explore terrain in first-person VR, are linked to improved conceptual retention, especially for spatially distributed information.

For university students, immersive systems fostered nuanced, self-constructed explanations, especially in river morphology. Elementary school students gained affective and perceptual benefits, with embodied sensations enhancing retention and discussion. Overall, immersive technologies, grounded in these theories, promote engagement and deeper spatial understanding when paired with reflection and active inquiry.

5.3 Practical Challenges and Instructional Design Considerations

While the system showcased pedagogical strengths, challenges in VR usability emerged, particularly for younger learners unfamiliar with navigation tools. Discomfort and disorientation, common in VR studies, were mitigated by pairing students to share a VR headset with mirrored visuals on a monitor, enabling collaborative discussion and reducing fatigue.

The paired-use approach proved effective for engagement and equitable access, offering a practical model for limited-resource settings. However, instructional scaffolding was vital, with pre-session guidance and structured tasks ensuring that immersive observations were aligned with curriculum goals. Teachers noted excitement often diverted focus, which required facilitation to emphasize meaningful inquiry.

Hardware availability remains a constraint. To scale, future iterations should integrate flexible modes, such as touchscreens and desktop platforms, to balance interactivity and accessibility. Immersive technologies must function as part of a comprehensive instructional ecosystem, rather than as standalone tools.

5.4 Implications for Curriculum and Future Development

The integration of VR and digital twin systems into geography education transforms learning by replacing static tools like maps with dynamic, embodied, and inquiry-driven experiences. VR enables experiential engagement, allowing learners to feel as if they are present in terrains and understand their influence on factors like climate and human settlement. Digital twins, using real-world data, allow exploration of seasonal and spatial dynamics over time (Catling & Willy, 2018).

This dual approach combines immersive presence with data accuracy, fostering exploration, hypothesis testing, and connecting geographic features to lived experience. While initially studied in professional training domains like construction, the cognitive and motivational benefits of data-driven, navigable environments apply equally to geography education. Sepasgozar (2020) highlights similar benefits in construction education, showing how digital twin systems enhance spatial understanding, motivation, and self-directed learning.

Future advancements should expand content coverage, improve accessibility, and train educators to integrate these tools into reflective, inquiry-based strategies, ensuring they support spatial thinking, empathy, and analytical reasoning across disciplines.

6. Conclusion

This study evaluated a Digital Twin Learning System integrating Virtual Reality (VR) and real-world data for immersive geography education. By allowing learners to explore regions like Hokkaido and Okinawa in spatially rich, interactive environments, the system aimed to make abstract geographic phenomena more tangible.

Two evaluations, one conducted with elementary school students and one with university students, revealed strong engagement, perceived clarity, and learning gains, particularly in vegetation knowledge among younger learners. University students demonstrated richer, personalized explanations, especially in river morphology, highlighting the system's ability to foster both comprehension and expressive skills.

The findings affirm that data-driven, immersive tools enhance spatial thinking, experiential learning, and learner agency. While measurable gains were most prominent in vegetation topics, subjective feedback and qualitative responses suggest that climate and terrain exploration also contributed to a richer sense of place and spatial awareness. By simulating seasonal dynamics and allowing first-person exploration, the system enabled learners to build meaningful connections between geographic features and lived experiences.

However, challenges like device usability, instructional scaffolding, and hardware access remain. Future work should address these barriers by developing curriculum-aligned modules, incorporating longitudinal weather datasets, and creating teacher training materials for effective implementation. These improvements would facilitate classroom adoption and maximize the system's educational potential.

With thoughtful integration, immersive technologies such as VR and digital twins can shift geography education from passive content delivery to active, inquiry-driven exploration. As the technology matures and becomes more accessible, it holds the potential to reshape how learners engage with place, scale, and environmental systems.

Column: The Digital Twin Classroom, Building a Bridge Between Data and Imagination

Imagine exploring Hokkaido's snowy valleys or Okinawa's subtropical, all from within the classroom. Digital twin technology turns this vision into reality, transforming geography education by making abstract concepts tangible.

A digital twin is a dynamic, data-driven replica of real-world places, integrating live or historical data. Combined with VR, it allows students to navigate environments, manipulate variables such as time or weather, and observe geographic processes firsthand.

This approach goes beyond traditional maps and charts, offering immersive experiences to foster spatial thinking and data literacy. Students interact with datasets, uncover patterns, and explore cause-effect relationships. They don't just learn that Hokkaido is colder than Okinawa, they discover the reasons behind it by examining altitude, latitude, and wind dynamics in the simulation.

Digital twins enable inquiry-based learning by bridging theoretical knowledge with lived experience. As these technologies become more accessible, they offer schools a cost-effective, immersive "field trip" into real environments, empowering a curious and data-literate generation of geographers.

Conclusion

Afterword: Shaping the Future of Learning and Interaction

As we conclude this exploration of Affective Learning, Affective Interaction, Serious Games, and XR and Beyond, it becomes evident that the fusion of emotion, interaction, immersion, and play is reshaping how we learn, interact, and solve problems. Each chapter in this book contributes to a broader narrative, weaving together cutting-edge research, innovative applications, and transformative ideas that redefine the role of technology in education and beyond.

Bridging Emotion and Learning

In the realm of Affective Learning, we have seen how intelligent systems can respond to and leverage human emotions to enhance education. From personalized tutoring systems that adapt to students' emotional states to avatars that bring online learning to life, these innovations highlight the importance of emotional engagement in driving meaningful learning outcomes. The incorporation of emotions into educational platforms is not merely about improving engagement; it is about creating systems that genuinely understand and support learners as human beings.

Interaction as a Catalyst for Change

The chapters on Affective Interaction delve deeper into the potential of emotional connections to drive behavior change and foster deeper learning. Pet-like artifacts with emotional expression encourage positive habits, while observation-based systems adapt to students' behaviors in real-time, creating personalized and effective learning experiences. Moreover, robots capable of empathic interactions push the boundaries of human-computer collaboration, offering a glimpse into a future where machines are not just tools but also partners in learning and growth.

Serious Games and XR: Play and Immersion with Purpose

The chapters on Serious Games demonstrate how gaming transcends entertainment to tackle societal challenges and impart crucial skills. From teaching responsible online behavior and anti-bullying awareness to training athletes in physical and

DOI: 10.1201/9781003782735-21

cognitive skills, these works illustrate the versatility and depth of educational games.

Complementing these efforts, the XR and Beyond section explores how virtual reality, mixed reality, and digital twins create deeply immersive learning environments. These chapters reveal how learners can visualize abstract concepts, simulate real-world systems, and experience spatial learning in entirely new ways. Together, serious games and XR technologies offer a compelling vision of the future—one in which learning is interactive, adaptive, and fully immersive.

A Vision for the Future

As we reflect on these chapters, a common theme emerges: the seamless integration of technology with human experience. This book is not just a collection of research; it is a call to action for educators, researchers, and technologists to envision and create the next generation of learning systems. The convergence of affective computing, serious games, and XR signals the beginning of a new era—one where learning is no longer confined to the classroom, but becomes an integral part of life, enriched by emotion, interaction, and immersive experience.

In the years to come, we anticipate even greater advancements. Imagine games that dynamically adapt to a player's emotions in real-time, creating deeply personalized learning experiences. Picture robots that not only assist with tasks but also inspire and motivate learners through genuine emotional understanding. Envision virtual environments enhanced by XR, where students can explore scientific concepts, practice skills in lifelike simulations, and learn through rich sensory experiences powered by digital twins and real-time interaction.

Beyond Education

The implications of these innovations extend far beyond the classroom. Affective technologies, serious games, and XR have the potential to revolutionize fields as diverse as healthcare, corporate training, and even disaster response. By tapping into the power of emotion and interaction, we can create systems that are not only efficient but also empathetic—systems that understand us, adapt to us, and grow with us.

Final Reflections

As we close this journey, we are reminded of the immense potential that lies at the intersection of technology, emotion, and learning. This book is but a stepping stone in an ongoing exploration, offering a glimpse into what is possible when we harness the power of human connection and technological innovation. The future of education, and indeed society itself, will be shaped by these advancements. It is our hope that the ideas and insights presented here will inspire further exploration, innovation, and collaboration in this exciting field.

Let us move forward with curiosity, creativity, and a commitment to harnessing the power of technology to create a better, more connected world, where learning is not just a task but a transformative experience that enriches lives and builds futures.

Acknowledgments

The Kaoru Sumi Laboratory, based in Japan at Future University Hakodate, focuses on a wide range of research areas including affective computing, persuasive technology, Human-Agent Interaction, the Metaverse, Interactive Digital Storytelling, Serious Games, Intelligent Systems, Artificial Intelligence, and Educational Technologies.

I would like to express my deepest appreciation to all contributors from the Kaoru Sumi Laboratory, whose research has provided the foundation for the chapters in this volume.

Individual Chapter Contributions

Chapter 1 was written and contributed by Dr. Thomas James Tiam-Lee of the College of Computer Studies, De La Salle University (Philippines). The work is based on his doctoral research, which I had the privilege to supervise. He joined the lab from the Philippines and engaged in close collaboration during his studies. His research received multiple awards at international conferences, underscoring its academic impact and excellence. I am sincerely grateful for his substantial contributions.

Chapter 2 draws upon undergraduate thesis research by Ms. Hina Nozawa. Despite conducting her study under remote conditions, she demonstrated resilience and academic rigor, for which I offer my heartfelt appreciation.

Chapter 3 builds in part on research by Mr. Shusuke Sato, including his undergraduate thesis and later collaborative projects. His dedication contributed greatly to the chapter and was recognized with an international conference award. I truly value his efforts.

Chapter 4 reflects the work of Ms. Rio Harada, who was involved in both undergraduate research and subsequent collaborations. Her work was honored at a domestic academic workshop, reflecting its practical relevance and quality. I appreciate her contributions deeply.

Chapter 5 is based on research by Dr. Ahmed Salem, encompassing his doctoral studies and subsequent collaborative publications. He joined the lab from Egypt and worked diligently throughout his degree. He has continued to contribute to ongoing projects after graduation, demonstrating exceptional commitment to research.

Chapter 6 was written by Dr. Nitchan Jianwattanapaisarn of the Interaction Science Laboratories, ATR (Japan). The chapter is based on his doctoral work, which I supervised. Originally from Thailand, he conducted his research with sincerity and focus. He now continues his academic journey in Japan at a leading research institution. I am grateful for his valuable contributions.

Chapter 7 was authored by Dr. Pinkie Anggia, based on research during her doctoral studies under my supervision. Her work brought an international and cross-cultural dimension to the project, which enriched the results. I am thankful for her insightful and rigorous contributions.

Chapter 8 is rooted in research by Mr. Kodai Kasai, who completed an undergraduate thesis and joined collaborative efforts thereafter. His work received an award at an application development contest, demonstrating its innovation and practical value.

Chapter 9 incorporates research by Ms. Ayaka Kazuhara. Her undergraduate thesis, recognized with the highest award at an application contest, showcased her creativity and technical excellence.

Chapter 10 draws upon the thesis of Mr. Ryoma Tanabe. His project was awarded an Encouragement Prize at a development contest, highlighting its originality and promise. I appreciate his effort and perspective.

Chapter 11 builds on contributions by Mr. Yuki Tsukamoto, spanning both undergraduate and master's theses, as well as academic publications. His work, awarded at a domestic academic conference, demonstrates strong scholarly merit.

Chapter 12 includes research by Mr. Ryo Okuyama, who brought dedication and a sports background to his work on virtual training. His practical perspective, informed by his experience as a handball player, added unique value.

Chapter 13 is based on research by Mr. Shogo Hirai. His careful and sincere approach to both his undergraduate and master's research resulted in significant contributions, for which I am truly grateful.

Chapter 14 draws upon work by Ms. Himari Kanazawa. She demonstrated strong technical ability and versatility, and has since begun her professional career in the metaverse industry.

Chapter 15 builds on research by Mr. Shun Furuichi. His continued dedication to his studies and collaborative work is commendable, and I look forward to his future accomplishments.

Chapter 16 draws from undergraduate research by Mr. Aito Nio. His diligence and perseverance were evident throughout the project, and his work is sincerely appreciated.

Collective Contributions and Institutional Support

Through close collaboration with these contributors, many research ideas were born, and their outcomes have seeded future innovations in the field.

I would also like to express my heartfelt thanks to the elementary and junior high schools in Hakodate City and to the students who participated in our user studies. Their cooperation was essential to evaluating the educational technologies discussed in this volume.

I am especially grateful to the editorial and production teams for their patience and support throughout the publication process. Their professionalism made it possible to bring this volume to completion, despite delays in manuscript submission.

References

Chapter 1

Arnold, K.E. and Pistilli, M.D. (2012, April). Course signals at Purdue: Using learning analytics to increase student success. In *Proceedings of the 2nd International Conference on Learning Analytics and Knowledge* (pp. 267–270). ACM.

Baker, R.S. (2016). Stupid tutoring systems, intelligent humans. *International Journal of Artificial Intelligence in Education*, 26(2), 600–614.

Barros, J.P., Estevens, L., Dias, R., Pais, R. and Soeiro, E. (2003). Using lab exams to ensure programming practice in an introductory programming course. *ACM SIGCSE Bulletin*, 35(3), 16–20.

Bloom, B.S. (1984). The 2 sigma problem: The search for methods of group instruction as effective as one-to-one tutoring. *Educational Researcher*, 13(6), 4–16.

Bosch, N., Chen, Y. and D'Mello, S. (2014, June). It's written on your face: Detecting affective states from facial expressions while learning computer programming. In *International Conference on Intelligent Tutoring Systems* (pp. 39–44). Springer, Cham.

Bosch, N. and D'Mello, S. (2017). The affective experience of novice computer programmers. *International Journal of Artificial Intelligence in Education*, 27(1), 181–206.

Chen, H.T.T. (2019). Investigating the effects of web-based instant response system on learning and teaching in pre-service teacher courses. In M. Chang, D. Sampson and N.-S. Chen (Eds.), *Shaping the future of education, communication and technology* (pp. 141–151). Springer.

Cho, M.H. and Heron, M.L. (2015). Self-regulated learning: The role of motivation, emotion, and use of learning strategies in students' learning experiences in a self-paced online mathematics course. *Distance Education*, 36(1), 80–99.

Daniels, L.M., Stupnisky, R.H., Pekrun, R., Haynes, T.L., Perry, R.P. and Newall, N. E. (2009). A longitudinal analysis of achievement goals: From affective antecedents to emotional effects and achievement outcomes. *Journal of Educational Psychology*, 101(4), 948–963.

Ekman, P. and Friesen, W.V. (2003). Unmasking the face: A guide to recognizing emotions from facial clues. Ishk.

Feidakis, M. (2016). A review of emotion-aware systems for e-learning in virtual environments. In D. Ifenthaler, N. Bellin-Mularski and D.-K. Mah (Eds.), *Formative assessment, learning data analytics and gamification* (pp. 217–242). Academic Press.

Grafsgaard, J.F., Boyer, K.E. and Lester, J.C. (2011, October). Predicting facial indicators of confusion with hidden Markov models. In *International Conference on Affective Computing and Intelligent Interaction* (pp. 97–106). Springer.

Holstein, K., McLaren, B.M. and Aleven, V. (2018, June). Student learning benefits of a mixed-reality teacher awareness tool in AI-enhanced classrooms. In *International Conference on Artificial Intelligence in Education* (pp. 154–168). Springer.

Mega, C., Ronconi, L. and De Beni, R. (2014). What makes a good student? How emotions, self-regulated learning, and motivation contribute to academic achievement. *Journal of Educational Psychology*, 106(1), 121–131.

Mori, M., MacDorman, K.F. and Kageki, N. (2012). The uncanny valley [From the field]. *IEEE Robotics & Automation Magazine*, 19(2), 98–100.

Nkambou, R., Mizoguchi, R. and Bourdeau, J. (Eds.). (2010). *Advances in intelligent tutoring systems* (Vol. 308). Springer.

Ocumpaugh, J. (2015). Baker Rodrigo Ocumpaugh Monitoring Protocol (BROMP) 2.0 Technical and Training Manual. Teachers College, Columbia University and Ateneo Laboratory for the Learning Sciences.

Rodrigo, M.M.T., Baker, R.S., Jadud, M.C., Amarra, A.C.M., Dy, T., Espejo-Lahoz, M.B.V. and Tabanao, E.S. (2009, July). Affective and behavioral predictors of novice programmer achievement. In *ACM SIGCSE Bulletin* (Vol. 41, No. 3, pp. 156–160). ACM.

Tiam-Lee, T.J. and Sumi, K. (2017). A comparison of Filipino and Japanese facial expressions and hand gestures in relation to affective states in programming sessions. In *Workshop on Computation: Theory and Practice.*

Tiam-Lee, T.J. and Sumi, K. (2018a, June). Adaptive feedback based on student emotion in a system for programming practice. In *International Conference on Intelligent Tutoring Systems* (pp. 243–255). Springer, Cham.

Tiam-Lee, T.J. and Sumi, K. (2018b). Generating abstract and real-world coding exercises with adjustable difficulty. In *International Conference on Computers in Education.*

Tiam-Lee, T.J. and Sumi, K. (2019, June). Analysis and prediction of student emotions while doing programming exercises. In *International Conference on Intelligent Tutoring Systems* (pp. 24–33). Springer, Cham.

VanLehn, K. (2011). The relative effectiveness of human tutoring, intelligent tutoring systems, and other tutoring systems. *Educational Psychologist*, 46(4), 197–221.

Chapter 2

Bagès, C., Verniers, C. and Martinot, D. (2016). Virtues of a hardworking role model to improve girls' mathematics performance. *Psychology of Women Quarterly*, 40(1), 55–64. https://doi.org/10.1177/0361684315608842.

Bandura, A. (1977). Self-efficacy: Toward a unifying theory of behavioral change. *Psychological Review*, 84(2), 191–215. https://doi.org/10.1037/0033-295X.84.2.191.

Baylor, A.L., Kim, Y. (2004). Pedagogical Agent Design: The Impact of Agent Realism, Gender, Ethnicity, and Instructional Role. In: Lester, J.C., Vicari, R.M., Paraguaçu, F. (eds) Intelligent Tutoring Systems. ITS 2004. Lecture Notes in Computer Science, vol 3220. Springer, Berlin, Heidelberg. https://doi.org/10.1007/978-3-540-30139-4_56

Bem, D.J. (1972). Self-perception theory. In L. Berkowitz (Ed.), *Advances in experimental social psychology* (Vol. 6, pp. 1–62). Academic Press.

Biocca, F., Harms, C. and Gregg, J. (2001). The Networked Minds Measure of Social Presence: Pilot Test of the Factor Structure and Concurrent Validity. *Proceedings of the Fourth Annual International Workshop on Presence* (PRESENCE 2001), 1–9.

Chang, F., Luo, M., Walton, G., Aguilar, L. and Bailenson, J. (2019). Stereotype threat in virtual learning environments: Effects of avatar gender and sexist behavior on women's math learning outcomes. *Cyberpsychology, Behavior, and Social Networking*, 22(10), 640–648. https://doi.org/10.1089/cyber.2019.0106.

D'Mello, S. and Graesser, A. (2012). Dynamics of affective states during complex learning. *Learning and Instruction*, 22(2), 145–157. https://doi.org/10.1016/j.learninstruc.2011.10.001.

Hudlicka, E. (2003). To feel or not to feel: The role of affect in human–computer interaction. *International Journal of Human-Computer Studies*, 59(1–2), 1–32. https://doi.org/10.1016/S1071-5819(03)00047-8.

Kao, D. and Harrell, D.F. (2017). MazeStar: A platform for studying virtual identity and computer science education, *Proceedings of the 12th International Conference on the Foundations of Digital Games*.

Kim, Y. and Baylor, A.L. (2006). A social-cognitive framework for pedagogical agents as learning companions. *Educational Technology Research and Development*, 54(6), 569–596. https://doi.org/10.1007/s11423-006-0637-3.

Krämer, N.C., Simons, N. and Kopp, S. (2007). The effects of an embodied agent's nonverbal behavior on users' evaluation and behavioral mimicry. In C. Pelachaud, J.-C. Martin, E. André, G. Chollet, K. Karpouzis, & D. Pelé (Eds.), *Intelligent Virtual Agents* (pp. 238–251). Springer.

Makransky, G. and Mayer, R.E. (2022). Benefits of Taking a Virtual Field Trip in Immersive Virtual Reality: Evidence for the Immersion Principle in Multimedia Learning. *Educational Psychology Review*, 34, 1771–1798.

McQuiggan, S.W., Mott, B.W. and Lester, J.C. (2008). Modeling self-efficacy in intelligent tutoring systems: An inductive approach. *User Modeling and User-Adapted Interaction*, 18(1–2), 81–123.

Moreno, R., Mayer, R.E., Spires, H.A. and Lester, J.C. (2010). The case for social agency in computer-based teaching: Do students learn more deeply when they interact with animated pedagogical agents? *Cognition and Instruction*, 19(2), 177–213. https://doi.org/10.1207/S1532690XCI1902_02

Oh, C.S., Bailenson, J.N. and Welch, G.F. (2018). A systematic review of social presence: Definition, antecedents, and implications. *Frontiers in Robotics and AI*, 5, 114. https://doi.org/10.3389/frobt.2018.00114

Picard, R.W. (1997). Affective computing. MIT Press.

Rosenberg-Kima, R.B., Baylor, A.L., Plant, E.A. and Doerr, C.E. (2008). Interface agents as social models for female students: The effects of agent visual presence and appearance on beliefs, self-efficacy, and learning. *Journal of Educational Psychology*, 100(2), 272–281.

Schwarzer, R. and Jerusalem, M. (1995). Generalized Self-Efficacy Scale. In J. Weinman, S. Wright and M. Johnston (Eds.), *Measures in health psychology: A user's portfolio* (pp. 35–37). NFER-Nelson.

Short, J., Williams, E. and Christie, B. (1976). *The social psychology of telecommunications*. John Wiley & Sons.

Steele, C.M. (2010). Whistling Vivaldi: How stereotypes affect us and what we can do. W.W. Norton & Company.

Tajfel, H. and Turner, J.C. (2004). The Social Identity Theory of Intergroup Behavior. In J.T. Jost & J. Sidanius (Eds.), *Political psychology: Key readings* (pp. 276–293). Psychology Press. https://doi.org/10.4324/9780203505984-16

Yee, N. and Bailenson, J. (2007). The Proteus effect: The effect of transformed self-representation on behavior. *Human Communication Research*, 33(3), 271–290. https://doi.org/10.1111/j.1468-2958.2007.00299.x.

Chapter 3

Anne, P. M. and Huntley, C. (2004). Dramatica: A New Theory of Story. *Dramatica: A new theory of story*.

Booth, M. (2009). The AI systems of Left 4 Dead. *Artificial Intelligence and Interactive Digital Entertainment Conference (AIIDE)*.

Brierley, B., Medford, N., Shaw, P. and David, A. (2007). Emotional memory for words: Separating content and context. *Cognition & Emotion*, 21(3), 495–521. https://doi.org/10.1080/02699930600684963

Cavazza, M., Pizzi, D., Charles, F., Vogt, T. and André, E. (2009). Emotional input for character-based interactive storytelling. *Proceedings of the Eighth International Conference on Autonomous Agents and Multiagent Systems (AAMAS 2009)*, 10–15.

Chang, H.M. and Soo, V.W. (2009). Planning-based narrative generation in simulated game universes. *IEEE Transactions on Computational Intelligence and AI in Games*, 1(3), 200–213. https://doi.org/10.1109/TCIAIG.2009.2034638

Dehn, N. (1981). Story generation after TALE-SPIN. *Proceedings of the 7th International Joint Conference on Artificial Intelligence (IJCAI)*, 16–18.

D'Mello, S. and Graesser, A. (2013). AutoTutor and affective AutoTutor: Learning by talking with cognitively and emotionally intelligent computers that talk back. *ACM Transactions on Interactive Intelligent Systems*, 2(4), 1–39. https://doi.org/10.1145/2395123.2395128

Eger, M., Potts, C.M., Barot, C. and Young, R.M. (2015). Plotter: Operationalizing the master book of all plots. *Proceedings of the AIIDE Conference.*

Ekman, P. and Friesen, W.V. (1977). Facial action coding system (FACS). *Consulting Psychologists Press.*

Ferré, P., Fraga, I., Comesaña, M. and Sánchez-Casas, R. (2015). Memory for emotional words: The role of semantic relatedness, encoding task and affective valence. *Cognition & Emotion*, 29(8), 1401–1410. https://doi.org/10.1080/02699931.2014.982515

Gilroy, S., Porteous, J., Charles, F. and Cavazza, M. (2012). Exploring passive user interaction for adaptive narratives. *Proceedings of the International Conference on Intelligent User Interfaces (IUI 2012)*, 119–128. https://doi.org/10.1145/2166966.2166990

Hernandez, S.P., Bulitko, V. and Hilaire, E.S. (2014). Emotion-based interactive storytelling with artificial intelligence. *Proceedings of the 10th AAAI Conference on Artificial Intelligence and Interactive Digital Entertainment (AIIDE 2014)*, 146–152.

Immordino-Yang, M.H. and Damasio, A. (2007). We feel, therefore we learn: The relevance of affective and social neuroscience to education. *Mind, Brain, and Education*, 1(1), 3–10. https://doi.org/10.1111/j.1751-228X.2007.00004.x

Kapp, K.M. (2012). The gamification of learning and instruction: game-based methods and strategies for training and education. John Wiley & Sons.

Kaptein, F. and Broekens, J. (2015). The affective storyteller: Using character emotion to influence narrative generation. *Proceedings of the International Conference on Affective Computing and Intelligent Interaction* (ACII 2015), 352–355. https://doi.org/10.1007/978-3-319-21996-7_38

Kolb, D. A. (2014). Experiential learning: Experience as the source of learning and development. FT press.

Kotsia, I., Zafeiriou, S., Goudelis, G., Patras, I. and Karpouzis, K. (2016). Multimodal sensing in affective gaming. *Emotion in Games: Theory and Praxis*, 59-84.

León, C. and Gervás, P. (2014). Creativity in story generation from the ground up: Non-deterministic simulation driven by narrative. *Proceedings of the International Conference on Computational Creativity (ICCC 2014).*

Lopes, P., Liapis, A. and Yannakakis, G. (2015). Targeting horror via level and soundscape generation. In *Proceedings of the AAAI Conference on Artificial Intelligence and Interactive Digital Entertainment* (Vol. 11, No. 1, pp. 37-43).

Magdin, M. and Prikler, F. (2017). Real-time facial expression recognition using webcam and SDK Affectiva. *International Journal of Interactive Multimedia and Artificial Intelligence*, 1(2), 1–7. https://doi.org/10.9781/ijimai.2017.11.002

Mateas, M. and Stern, A. (2003). Mateas, M. and Stern, A. (2003). Façade: An Experiment in Building a Fully-Realized Interactive Drama. *Proceedings of the ACM SIGCHI Conference on Human Factors in Computing Systems (CHI 2003).*

O'Neill, B., Riedl, M. (2016). Emotion-Driven Narrative Generation. In: Karpouzis, K., Yannakakis, G. (eds) Emotion in Games. *Socio-Affective Computing*, Vol 4. Springer, Cham. https://doi.org/10.1007/978-3-319-41316-7_10.

Pekrun, R. (2006). The control-value theory of achievement emotions: Assumptions, corollaries, and implications for educational research and practice. *Educational psychology review*, 18, 315-341.

Picard, R.W. (1997). *Affective computing*. MIT Press.
Plass, J.L., Mayer, R.E. and Homer, B.D. (2020). *Handbook of game-based learning*. MIT Press.
Pérez y Pérez, R. (2014). From MEXICA to MEXICA-Impro: The evolution of a computer model for plot generation. In *Computational Creativity Research: Towards Creative Machines* (pp. 267–284). Paris: Atlantis Press.
Rashkin, H., Celikyilmaz, A., Choi, Y. and Gao, J. (2020). PlotMachines: Outline-conditioned generation with dynamic plot state tracking. arXiv preprint arXiv:2004.14967.
Schmidt, S.R. (2012). Memory for emotional words in sentences: The importance of emotional contrast. *Cognition & Emotion*, 26(6), 1015–1035. https://doi.org/10.1080/02699931.2011.631986.
Sousa, R. (2000). Book Reviews: Artificial intelligence and literary creativity: Inside the mind of BRUTUS, a storytelling machine. *Computational Linguistics*, 26(4).
Sumi, K. and Sato, S. (2022). Experiences of game-based learning and reviewing history of the experience using player's emotions. *Frontiers in Artificial Intelligence*, 5, Article 874106. https://doi.org/10.3389/frai.2022.874106.
Yannakakis, G.N. and Togelius, J. (2011). Experience-driven procedural content generation. *IEEE Transactions on Affective Computing*, 2(3), 147–161. https://doi.org/10.1109/T-AFFC.2011.6.

Chapter 4

Batson, C.D. (1991). The Altruism Question: Toward A Social-psychological Answer (1st ed.). *Psychology Press*. https://doi.org/10.4324/9781315808048.
Breazeal, C. (2003). Emotion and sociable humanoid robots. *International Journal of Human-Computer Studies*, 59(1–2), 119-155. https://doi.org/10.1016/S1071-5819(03)00018-1.
Davis, M.H. (1996). Empathy: A Social Psychological Approach (1st ed.). *Routledge*. https://doi.org/10.4324/9780429493898.
D'Mello, S.K. and Graesser, A.C. (2012). *AutoTutor and affective AutoTutor: Learning by talking with cognitively and emotionally intelligent computers that talk back.* ACM Transactions on Interactive Intelligent Systems (TiiS), 2(4), 1–39. https://doi.org/10.1145/2395123.2395128.
Fogg, B.J. (2002). Persuasive technology: using computers to change what we think and do. Ubiquity 2002, December, Article 5 (December 1–December 31, 2002), 32 pages. https://doi.org/10.1145/764008.763957.
Fujita, M. (2000). AIBO: Toward the era of digital creatures. *The International Journal of Robotics Research*, 20(10), 781–794. https://doi.org/10.1177/02783640122068092.
Heerink, M., Kröse, B., Evers, V. and Wielinga, B. (2010). Assessing acceptance of assistive social agent technology by older adults: The Almere model. *International Journal of Social Robotics*, 2(4), 361–375. https://doi.org/10.1007/s12369-010-0068-5.
Lakatos G, Gácsi M, Konok V, Brúder I, Bereczky B, Korondi P, et al. (2014). *Emotion Attribution to a Non-Humanoid Robot in Different Social Situations*. PLoS ONE 9(12): e114207. https://doi.org/10.1371/journal.pone.0114207.
Maginnity, M.E. and Grace, R.C. (2014). Visual perspective taking by dogs (Canis familiaris) in a Guesser-Knower task: Evidence for canine theory of mind? *Animal Cognition*, 17(6), 1375–1392. https://doi.org/10.1007/s10071-014-0773-9.
Miklósi, Á., Polgárdi, R., Topál, J. and Csányi, V. (2000). Intentional behavior in dog-human communication: An experimental analysis of "showing" behavior in the dog. *Animal Cognition*, 3(3), 159-166. https://doi.org/10.1007/s100710000072.
Picard, R.W. (1997). *Affective computing*. MIT Press.
Robinson, H., MacDonald, B. and Broadbent, E. (2014). The role of healthcare robots for older people at home: A review. *International Journal of Social Robotics*, 6(4), 575–591. https://doi.org/10.1007/s12369-014-0242-2.

Shibata, T. and Wada, K. (2011). *Robot therapy: A new approach for mental healthcare of the elderly – A mini-review. Gerontology*, 57(4), 378–386. https://doi.org/10.1159/000319015.

Tamura, T., Yonemitsu, S., Itoh, A., Oikawa, D., Kawakami, A., Higashi, Y., Fujimo, H. and Nakajima, K. (2004). Is an entertainment robot useful in the care of elderly people with severe dementia? *The Journals of Gerontology: Series A*, 59(1), M83-M85. https://doi.org/10.1093/gerona/59.1.M83.

Wada, K., Shibata, T., Saito, T., Sakamoto, K. and Tanie, K. (2005). Robot-assisted activity for elderly people and nurses at a day service center. *Proceedings of the IEEE*, 92(11), 1780–1788. https://doi.org/10.1109/JPROC.2004.835378.

Wada, K. and Shibata, T. (2007). Living with seal robots – Its sociopsychological and physiological influences on the elderly at a care house. *IEEE Transactions on Robotics*, 23(5), 972–980. https://doi.org/10.1109/TRO.2007.906261.

Xu, B. and Chen, N.-S. (2020). Effects of teacher role on student engagement in WeChat-based online discussion learning. *Computers & Education*, 157, 103956. https://doi.org/10.1016/j.compedu.2020.103956.

Yamaji, Y., Miyake, T., Yoshiike, Y., De Silva, P.R.S. and Okada, M. (2011). STB: child-dependent sociable trash box. *International Journal of Social Robotics 3*, 359–370 (2011). https://doi.org/10.1007/s12369-011-0114-y.

Chapter 5

Bartneck, C. and Saerbeck, M. (2010). Expressive robots in education: Varying the degree of social supportive behavior of a robotic tutor. *Proceedings of the SIGCHI Conference on Human Factors in Computing Systems*, 1613–1622. https://doi.org/10.1145/1753326.1753567.

Bekele, E., Crittendon, J.A., Swanson, A., Sarkar, N., Warren, Z. E. and Weitlauf, A.S. (2014). Pilot clinical application of an adaptive robotic system for young children with autism. *Autism*, 18(5), 598–608. https://doi.org/10.1177/1362361313479454.

Belpaeme, T., Kennedy, J., Ramachandran, A., Scassellati, B. and Tanaka, F. (2018). Social robots for education: A review. *Science Robotics*, 3(21), eaat5954. https://doi.org/10.1126/scirobotics.aat5954.

Bender, E.M., Gebru, T., McMillan-Major, A. and Shmitchell, S. (2021). On the Dangers of Stochastic Parrots: Can Language Models Be Too Big? In Proceedings of the 2021 ACM Conference on Fairness, Accountability, and Transparency (pp. 610–623). *Association for Computing Machinery*. https://doi.org/10.1145/3442188.3445922.

Brink, K.A. and Wellman, H.M. (2020). Robot teachers for children? Young children trust robots depending on their perceived accuracy and agency. *Developmental Psychology*, 56(7), 1268–1277. https://doi.org/10.1037/dev0000884

Buolamwini, J. and Gebru, T. (2018). Gender Shades: Intersectional Accuracy Disparities in Commercial Gender Classification. *Proceedings of Machine Learning Research*, 81, 77–91.

Cabibihan, J.-J., Javed, H., Ang, M. and Aljunied, S.M. (2013). Why robots? A survey on the roles and benefits of social robots in the therapy of children with autism. *International Journal of Social Robotics*, 5(4), 593–618. https://doi.org/10.1007/s12369-013-0202-2.

Calo, R. (2014). The case for a federal robotics commission. Brookings Institution. https://www.brookings.edu/articles/the-case-for-a-federal-robotics-commission/.

Cowie, R., Douglas-Cowie, E., Savvidou, S., McMahon, E., Sawey, M. and Schröder, M. (2000). 'FEELTRACE': An instrument for recording perceived emotion in real time. In *Proceedings of the ISCA Workshop on Speech and Emotion* (pp. 19–24). ISCA Archive.

Cramer, H.S.M., Kemper, N.A., Amin, A. and Evers, V. (2009). The effects of robot touch and proactive behaviour on perceptions of human-robot interactions.

Davenport, T. and Kalakota, R. (2019). The potential for artificial intelligence in healthcare. *Future Healthcare Journal*, 6(2), 94–98. https://doi.org/10.7861/futurehosp.6-2-94.

Esposito, R., Rossi, A. and Rossi, S. (2024). Deception in HRI and its Implications: a Systematic Review. ACM Transactions on Human-Robot Interaction.

FitzGerald, E., Jones, A., Kucirkova, N. and Scanlon, E. (2018). A literature synthesis of personalised technology-enhanced learning: What works and why. *Research in Learning Technology*, 26. https://doi.org/10.25304/rlt.v26.2095.

Gordon, G., Breazeal, C. and Engel, S. (2015). Can children catch curiosity from a social robot? In *Proceedings of the 10th ACM/IEEE International Conference on Human-Robot Interaction* (pp. 91–98). https://doi.org/10.1145/2696454.2696469.

Howard, A. and Borenstein, J. (2017). The ugly truth about ourselves and our robot creations: The problem of bias and social inequity. *Science and Engineering Ethics*, 24(5), 1521–1536. https://doi.org/10.1007/s11948-017-9975-2.

In Proceedings of the 4th ACM/IEEE International Conference on Human-Robot Interaction (HRI '09) (pp. 275–276). Association for Computing Machinery. https://doi.org/10.1145/1514095.1514173.

Ji, Z., Lee, N., Frieske, R., Yu, T., Su, D., Xu, Y., Ishii, E., Bang, Y., Chen, D., Dai, W., Chan, H.S., Madotto, A. and Fung, P. (2023). Survey of hallucination in natural language generation. arXiv preprint arXiv:2202.03629. https://arxiv.org/abs/2202.03629.

Kanda, T., Hirano, T., Eaton, D. and Ishiguro, H. (2004). Interactive robots as social partners and peer tutors for children: A field trial. *Human–Computer Interaction*, 19(1 & 2), 61–84. https://doi.org/10.1207/s15327051hci1901&2_4.

Kennedy, J., Baxter, P. and Belpaeme, T. (2015). The robot who tried too hard: Social behaviour of a robot tutor can negatively affect child learning. In *Proceedings of the 10th ACM/IEEE International Conference on Human-Robot Interaction* (pp. 267–274). https://doi.org/10.1145/2696454.2696457.

Kory-Westlund, J.M. and Breazeal, C. (2019a). A long-term study of young children's rapport, social emulation, and language learning with a peer-like robot playmate in preschool. *Frontiers in Robotics and AI*, 6, 81. https://doi.org/10.3389/frobt.2019.00081.

Kory-Westlund, J.M. and Breazeal, C. (2019b). Exploring the effects of a social robot's speech entrainment and backstory on young children's emotion, rapport, relationship, and learning. *Frontiers in Robotics and AI*, 6, 54. https://doi.org/10.3389/frobt.2019.00054.

Leite, I., Castellano, G., Pereira, A., Martinho, C. and Paiva, A. (2014). Empathic robots for long-term interaction: evaluating social presence, engagement and perceived support in children. *International Journal of Social Robotics*, 6, 329–341.

Leite, I., Martinho, C. and Paiva, A. (2013). Social robots for long-term interaction: A survey. *International Journal of Social Robotics*, 5(2), 291–308. https://doi.org/10.1007/s12369-013-0178-y.

Leyzberg, D., Ramachandran, A. and Scassellati, B. (2018). The effect of personalization in longer-term robot tutoring. *ACM Transactions on Human-Robot Interaction*, 7(3), Article 19, 1–19. https://doi.org/10.1145/3283453.

Leyzberg, D., Spaulding, S. and Scassellati, B. (2014). Personalizing robot tutors to individuals' learning differences. In *Proceedings of the 2014 ACM/IEEE International Conference on Human-Robot Interaction* (pp. 423–430). https://doi.org/10.1145/2559636.2559671.

Luckin, R., Holmes, W., Griffiths, M. and Forcier, L.B. (2016). Intelligence Unleashed: An Argument for AI in Education.

Moise, I.M., Staicu, A.M., Dascălu, M.I. and Trausan-Matu, S. (2024). Towards integrating automatic emotion recognition in education: A deep learning model based on 5 EEG channels. Education and Information Technologies. *Advance online publication*. https://doi.org/10.1007/s44196-024-00638-x.

Ng, D.T.K., Leung, J.K.L., Chu, S.K.W. and Qiao, M.S. (2021). Conceptualizing AI literacy: An exploratory review. Computers and Education: *Artificial Intelligence*, 2, 100041. https://doi.org/10.1016/j.caeai.2021.100041.

Pennisi, P., Tonacci, A., Tartarisco, G., Billeci, L., Ruta, L., Gangemi, S. and Pioggia, G. (2015). Autism and social robotics: A systematic review. *Autism Research*, 9(2), 165–183. https://doi.org/10.1002/aur.1527.

Reich-Stiebert, N. and Eyssel, F. (2016). Robots in the classroom: What teachers think about teaching and learning with education robots. In A. Agah, J.J. Cabibihan, A.M. Howard, M.A. Salichs and H. He (Eds.), *Social Robotics: ICSR 2016* (pp. 671–680). Springer. https://doi.org/10.1007/978-3-319-47437-3_66.

Rosenthal-von der Pütten, A.M. and Bock, N. (2018). Development and validation of the self-efficacy in human-robot-interaction scale (SE-HRI). *ACM Transactions on Human-Robot Interaction*, 7(3), Article 14. https://doi.org/10.1145/3139352.

Saerbeck, M., Schut, T., Bartneck, C. and Janse, M.D. (2010). Expressive robots in education: Varying the degree of social supportive behavior of a robotic tutor. In *Proceedings of the SIGCHI Conference on Human Factors in Computing Systems* (pp. 1613–1622). https://doi.org/10.1145/1753326.1753567.

Salem, A. and Sumi, K. (2024). Deception detection in educational AI: Challenges for Japanese middle school students in interacting with generative AI robots. *Frontiers in Artificial Intelligence, 7, AI for Human Learning and Behavior Change*. https://doi.org/10.3389/frai.2024.1493348.

Scassellati, B., Admoni, H. and Mataric, M. (2012). Robots for use in autism research. *Annual Review of Biomedical Engineering*, 14, 275–294. https://doi.org/10.1146/annurev-bioeng-071811-150036.

Sharkey, A. (2016). Should we welcome robot teachers? *Ethics and Information Technology*, 18(4), 283–297. https://doi.org/10.1007/s10676-016-9387-z.

Smuha, N.A. (2021). From a 'race to AI' to a 'race to AI regulation': Regulatory competition for artificial intelligence. *Law, Innovation and Technology*, 13(1), 57–84. https://doi.org/10.1080/17579961.2021.1898300.

Tiam-Lee, T.J. and Sumi, K. (2019). Analysis and prediction of student emotions while doing programming exercises. In A. Coy, Y. Hayashi and M. Chang (Eds.), Intelligent Tutoring Systems: 15th International Conference, ITS 2019, Kingston, Jamaica, June 3–7, 2019, Proceedings (Lecture Notes in Computer Science, Vol. 11528, pp. 24–33). Springer. https://doi.org/10.1007/978-3-030-22244-4_4.

Vosoughi, S., Roy, D. and Aral, S. (2018). The spread of true and false news online. *Science*, 359(6380), 1146–1151. https://doi.org/10.1126/science.aap9559.

Woolf, B.P., Burleson, W., Arroyo, I., Dragon, T., Cooper, D.G. and Picard, R. (2009). Affect-aware tutors: Recognizing and responding to student affect. *International Journal of Learning Technology*, 4(3), 129–164. https://doi.org/10.1504/IJLT.2009.028804.

Xie, H., Chu, H.-C., Hwang, G.-J. and Wang, C.-C. (2019). Trends and development in technology-enhanced adaptive/personalized learning: A systematic review of journal publications from 2007 to 2017. *Computers & Education*, 140, 103599. https://doi.org/10.1016/j.compedu.2019.103599.

Zawacki-Richter, O., Marín, V. I., Bond, M. and Gouverneur, F. (2019). Systematic review of research on artificial intelligence applications in higher education – Where are the educators? *International Journal of Educational Technology in Higher Education*, 16, 39. https://doi.org/10.1186/s41239-019-0171-0.

Chapter 6

Jianwattanapaisarn, N. (2022). Human gait analysis of different emotions in real-time video viewing (Doctoral dissertation, Future University Hakodate).

Jianwattanapaisarn, N., Sumi, K., Utsumi, A., Khamsemanan, N. and Nattee, C. (2022). Emotional characteristic analysis of human gait while real-time movie viewing. *Frontiers in Artificial Intelligence*, 5, 989860.

Killeen, T., Elshehabi, M., Filli, L., Hobert, M.A., Hansen, C., Rieger, D. and Maetzler, W. (2018). Arm swing asymmetry in overground walking. *Scientific Reports*, 8(1), 12803.

Kuhtz-Buschbeck, J.P., Brockmann, K., Gilster, R., Koch, A. and Stolze, H. (2008). Asymmetry of arm-swing not related to handedness. *Gait & Posture*, 27(3), 447–454.

Chapter 7

Anggia, P. and Sumi, K. (2023). Persuasion-building fundamental premises and implications for conversational agents: A conceptual model in captology. In A. Meschtscherjakov, C. Midden, & J. Ham (Eds.), Persuasive Technology (Vol. 13832). Springer, Cham.

Anggia, P. and Sumi, K. (2023). Towards a new approach to increasing the persuasion of product marketing: An experimental study. Journal of Robotics, Networking and Artificial Life.

Anggia, P. and Sumi, K. (2024). Persuasive emotional and cultural elicitation in health marketing content: A cross-cultural experimental study. In Proceedings of the 1st IEEE International Workshop on Interactive Systems, Affective Computing Technologies and Applications (ISAC 2024), The 48th IEEE International Conference on Computers, Software, and Applications (COMPSAC 2024), Osaka.

Babin, B.J. and Attaway, J.S. (2000). Atmospheric affect as a tool for creating value and gaining share of customer. *Journal of Business Research*, 49(2), 91–99.

Bagozzi, R.P., Gopinath, M. and Nyer, P.U. (1999). The role of emotions in marketing. *Journal of the Academy of Marketing Science*, 27, 184–206.

Barrick, M.R. and Mount, M.K. (1991). The big five personality dimensions and job performance: A meta-analysis. *Personnel Psychology*, 44(1), 1–26.

Bawack, R. E., Wamba, S. F., & Carillo, K. D. A. (2021). Exploring the role of personality, trust, and privacy in customer experience performance during voice shopping: Evidence from SEM and fuzzy set qualitative comparative analysis. International Journal of Information Management, 58, 102309.

Dennis, C., Newman, A., Michon, R., Brakus, J. J., & Wright, L. T. (2010). The mediating effects of perception and emotion: Digital signage in mall atmospherics. Journal of Retailing and Consumer Services, 17(3).

Floh, A., & Madlberger, M. (2013). The role of atmospheric cues in online impulse-buying behavior. Journal Name, 12(6).

Fogg, B. J. (2002). Persuasive technology: Using computers to change what we think and do. Ubiquity, 2002(December), 2.

Gerber, A.S., Huber, G.A., Doherty, D., Dowling, C.M. and Panagopoulos, C. (2013). Big five personality traits and responses to persuasive appeals: Results from voter turnout experiments. *Political Behavior*, 35(4), 687–728.

Guo, J., Wang, X. and Wu, Y. (2020). Positive emotion bias: Role of emotional content from online customer reviews in purchase decisions. *Journal of Retailing and Consumer Services*, 52, 101891. https://doi.org/10.1016/j.jretconser.2019.101891.

Meyer, E. (2014). The culture map: Breaking through the invisible boundaries of global business. Public Affairs Books.

Sumi, K. (2010). Learning story marketing through practical experience of story creation system. In *Joint International Conference on Interactive Digital Storytelling* (pp. 98–110). Springer.

Sumi, K. and Nagata, M. (2010). Evaluating a virtual agent as persuasive technology. In J. Csapó & A. Magyar (Eds.), *Psychology of Persuasion*. Nova Science Publishers.

Thomas, S., Ferstl, Y., McDonnell, R. and Ennis, C. (2022). Investigating how speech and animation realism influence the perceived personality of virtual characters and agents. In 2022 IEEE Conference on Virtual Reality and 3D User Interfaces (VR). IEEE.

Xu, W., Ishikawa, Y. and Legaspi, R. (2022). The utility of personality types for personalizing persuasion. In *International Conference on Persuasive Technology* (pp. 240–254). Springer.

Chapter 8

Alfieri, L., Brooks, P.J., Aldrich, N.J. and Tenenbaum, H. R. (2011). Does discovery-based instruction enhance learning? *Journal of Educational Psychology*, 103(1), 1–18. https://doi.org/10.1037/a0021017.

Boyd, d. (2014). It's complicated: The social lives of networked teens. Yale University Press.

Buckingham, D. (2007). Digital media literacies: Rethinking media education in the age of the Internet. *Research in Comparative and International Education*, 2(1), 43–55.

de Freitas, S. (2006). Learning in immersive worlds: A review of game-based learning. Joint Information Systems Committee (JISC).

Duggan, M. (2014). Online harassment. Pew Research Center. https://www.pewresearch.org/internet/2014/10/22/online-harassment/

Gentry, S.V., Gauthier, A., Ehrström, B.L., Wortley, D., Lilienthal, A., Tudor Car, L., Dauwels-Okutsu, S., Nikolaou, C.K., Zary, N., Campbell, J. and Car, J. (2019). Serious gaming and gamification education in health professions: Systematic review. *Journal of Medical Internet Research*, 21(3), e12994. https://doi.org/10.2196/12994.

Gibson, M. (2010). The Schillers of the suburbs – creativity and mediated sociality. *International Journal of Cultural Policy*, 17(5), 523–537. https://doi.org/10.1080/10286632.2010.531717.

Gillmor, D. (2010). Mediactive. Dan Gillmor.

Immordino-Yang, M.H. and Damasio, A. (2007). We feel, therefore we learn: The relevance of affective and social neuroscience to education. *Mind, Brain, and Education*, 1(1), 3–10. https://doi.org/10.1111/j.1751-228X.2007.00004.x.

Kellogg, R.T. (2007). Fundamentals of cognitive psychology. Sage Publications.

Kirschner, P.A., Sweller, J. and Clark, R.E. (2006). Why minimal guidance during instruction does not work: An analysis of the failure of constructivist, discovery, problem-based, experiential, and inquiry-based teaching. *Educational Psychologist*, 41(2), 75–86. https://doi.org/10.1207/s15326985ep4102_1.

Kolb, D.A. (1984). Experiential learning: Experience as the source of learning and development. Prentice Hall.

Livingstone, S. and Third, A. (2017). Children and young people's rights in the digital age: An emerging agenda. *New Media & Society*, 19(5), 657–670. https://doi.org/10.1177/1461444816686318.

Mayer, R.E. (2004). Should there be a three-strikes rule against pure discovery learning? The case for guided methods of instruction. *American Psychologist*, 59(1), 14–19. https://doi.org/10.1037/0003-066X.59.1.14

Nesi, J. and Prinstein, M.J. (2015). Using social media for social comparison and feedback-seeking: Gender and popularity moderate associations with depressive symptoms. *Journal of Abnormal Child Psychology*, 43(8), 1427–1438.

OECD. (2021). 21st-century readers: Developing literacy skills in a digital world. OECD Publishing. https://doi.org/10.1787/a83d84cb-en.

Pekrun, R. (2006). The control-value theory of achievement emotions: Assumptions, corollaries, and implications for educational research and practice. *Educational Psychology Review*, 18(4), 315–341. https://doi.org/10.1007/s10648-006-9029-9.

Reeves, T.C. and Hedberg, J.G. (2003). Interactive learning systems evaluation. Educational Technology Publications.

Sailer, M., Murböck, J. and Fischer, F. (2021). Digital learning in schools: What does it take beyond digital technology? Teaching and Teacher Education, 103, 103346. https://doi.org/10.1016/j.tate.2021.103346.

Schrier, K. and Gibson, D. (Eds.). (2011). Designing Games for Ethics: Models, Techniques and Frameworks. IGI Global. https://doi.org/10.4018/978-1-60960-120-1.

Sousa, D.A. (2022). How the brain learns. Corwin Press.

Zeigarnik, B. (1927). Über das Behalten von erledigten und unerledigten Handlungen. *Psychologische Forschung*, 9(1), 1–85.

Chapter 9

Bowers, P.N. and Kirby, J.R. (2010). Effects of morphological instruction on vocabulary acquisition. *Reading and Writing*, 23(5), 515–537. https://doi.org/10.1007/s11145-009-9172-z.

Butler, Y.G. (2005). Comparative perspectives towards communicative activities among elementary school teachers in South Korea, Japan and Taiwan. *Language Teaching Research*, 9(4), 423–446.

Cameron, L. (2001). Teaching languages to young learners. Cambridge University Press.

Carlisle, J.F. (2000). Awareness of the structure and meaning of morphologically complex words: Impact on reading. *Reading and Writing*, 12(3), 169–190.

Carlisle, J.F. (2003). Morphology matters in learning to read: A commentary. *Reading Psychology*, 24(3–4), 291–322.

Clark, R.C. and Mayer, R.E. (2016). E-learning and the science of instruction: Proven guidelines for consumers and designers of multimedia learning (4th ed.). Wiley.

Devonshire, V., Morris, P. and Fluck, M. (2013). Spelling and reading development: The effect of teaching children multiple levels of representation in their orthography. *Learning and Instruction*, 25, 85–94. https://doi.org/10.1016/j.learninstruc.2012.11.007.

Fauconnier, G. and Turner, M. (2002). The way we think: Conceptual blending and the mind's hidden complexities. Basic Books.

Immordino-Yang, M. H. and Damasio, A. (2007). We feel, therefore we learn: The relevance of affective and social neuroscience to education. *Mind, Brain, and Education*, 1(1), 3–10. https://doi.org/10.1111/j.1751-228X.2007.00004.x.

Kellogg, R.T. (2007). Fundamentals of cognitive psychology. Sage Publications.

Kieffer, M.J. and Lesaux, N. K. (2007). Breaking down words to build meaning: Morphology, vocabulary, and reading comprehension in the urban classroom. *The Reading Teacher*, 61(2), 134–144.

Lakoff, G. and Johnson, M. (1980). Metaphors we live by. University of Chicago Press.

Mayer, R.E. (2009). Multimedia learning (2nd ed.). Cambridge University Press.

Nagy, W.E., Berninger, V.W. and Abbott, R.D. (2006). Contributions of morphology beyond phonology to literacy outcomes of upper elementary and middle-school students. *Journal of Educational Psychology*, 98(1), 134–147. https://doi.org/10.1037/0022-0663.98.1.134.

Nakata, Y. (2011). Teachers' readiness for promoting learner autonomy: A study of Japanese EFL high school teachers. *Teaching and Teacher Education*, 27(5), 900–910.

Nation, I.S.P. (2001). Learning vocabulary in another language. Cambridge University Press.

Paivio, A. (1971). Imagery and verbal processes. Psychology Press. https://doi.org/10.4324/9781315798868.

Paivio, A. (1986). Mental representations: A dual-coding approach. Oxford University Press.

Pearson, P.D. and Gallagher, M.C. (1983). The instruction of reading comprehension. *Contemporary Educational Psychology*, 8(3), 317–344.

Piaget, J. and Inhelder, B. (1969). The psychology of the child (H. Weaver, Trans.). Basic Books. (Original work published 1966).

Plass, J.L., Chun, D.M., Mayer, R.E. and Leutner, D. (1998). Supporting visual and verbal learning preferences in a second-language multimedia learning environment. *Journal of Educational Psychology*, 90(1), 25.

Rumelhart, D.E. (1980). Schemata: The building blocks of cognition. In R.J. Spiro, B.C. Bruce and W.F. Brewer (Eds.), **Theoretical issues in reading comprehension** (pp. 33–58). Lawrence Erlbaum Associates.

Zeigarnik, B. (1927). Über das Behalten von erledigten und unerledigten Handlungen. *Psychologische Forschung*, 9(1), 1–85.

Chapter 10

Baumeister, R.F., Stillwell, A.M. and Heatherton, T.F. (1994). Guilt: An interpersonal approach. *Psychological Bulletin*, 115(2), 243–267. https://doi.org/10.1037/0033-2909.115.2.243.

Bertrand, P., Guegan, J., Robieux, L., McCall, C.A. and Zenasni, F. (2018). Learning empathy through virtual reality: Multiple strategies for training empathy-related abilities using body ownership illusions in embodied virtual reality. *Frontiers in Robotics and AI*, 5, 26. https://doi.org/10.3389/frobt.2018.00026.

Chaplin, T.M. and Aldao, A. (2013). Gender differences in emotion expression in children: A meta-analytic review. *Psychological Bulletin*, 139(4), 735–765. https://doi.org/10.1037/a0030737.

Eisenberg, N., Spinrad, T.L. and Sadovsky, A. (2006). Empathy-related responding in children. In M. Killen and J.G. Smetana (Eds.), *Handbook of moral development* (pp. 517–549). Lawrence Erlbaum Associates.

First person experience of body transfer in virtual reality. *PLOS ONE*, 5(5), e10564. https://doi.org/10.1371/journal.pone.0010564.

Fogg, B.J. (2003). Persuasive technology: Using computers to change what we think and do. Morgan Kaufmann.

Gee, J.P. (2003). What video games have to teach us about learning and literacy. Palgrave Macmillan.

Haidt, J. (2001). The emotional dog and its rational tail: A social intuitionist approach to moral judgment. *Psychological Review*, 108(4), 814–834. https://doi.org/10.1037/0033-295X.108.4.814.

Kilteni, K., Groten, R. and Slater, M. (2012). The sense of embodiment in virtual reality. *Presence: Teleoperators and Virtual Environments*, 21(4), 373–387. https://doi.org/10.1162/PRES_a_00124.

Kolb, D.A. (1984). Experiential learning: Experience as the source of learning and development. Prentice Hall.

Oinas-Kukkonen, H. and Harjumaa, M. (2009). Persuasive systems design: Key issues, process model, and system features. *Communications of the Association for Information Systems*, 24(1), Article 28. https://doi.org/10.17705/1CAIS.02428.

Pérez, J., Castro, M., Awad, E. and López, G. (2023). Virtual harassment, real understanding: Using a serious game and Bayesian networks to study cyberbullying. arXiv preprint, arXiv:2309.08428. https://arxiv.org/abs/2309.08428.

Slater, M., Spanlang, B., Sanchez-Vives, M. V., & Blanke, O. (2010).

Veenstra, R. and Huitsing, G. (2021). Social network approaches to bullying and victimization. *In The Wiley Blackwell Handbook of Bullying* (pp. 196–214). Wiley Blackwell. https://doi.org/10.1002/9781118482650.ch11.

Chapter 11

Bandura, A. (1997). Self-efficacy: The exercise of control. W.H. Freeman.

Csikszentmihalyi, M. (1990). Flow: The Psychology of Optimal Experience. Harper & Row.

Deci, E.L. and Ryan, R.M. (2000). The "what" and "why" of goal pursuits: Human needs and the self-determination of behavior. *Psychological Inquiry*, 11(4), 227–268. https://doi.org/10.1207/S15327965PLI1104_01.

Deterding, S., Dixon, D., Khaled, R. and Nacke, L. (2011). From game design elements to gamefulness: Defining "gamification." In *Proceedings of the 15th International Academic MindTrek Conference* (pp. 9–15). ACM. https://doi.org/10.1145/2181037.2181040

Domínguez, A., Saenz-de-Navarrete, J., de-Marcos, L., Fernández-Sanz, L., Pagés, C. and Martínez-Herráiz, J.-J. (2013). Gamifying learning experiences: Practical implications and outcomes. *Computers & Education*, 63, 380–392.

Fleisig, G.S., Andrews, J.R., Dillman, C.J. and Escamilla, R.F. (1995). Kinetics of baseball pitching with implications about injury mechanisms. *The American journal of sports medicine*, 23(2), 233–239.

Gallagher, S. (2006). How the body shapes the mind. Clarendon press.

Gee, J.P. (2003). What video games have to teach us about learning and literacy. *Computers in Entertainment (CIE)*, 1(1), 20.

Hamari, J., Koivisto, J. and Sarsa, H. (2014). Does gamification work? A literature review of empirical studies on gamification. In *Proceedings of the 47th Hawaii International Conference on System Sciences* (pp. 3025–3034). IEEE. https://doi.org/10.1109/HICSS.2014.377

Haggard, P. and Tsakiris, M. (2009). The experience of agency: Feelings, judgments, and responsibility. *Current Directions in Psychological Science*, 18(4), 242–246. https://doi.org/10.1111/j.1467-8721.2009.01644.x.

Hattie, J. and Timperley, H. (2007). The power of feedback. *Review of Educational Research*, 77(1), 81–112.

Haywood, K.M. and Getchell, N. (2019). Life Span Motor Development (7th ed.). Human Kinetics.

Janelle, C.M., Fawver, B. and Beatty, G.F. (2018). "Emotions and Sport Performance." In G. Tenenbaum & B. Eklund (Eds.), *Handbook of Sport Psychology* (4th ed.). Wiley.

López-Bueno R, López-Sánchez GF, Casajús JA, Calatayud J, Gil-Salmerón A, Grabovac I, Tully MA, Smith L. Health-Related Behaviors Among School-Aged Children and Adolescents During the Spanish Covid-19 Confinement. *Front Pediatr*. 2020 Sep 11;8:573. doi: 10.3389/fped.2020.00573. PMID: 33042917; PMCID: PMC7516648.

Mousavi, S.A., Parvizi, N. and Hajhasan Tehrani, A. (2024). "Kinematic of dart-throwing: virtual reality (functional and structural constraints) vs. real-world." *Computer Methods in Biomechanics and Biomedical Engineering: Imaging & Visualization*.

Lange, B., Flynn, S.M. and Rizzo, A.S. (2009). Initial usability assessment of off-the-shelf video game consoles for clinical game-based motor rehabilitation. *Physical Therapy Reviews*, 16(5), 324–330.

Mekler, E.D., Brühlmann, F., Tuch, A.N. and Opwis, K. (2017). Towards understanding the effects of individual gamification elements on intrinsic motivation and performance. *Computers in human behavior*, 71, 525–534.

Michael, D.R. and Chen, S.L. (2005). *Serious games: Games that educate, train, and inform*. Muska & Lipman/Premier-Trade.

Ministry of Education, Culture, Sports, Science and Technology [MEXT]. (2013). *Annual Report on Physical Strength and Athletic Ability of Japanese Children* [in Japanese]. Tokyo: MEXT.

Ntoumanis, N. (2010). A self-determination approach to the understanding of motivation in physical education. *British Journal of Educational Psychology*, 71(2), 225–242. https://doi.org/10.1348/000709901158497.

Plass, J.L., Homer, B.D. and Kinzer, C.K. (2015). Foundations of game-based learning. *Educational Psychologist*, 50(4), 258–283.

Robinson, L.E., Stodden, D.F., Barnett, L.M., Lopes, V.P., Logan, S.W., Rodrigues, L.P. and D'Hondt, E. (2015). Motor competence and its effect on positive developmental trajectories of health. *Sports Medicine*, 45(9), 1273–1284.

Ryan, R.M. and Deci, E.L. (2000). Self-determination theory and the facilitation of intrinsic motivation, social development, and well-being. *American psychologist*, 55(1), 68.

Schmidt, R.A. and Wrisberg, C.A. (2008). *Motor learning and performance: A situation-based learning approach. Human kinetics.*

Shams, L. and Seitz, A.R. (2008). Benefits of multisensory learning. *Trends in Cognitive Sciences*, 12(11), 411–417.

Sigrist, R., Rauter, G., Riener, R. and Wolf, P. (2013). Augmented visual, auditory, haptic, and multimodal feedback in motor learning: A review. *Psychonomic Bulletin & Review*, 20, 21–53.

Stodden, D.F., Goodway, J.D., Langendorfer, S.J., Roberton, M.A., Rudisill, M.E., Garcia, C. and Garcia, L.E. (2008). A developmental perspective on the role of motor skill competence in physical activity. *Quest*, 60(2), 290–306.

Sumi, K. and Tsukamoto, Y. (2016). A throw training system utilizing visual and sound effects. In A. L. Brooks, R. Lukosch, & A. Verbraeck (Eds.), *Entertainment Computing and Serious Games. INTETAIN 2016. Lecture Notes of the Institute for Computer Sciences, Social Informatics and Telecommunications Engineering* (Vol. 179, pp. 169–174). Springer. https://doi.org/10.1007/978-3-319-49616-0_13.

Susi, T., Johannesson, M. and Backlund, P. (2007). Serious games: An overview. Technical Report, University of Skövde, Sweden.

Veldman, S.L.C., Jones, R.A. and Okely, A.D. (2023). COVID-19 and its impact on child physical activity: Global insights. *Pediatric Exercise Science*, 35(1), 1–10.

Weiss, M.R. (2000). Motivating kids in physical activity. *President's Council on Physical Fitness and Sports Research Digest*, 3(11), 1–8.

World Health Organization. (2019). *Guidelines on physical activity, sedentary behaviour and sleep for children under 5 years of age*. https://www.who.int/publications/i/item/9789241550536.

Wang, L. and Qiu, S. (2019). "AI Coach: Deep Human Pose Estimation and Analysis for Personalized Athletic Training Assistance." In *Proceedings of the 27th ACM International Conference on Multimedia*, 374–382.

Zhang, T., Li, J. and Wang, S. (2024). Artificial intelligence in physical education: comprehensive review and outlook. *Frontiers in Public Health*, 12, https://doi.org/10.3389/fpubh.2024.1484848.

Chapter 12

Bard, C. and Fleury, M. (1976). Analysis of visual search activity during sport problem situations. *Journal of Human Movement Studies*, 2, 214–222.

Eccles, D.W. and Tenenbaum, G. (2004). Why an expert team is more than a team of experts: A social-cognitive conceptualization of team coordination and communication in sport. *Journal of Sport and Exercise Psychology*, 26(4), 542–560. https://doi.org/10.1123/jsep.26.4.542.

Endsley, M.R. (1995). Toward a theory of situation awareness in dynamic systems. *Human Factors*, 37(1), 32–64. https://doi.org/10.1518/001872095779049543.

Farrow, D., Abernethy, B. and Jackson, R.C. (1998). The utility of perceptual training in ball sports. *Journal of Sports Sciences*, 16(2), 153–160.

Faubert, J. (2013). Professional athletes have extraordinary skills for rapidly learning complex and neutral dynamic visual scenes. *Scientific Reports*, 3, 1154. https://doi.org/10.1038/srep01154.

Kittel, A., Larkin, P. and Elsworthy, N. (2024). The use of extended reality technologies in sport perceptual-cognitive skill training: A systematic scoping review. *Sports Medicine - Open*, 10, 10. https://doi.org/10.1186/s40798-024-00653-4.

Kredel, R., Hernandez, J., Hossner, E.-J. and Zahno, S. (2023). Eye-tracking technology and the dynamics of natural gaze behavior in sports: An update 2016–2022. *Frontiers in Psychology*, 14, 1130051. https://doi.org/10.3389/fpsyg.2023.1130051.

Legault, I. and Faubert, J. (2012). Perceptual-cognitive training improves biological motion perception: Evidence for transferability of training in healthy aging. *NeuroReport*, 23(8), 469–473. https://doi.org/10.1097/WNR.0b013e328353e48a.

Mann, D.L., Williams, A.M., Ward, P. and Janelle, C.M. (2007). Perceptual-cognitive expertise in sport: A meta-analysis. *Journal of Sport and Exercise Psychology*, 29(4), 457–478. https://doi.org/10.1123/jsep.29.4.457

Richlan, F., Weiß, M., Kastner, P. and Braid, J. (2023). Virtual training, real effects: A narrative review on sports performance enhancement through interventions in virtual reality. *Frontiers in Psychology*, 14, 1240790. https://doi.org/10.3389/fpsyg.2023.1240790.

Romeas, T., Guldner, A. and Faubert, J. (2016). 3D-Multiple Object Tracking training task improves passing decision-making accuracy in soccer players. *Psychology of Sport and Exercise*, 22, 1–9. https://doi.org/10.1016/j.psychsport.2015.06.002.

Shelton, A.L. and Gabrieli, J.D.E. (2002). Neural correlates of encoding space from route and survey perspectives. *Journal of Neuroscience*, 22(7), 2711–2717. https://doi.org/10.1523/JNEUROSCI.22-07-02711.2002.

Shepard, R.N. and Metzler, J. (1971). Mental rotation of three-dimensional objects. *Science*, 171(3972), 701–703. https://doi.org/10.1126/science.171.3972.701.

Shimizu, S. and Sumi, K. (2019). Sports training system for visualizing bird's-eye view from first-person view. In *Proceedings of the IEEE Conference on Virtual Reality* (VR 2019), Osaka, Japan.

Sumi, K. and Okuyama, R. (2024). Training system for converting current visual information to bird's eye view. *Frontiers in Psychology*, 15, Movement Science. https://doi.org/10.3389/fpsyg.2024.1504838.

Vickers, J.N. (2007). Perception, cognition, and decision training: The quiet eye in action. *Human Kinetics*.

Williams, A.M., Ward, P., Knowles, J.M. and Smeeton, N.J. (2002). Anticipation skill in a real-world task: Measurement, training, and transfer in tennis. *Journal of Experimental Psychology: Applied*, 8(4), 259–270.

Chapter 13

Ahn, L.V. and Dabbish, L.A. (2008). Designing games with a purpose. *Commun.* ACM, 51, 58–67.

Coyne, B. and Sproat, R. (2001). WordsEye: An automatic text-to-scene conversion system. *Proceedings of the 28th Annual Conference on Computer Graphics and Interactive Techniques (SIGGRAPH)*, 487–496. https://doi.org/10.1145/383259.383317

Hirai, S. and Sumi, K. (2019). Collecting visual effect linked data using GWAP. In A. El Rhalibi et al. (Eds.), E-Learning and Games. Edutainment 2018 (Lecture Notes in Computer Science, vol. 11462). Springer, Cham. https://doi.org/10.1007/978-3-030-23712-7_39.

Kim, G., Kwon, T. and Ye, J. (2021). DiffusionCLIP: Text-guided diffusion models for robust image manipulation. In *2022 IEEE/CVF Conference on Computer Vision and Pattern Recognition (CVPR)*, 2416–2425.

Lenat, D.B. (1995). CYC: A large-scale investment in knowledge infrastructure. *Communications of the ACM*, 38(11), 33–38. https://doi.org/10.1145/219717.219745.

Lieberman, H., Paternò, F. and Wulf, V. (Eds.). (2006). End user development. *Human–Computer Interaction Series*, vol. 9. Springer, Dordrecht. https://doi.org/10.1007/1-4020-5386-X.

Liu, H. and Singh, P. (2004). ConceptNet—a practical commonsense reasoning tool-kit. *BT Technology Journal*, 22(4), 211–226. https://doi.org/10.1023/B:BTTJ.0000047600.45421.6d

Madden, T.J., Hewett, K. and Roth, M.S. (2000). Managing images in different cultures: A cross-national study of color meanings and preferences. *Journal of International Marketing*, 8(4), 90–107. https://doi.org/10.1509/jimk.8.4.90.19795.

Miller, G.A. (1995). WordNet: A lexical database for English. *Communications of the ACM*, 38(11), 39–41. https://doi.org/10.1145/219717.219748

Nagamachi, M. (1995). Kansei engineering: A new ergonomic consumer-oriented technology for product development. *International Journal of Industrial Ergonomics*, 15(1), 3–11. https://doi.org/10.1016/0169-8141(94)00052-5.

Norman, D.A. (2002). Emotion & design: Attractive things work better. *Interactions*, 9(4), 36–42. https://doi.org/10.1145/543434.543435.

OpenAI. (2024). Sora: Multimodal video generation system. Retrieved from https://openai.com.

Picard, R.W. (1997). Affective computing. MIT Press. https://affect.media.mit.edu/projectpages/affectbook.html.

Ramesh, A., Dhariwal, P., Nichol, A., Chu, C. and Chen, M. (2022). Hierarchical text-conditional image generation with CLIP latents. *arXiv preprint*. https://arxiv.org/abs/2204.06125.

Rombach, R., Blattmann, A., Lorenz, D., Esser, P. and Ommer, B. (2022). High-resolution image synthesis with latent diffusion models. In *Proceedings of the IEEE/CVF Conference on Computer Vision and Pattern Recognition (CVPR)*, 10684–10695. https://arxiv.org/abs/2112.10752

Saharia, C., Chan, W., Saxena, S., Li, L., Whang, J., Denton, E. and Salimans, T. (2022). Photorealistic text-to-image diffusion models with deep language understanding. *arXiv preprint*. https://arxiv.org/abs/2205.11487.

Singer, J., Arbour, D., Odena, A. and Sohl-Dickstein, J. (2022). Text-to-image generation using CLIP-guided diffusion. *arXiv preprint*. https://arxiv.org/abs/2112.05144.

Singh, P., Lin, T., Mueller, E.T., Lim, G., Perkins, T. and Li Zhu, W. (2002). Open Mind Common Sense: Knowledge acquisition from the general public. In R. Meersman & Z. Tari (Eds.), On the Move to Meaningful Internet Systems 2002: CoopIS, DOA, and ODBASE (Lecture Notes in Computer Science, vol. 2519). Springer, Berlin, Heidelberg. https://doi.org/10.1007/3-540-36124-3_77.

Sumi, K. (2005). Automatic conversion from E-content into virtual storytelling. In G. Subsol (Ed.), *Virtual Storytelling* (LNCS, vol. 3805, pp. 262–271). Springer.

Sumi, K. (2007). Anime de Blog for collecting animation data. In M. Cavazza & S. Donikian (Eds.), *Virtual Storytelling* (LNCS, vol. 4871, pp. 139–149). Springer.

Sumi, K. (2009). Interactive storytelling system using recycle-based story knowledge. In I. Iurgel, N. Zagalo, & P. Petta (Eds.), *Interactive Storytelling* (LNCS, vol. 5915, pp. 74–85). Springer.

Valdez, P. and Mehrabian, A. (1994). Effects of color on emotions. Journal of Experimental Psychology: General, 123(4), 394–409. https://doi.org/10.1037/0096-3445.123.4.394.

Villegas, R., Yang, T.-J., Gong, K., Zhang, L., Ye, Y., Wang, X. and Lee, H. (2022). Phenaki: Variable-length video generation from open-domain textual descriptions. *arXiv preprint*. https://arxiv.org/abs/2210.02399.

Zhang, C., Zhang, C., Zhang, M., Kweon, I.S. and Kim, J. (2023). Text-to-image diffusion models in generative AI: A survey. *arXiv preprint*. https://arxiv.org/abs/2303.07909.

Chapter 14

Adams, N., Wainman, B., King, J.A. and Nonis, D. (2022). Mixed reality results in vocational education: a case study with HoloLens 2. *Research in Learning Technology*, 30, 1–12. https://doi.org/10.25304/rlt.v30.2803.

Annetta, L.A., Folta, E., Cheng, Y. and Holmes, S.Y. (2024). Enhancing science and literacy outcomes through immersive mixed reality environments. *Computers & Education: X Reality*, 5, 100093. https://doi.org/10.1016/j.cexr.2024.100093.

Azzam, I., Breidi, F., Aqlan, F., Garcia, J.M. and Asunda, P. (2024, June). Board 342: On the Development of Spatial Visual Abilities among STEM Students via Interactive Mixed Reality Modules. *Paper presented at the 2024 ASEE Annual Conference & Exposition, Portland, Oregon.* https://peer.asee.org/46924.

Banjar, A., Xu, X., Iqbal, M.Z. and Campbell, A. (2023). A systematic review of the experimental studies on the effectiveness of mixed reality in higher education between 2017 and 2021. *Computers & Education: X Reality*, 3, 100034. https://doi.org/10.1016/j.cexr.2023.100034.

Barsalou, L.W. (2008). Grounded cognition. *Annual Review of Psychology*, 59, 617–645. https://doi.org/10.1146/annurev.psych.59.103006.093639.

Battista, M.T. (2007). The development of geometric and spatial thinking. In F.K. Lester Jr. (Ed.), *Second Handbook of Research on Mathematics Teaching and Learning* (pp. 843–908). Charlotte, NC: Information Age.

Boakes, N.J. (2009). The impact of origami-mathematics lessons on achievement and spatial ability of middle-school students. *ERIC Document Reproduction Service*, ED506182.

Clements, D.H. and Battista, M.T. (1992). Geometry and spatial reasoning. Handbook of research on mathematics teaching and learning: *A project of the National Council of Teachers of Mathematics*, 420–464.

Clements, D.H. and Sarama, J. (2011). Early childhood mathematics intervention. *Science*, 333(6045), 968–970.

Cohen, C.A. and Hegarty, M. (2007). Sources of difficulty in imagining cross sections of 3D objects. *Proceedings of the Cognitive Science Society*, 29.

Fonkalsrud, B., Røising, H., Bakke, I. and Rystedt, H. (2025). Midwifery students' perceptions of a mixed reality fetal anatomy lesson using the HoloLens: A qualitative study. *Nurse Education in Practice*, 74, 103640.

Goagoses, N., Winschiers-Theophilus, H., Auala, S., Kandjinga, L. and Bidwell, N.J. (2024). Teachers and students envisioning mixed reality remote learning: A qualitative exploration on fostering academic engagement. *Technology, Knowledge and Learning*. Advance online publication. https://doi.org/10.1007/s10758-024-09797-4.

Huang, S., Tarng, W. and Ou, K. (2023). Effectiveness of AR Board Game on Computational Thinking and Programming Skills for Elementary School Students. *Syst.*, 11, 25.

Jones, K. (2012). Geometrical and spatial reasoning: Challenges for research in mathematics education. In H. Pinto, H. Jacinto, A. Henriques, A. Silvestre, & C. Nunes (Eds.), *Atas do XXIII Seminário de Investigação em Educação Matemática (SIEM XXIII)* (pp. 3–10). Associação de Professores de Matemática. Retrieved from https://eprints.soton.ac.uk/446098/

Lave, J. and Wenger, E. (1991). Situated learning: Legitimate peripheral participation. Cambridge University Press.

Maas, M.J. and Hughes, J.M. (2020). Virtual, augmented and mixed reality in K–12 education: A review of the literature. *Technology, Pedagogy and Education*, 29(2), 231–249. https://doi.org/10.1080/1475939X.2020.1737210.

Mix, K.S. and Cheng, Y.L. (2012). The relation between space and math: Developmental and educational implications. *Advances in Child Development and Behavior*, 42, 197–243.

Newcombe, N.S. (2010). Picture this: Increasing math and science learning by improving spatial thinking. *American Educator*, 34(2), 29–35.

Norman, D.A. (1988). *The design of everyday things*. Basic Books.

Ogunseiju, O.R., Akanmu, A.A., Bairaktarova, D., Bowman, D. and Jazizadeh, F. (2024). Cognitive Load within Mixed Reality Learning Environment in Construction Education. *Construction Research Congress 2024*.

Paivio, A. (1986). *Mental representations: A dual coding approach*. Oxford University Press.

Piaget, J. (1964). Development and learning. In R.E. Ripple & V. N. Rockcastle (Eds.), *Piaget Rediscovered* (pp. 7–20). Ithaca, NY: Cornell University Press.

Rohendi, D., Septian, S.Y. and Sutarno, H. (2018). The Use of Geometry Learning Media Based on Augmented Reality for Junior High School Students. *IOP Conference Series: Materials Science and Engineering*, 306.

Shneiderman, B. (1998). Designing the user interface: Strategies for effective human-computer interaction (3rd ed.). Addison-Wesley.

Sweller, J. (1988). Cognitive load during problem solving: Effects on learning. *Cognitive Science*, 12(2), 257–285. https://doi.org/10.1207/s15516709cog1202_4

Uttal, D.H., Meadow, N.G., Tipton, E., Hand, L.L., Alden, A.R. and Warren, C. (2013). The malleability of spatial skills: A meta-analysis of training studies. *Psychological Bulletin*, 139(2), 352–402. https://doi.org/10.1037/a0028446.

Wilson, M. (2002). Six views of embodied cognition. *Psychonomic Bulletin & Review*, 9(4), 625–636. https://doi.org/10.3758/BF03196322.

Wood, D., Bruner, J.S. and Ross, G. (1976). The role of tutoring in problem solving. *Journal of Child Psychology and Psychiatry*, 17(2), 89–100. https://doi.org/10.1111/j.1469-7610.1976.tb00381.x.

Chapter 15

Bacca, J., Baldiris, S.M., Fabregat, R., Graf, S. and Kinshuk (2014). Augmented Reality Trends in Education: A Systematic Review of Research and Applications. *J. Educ. Technol. Soc.*, 17, 133–149.

Battista, M.T. (2007). The development of geometric and spatial thinking. In F.K. Lester Jr. (Ed.), *Second handbook of research on mathematics teaching and learning* (pp. 843–908). National Council of Teachers of Mathematics.

Dede, C. (2009). Immersive interfaces for engagement and learning. *Science*, 323(5910), 66–69. https://doi.org/10.1126/science.1167311.

Clark, J.M. and Paivio, A. (1991). Dual coding theory and education. *Educational Psychology Review*, 3, 149–210.

Clements, D.H. and Battista, M.T. (1992). Geometry and spatial reasoning. In D. A. Grouws (Ed.), *Handbook of research on mathematics teaching and learning* (pp. 420–464). New York: Macmillan.

Csikszentmihalyi, M. (1990). *Flow: The Psychology of Optimal Experience*. Harper & Row.

Faridan, M., Kumari, B. and Suzuki, R. (2023). ChameleonControl: Teleoperating real human surrogates through mixed reality gestural guidance for remote hands-on classrooms. In *Proceedings of the 2023 CHI Conference on Human Factors in Computing Systems* (pp. 1–13). ACM. https://doi.org/10.1145/3544548.3581381

Fowler, C. (2015). Virtual reality and learning: Where is the pedagogy? *British Journal of Educational Technology*, 46(2), 412–422. https://doi.org/10.1111/bjet.12135.

Furuichi, S. and Sumi, K. (2024). Experiential learning system with generative art using virtual spaces. In *The 1st IEEE International Workshop on Interactive Systems, Affective Computing Technologies and Applications (ISAC 2024)*, The 48th IEEE International Conference on Computers, Software, and Applications (COMPSAC 2024). Osaka, Japan. https://doi.org/10.1109/COMPSAC61105.2024.00330.

Galanter, P. (2003). What is generative art? Complexity theory as a context for art theory. In *Proceedings of the International Conference on Generative Art*.

Grover, S. and Pea, R.D. (2013). Computational thinking in K–12: A review of the state of the field. *Educational Researcher*, 42(1), 38–43. https://doi.org/10.3102/0013189X12463051.

Guzdial, M. and Ericson, B. (2016). *Introduction to Computing and Programming in Python: A Multimedia Approach* (4th ed.). Pearson.

Henriksen, D. (2014). Full STEAM Ahead: Creativity in Excellent STEM Teaching Practices. *The STEAM Journal*, 1, 15.

Johnson-Glenberg, M.C. (2018). Immersive VR and Education: Embodied Design Principles That Include Gesture and Hand Controls. *Frontiers in Robotics and AI*, 5.

Messer, U. (2024). Co-creating art with generative artificial intelligence: Implications for artworks and artists. *Computers in Human Behavior: Artificial Humans*, 2(1), Article 100056. https://doi.org/10.1016/j.chbah.2024.100056

Milgram, P. and Kishino, F. (1994). A taxonomy of mixed reality visual displays. *IEICE Transactions on Information and Systems*, E77-D(12), 1321–1329.

Ogunseiju, O.R., Akanmu, A.A., Bairaktarova, D., Bowman, D. and Jazizadeh, F. (2024). Cognitive Load within Mixed Reality Learning Environment in Construction Education. *Construction Research Congress 2024*.

Papert, S. (1980). Mindstorms: Children, computers, and powerful ideas. Basic Books.

Presmeg, N.C. (1986). Visualization in high school mathematics education. *For the Learning of Mathematics*, 6(3), 42–46.

Rauth, I., Köppen, E., Jobst, B. and Meinel, C. (2010). Design thinking: An educational model towards creative confidence. In *DS 66-2: Proceedings of the 1st International Conference on Design Creativity* (ICDC 2010).

Resnick, M., Maloney, J., Monroy-Hernández, A., Rusk, N., Eastmond, E., Brennan, K. and Kafai, Y. B. (2009). Scratch: Programming for all. *Communications of the ACM*, 52(11), 60–67. https://doi.org/10.1145/1592761.1592779.

Schön, D.A. (1983). *The Reflective Practitioner: How Professionals Think in Action.* Basic Books.

Sorby, S.A. (2009). Educational research in developing 3-D spatial skills for engineering students. *International Journal of Science Education*, 31(3), 459–480. https://doi.org/10.1080/09500690802595839.

Uttal, D.H., Meadow, N.G., Tipton, E., Hand, L.L., Alden, A.R. and Warren, C. (2013). The malleability of spatial skills: A meta-analysis of training studies. *Psychological Bulletin*, 139(2), 352–402. https://doi.org/10.1037/a0028446.

Van Hiele, P.M. (1959). The child's thought and geometry. English translation of selected writings of Dina van Hiele-Geldof and Pierre M. van Hiele, 243–252.

Wilson, M. (2002). Six views of embodied cognition. *Psychonomic Bulletin & Review*, 9(4), 625–636. https://doi.org/10.3758/BF03196322.

Yakman, G. (2008). STEAM education: An overview of creating a model of integrative education. In *PATT-19 Proceedings: Research and Practice in Technology Education: Perspectives on Human Capacity and Development* (pp. 335–358). International Technology Education Association.

Chapter 16

Catling, S. and Willy, T. (2018). Understanding and teaching primary geography (2nd ed.). SAGE Publications.

Chin, K.Y., Wang, C.S. and Chen, Y. L. (2019). Effects of an augmented reality-based mobile system on students' learning achievements and motivation for a liberal arts course. *Interactive Learning Environments*, 27(7), 927–941.

Czimre, Mucsi, and Török (2024) conducted a systematic review highlighting the role of VR in improving geographical thinking, motivation, and spatial awareness. They found that interactive VR environments are more effective than passive videos in promoting inquiry and retention (Czimre et al., 2024).

Fuller, A., Fan, Z., Day, C. and Barlow, C. (2020). *Digital twin: Enabling technologies, challenges and open research. IEEE Access*, 8, 108952–108971. https://doi.org/10.1109/ACCESS.2020.2998358.

Grieves, M. and Vickers, J. (2017). Digital twin: Mitigating unpredictable, undesirable emergent behavior in complex systems. In F.-J. Kahlen, S. Flumerfelt, & A. Alves (Eds.), *Transdisciplinary perspectives on complex systems* (pp. 85–113). Springer. https://doi.org/10.1007/978-3-319-38756-7_4.

Ishikawa, T. and Kastens, K.A. (2005). Why some students have trouble with maps and other spatial representations. *Journal of Geoscience Education*, 53(2), 184–197. https://doi.org/10.5408/1089-9995-53.2.184.

Johnson-Glenberg, M.C. (2018). Immersive VR and education: Embodied design principles that include gesture and hand controls. *Frontiers in Robotics and AI*, 5, 81. https://doi.org/10.3389/frobt.2018.00081.

Kolb, D. A. (1984). Experiential learning: Experience as the source of learning and development. Prentice Hall.

Lambert, D. and Morgan, J. (2010). *Teaching geography* 11–18: A conceptual approach. Open University Press.

Maher, D. and Buchanan, R. (2021). 360 degree representation: Desktop virtual reality combined with analytics in the primary school classroom. *Technology, Pedagogy and Education*, 30(4), 609–622. https://doi.org/10.1080/1475939X.2021.1939770.

National Research Council. (2006). Learning to think spatially: GIS as a support system in the K–12 curriculum. The National Academies Press. https://doi.org/10.17226/11019.

Negri, E., Fumagalli, L. and Macchi, M. (2017). A review of the roles of digital twin in CPS-based production systems. *Procedia Manufacturing*, 11, 939–948. https://doi.org/10.1016/j.promfg.2017.07.198.

Rickinson, M., Dillon, J., Teamey, K., Morris, M., Choi, M.Y., Sanders, D. and Benefield, P. (2004). A review of research on outdoor learning. Shrewsbury: Field Studies Council.

Sepasgozar, S.M.E. (2020). Digital twin and web-based virtual gaming technologies for online education: A case of construction management and engineering. *Applied Sciences*, 10(13), 4678. https://doi.org/10.3390/app10134678.

Southgate, E. (2020). Virtual reality in curriculum and pedagogy: Evidence from secondary classrooms. Routledge. https://doi.org/10.4324/9780429291982.

Index